YALE CLASSICAL MONOGRAPHS, 2

TOWARD THE SOUL

An Inquiry into the Meaning of ψυχή before Plato

DAVID B. CLAUS

NEW HAVEN AND LONDON   YALE UNIVERSITY PRESS

Designed by James J. Johnson
and set in Monophoto Bembo type by
Asco Trade Typesetting Ltd., Hong Kong.
Printed in the United States of America by
Halliday Lithograph, West Hanover, Mass.

Library of Congress Cataloging in Publication Data

Claus, David B 1937–
  Toward the soul.

  (Yale classical monographs; 2)
  Bibliography: p.
  Includes indexes.
  1. Soul. 2. Psyche (The word)
3. Philosophy, Ancient. 4. Socrates.
5. Plato. I. Title. II. Series.
B187.S6C55   128'.1   80-25496
ISBN 0-300-02096-1

10 9 8 7 6 5 4 3 2 1

FOR

ERIC A. HAVELOCK

Contents

Acknowledgments

A portion of the research for this book was completed under grants from the National Endowment for the Humanities and Yale University. I wish to thank them here for their support.

I owe a great debt to many who have, at one time or another, helped in the preparation of the manuscript, especially to my former student Sharon Gallagher, for the many hours she gave to verifying the accuracy of the numbers in the text, and to Alice Oliver and Nancy Burson for patient typing.

Many scholars have been generous with their time and thoughtful criticisms as the work progressed, particularly my colleagues in the Yale Classics Department, Gordon Williams and Thomas Cole, and above all my good friend and teacher, Eric Havelock, to whom it gives me great pleasure to dedicate these pages. For his many kindnesses over the years of our friendship this book is but a small return.

Scripps College
July 1980

Citations and Quotations

Ancient titles and names discussed in the text are rendered in Latin except where English is customary (*Odyssey* for *Odysseia*) or where Latin is especially cumbersome (*Ranae* for *Frogs*). All abbreviations of ancient names are taken from the list in Liddell-Scott-Jones, *Greek-English Lexicon*. In a few cases I have introduced changes to avoid duplication: *Sept.* = *Septem*, Thuc. = Thucydides, *Tra.* = *Trachiniae*, *Pho.* = *Phoenissae*, Bacch. = Bacchylides, *Hr.* = *Heraclidae*. Modern abbreviations used in the text are LfrgE (*Lexikon des frühgriechischen Epos*), KR (G. S. Kirk and J. E. Raven, *The Presocratic Philosophers*, Cambridge, 1964), RE (*Realencyclopädie des klassischen Altertums*). English equivalents for Greek words and noun phrases are marked by a single quotation mark, as in the phrase '*soul*' *words*. Technically every occurrence of the word 'soul' could be so marked. I have avoided doing so except where it has seemed important to call attention to the use of the word as an equivalent for one or another of the ancient terms examined here.

Introduction

The changes in meaning exhibited by the word ψυχή during the archaic and classical periods are exceptionally important and dramatic. In Homer ψυχή signifies both the 'life' that is lost at death and 'shade' or 'wraith', as in the description of death in battle (*Il.* 5.296 [= 8.123] τοῦ δ' αὖθι λύθη ψυχή τε μένος τε) and in Achilles' exclamation at seeing the 'shade' of Patroclus (*Il.* 23.103–04 ὢ πόποι, ἦ ῥά τίς ἐστι καὶ εἰν Ἀΐδαο δόμοισι / ψυχὴ καὶ εἴδωλον, ἀτὰρ φρένες οὐκ ἔνι πάμπαν). After Homer ψυχή undergoes transformations in meaning that lead eventually to its use by Plato to designate the comprehensive personal 'soul'—the immortal and divine part of man, the self as a center or microcosm of his whole being, the seat of the rational intelligence and thus of moral choice, that which is not body and which is related to body as master is to slave.[1] Because ψυχή is the word that in time allows human life to be characterized as a composite of body and soul, its history is central to one of the most important and influential achievements of Greek thought.

For good reason, therefore, the questions raised by the development of ψυχή have invited substantial attention from scholars. First among these stands Erwin Rohde, whose late nineteenth-century literary and scholarly masterpiece, *Psyche: Seelenkult und Unsterblichkeitsglaube der Griechen*,[2] remains a text essential to the study of Greek religion and ethics. The way in which Rohde handled the semantic changes sustained by ψυχή, however, left much to be desired. His intent was to show that the Platonic description of the soul, or ψυχή, could be derived in the main from the introduction of ascetic religious values into Greece in the centuries after Homer, a phenom-

---

1. E.g., Plato *Phd.* 79e–81a; 107c–d; *Alc.* I 129a–130c.
2. Quoted throughout in the translation of W. B. Hillis.

enon manifested in the cult of Orphism and the reported philosophical
speculations of the early Pythagoreans. These beliefs he derived in turn
from the earlier practice of ecstatic Dionysian religion.³ But Rohde never
successfully explained how the one truly indispensable piece of evidence
for any theory of change in the idea of the soul in Greece, namely the
surviving occurrences of the word ψυχή, could be made to support his
thesis. Instead he borrowed from the animistic anthropology of his time the
hypothesis that certain ideas—here the so-called Doppelgänger—recur
from culture to culture as allegedly universal powers of human logic are
applied by primitive peoples to spontaneous mental events, like dreaming,
that can be taken as inevitable in human experience.⁴ By the same reasoning it could be assumed that more modern ideas of personality and self
would invariably follow any advance in civilization and scientific knowledge, and this assumption allowed Rohde to treat all uses of ψυχή after
Homer not clearly the result of Orphic or Pythagorean influence as
naturally implying a more comprehensive and rational idea of self. Thus,
in the Presocratic philosophers ψυχή became, in his view, a "collective
expression for all the powers of thought, desire, and will," ⁵ and in a single
footnote he extended this generalization to much of Greek literature after
Homer apart from texts directly influenced by Orphic or Pythagorean
ideas.⁶ Since the Platonic view of the soul encompasses both the rational
personality and the capacity for supernatural existence, however, this
magisterial treatment of the secular usage of ψυχή must be regarded as a
major omission in Rohde's argument. If in fact the ψυχή could be widely
recognized as the seat of "thought, desire, and will" in contexts not
influenced by Orphic and Pythagorean teachings, the details of that secular
development in the meaning of the word would be clearly important for

3. Rohde, pp. 254–55; p. 326.
4. Rohde's reliance on the principles of Spencerian anthropology is implicit but undeniable:
"The earlier age which handed down to the Greeks of Homer their beliefs about the soul cannot have
failed any more than other nations to observe the facts upon which a fantastic logic based the conclusion
of man's double personality" (p. 6). See Otto, pp. 15–21, and for an authoritative discussion of
animism, Evans-Pritchard, pp. 23–27.
5. Rohde, p. 365.
6. Chap. 11, n. 2: "Just this [θυμός] and more than this, the sum and substance of all the mental
powers in general, is what the word ψυχή means in the language of the philosophers (except those
affected by religious tendencies). They left out of account altogether that spiritual double of mankind
whom the popular psychology called the ψυχή, and were thus free to use the word to express the whole
psychical content of the human individual. From the fifth century onwards we find the word ψυχή used
commonly, and even regularly, in this sense in the vocabulary of non-philosophical poets and prose
writers. Only theologians and poets, or philosophers of a theological tendency, continued to use the
word in its ancient and primitive sense."

the Platonic idea of the soul and could not fairly be ignored. Equally important, the ascetic tradition about the ψυχή can hardly have furnished Plato as rich a starting point for his own ideas as that claimed for it by Rohde unless there had already come into being, before Plato, some significant connection between the conscious moral self and the super-natural soul, and this alignment is regularly implied in Rohde's descrip-tions of the earlier religious ideas.[7] Whether Rohde saw these alternative explanations of the history of ψυχή as complementary or contradictory cannot be decided; in any case, no consistent or detailed theory of semantic development can be extracted from *Psyche*.

In the wake of *Psyche*, however, much more systematic explanations for the observed changes in meaning of ψυχή have been put forward. The general case for the influence of afterlife ideas is stated concisely by Snell:

> The word denoting the eschatological soul was put to a new use, to designate the soul as a whole, and the word for corpse came to be employed for the living body; the reason for this must be that the element which provided man during his living days with emotions, perceptions, and thoughts was believed to survive in the *psyche*.[8]

This view is in accord, at least superficially, with evidence like that of Pindar's second *Olympian*, where salvation of some kind is promised to those who "keep the ψυχή from unjust acts."[9] A more rigorous application of this belief is attributed to the Pythagoreans as a consequence of the doctrine of metempsychosis, and it has seemed reasonable to many scholars to make such influence decisive for the history of ψυχή.[10] That Presocratic natural philosophy contributed to the development of ψυχή through epistemological speculation—a claim obviously true in some sense—is also widely accepted, and in the case of Heraclitus is well supported by

---

7. He asserts, for example (pp. 294–95), that Dionysian worship had "nothing whatever to do with morality or with what we should call the voice of conscience" and that this omission was filled by Orphism, which held that the "height of morality is the turning again towards god," that the soul is confined in the body in expiation of its "guilt," and that an etiological explanation of man's dual nature of good and evil is to be found in the myth of the sufferings of Dionysus (pp. 341–43). It is clear enough that in examining Greek doctrines of immortality Rohde felt he was thereby describing how a universally shared conception of the human psychological life began to have deeper significance for the Greeks by acquiring connotations of immortality and divinity.

8. Snell (1953), pp. 16–17; cf. Guthrie (1952), p. 3; Jaeger (1947), p. 72; Nilsson (1941), pp. 1–16.

9. Pi. O. 2.68–70.

10. Dodds, p. 139; Furley, p. 11; Snell (1953), chap. 1, n. 21; Long, p. 27; Adkins (1970), p. 101; Gulley, p. 196.

actual quotations. Some of these are distressingly enigmatic, but others are less so. In B 107, an example of the latter, Heraclitus appears to regard the ψυχή as the mental agent responsible for interpreting the information received through the senses:[11] "The eyes and ears are bad witnesses for men if they have barbarian ψυχαί." Sources outside religion and philosophical doctrine have also been suggested for the development of ψυχή. One recent study, which tries to place the idea of the self or soul in the changing sociology of archaic Greece, takes the view that by the fifth century the general climate of individuality was so compelling that a comprehensive idea of personality was inevitable, and this need simply seized upon ψυχή.[12] Finally, explanations of a purely linguistic nature have been proposed. The use of the word in early Greek lyric poetry in contexts like that of Hipponax 39 (κακοῖσι δώσω τὴν πολύστονον ψυχήν), which in contrast to Homeric practice implies that the word has acquired psychological value of some kind, is attributed to the post-Homeric analogy of ψυχή to θυμός.[13] Another view, less probable but still influential, is that the increase in psychological uses of ψυχή in later Greek tragedy—some examples of which, like Orestes 1180 (ἐπεὶ τὸ συνετόν γ' οἶδα σῇ ψυχῇ παρόν), may entail an explicit sense of rationality—results from the evolution of periphrastic constructions[14] and from an analogy occurring in the fifth century between ψυχή and other soul words having both a specific organic identity and a manifest role in the conscious psychological life.[15]

Each of these arguments has its perils. What we know of actual semantic value about the use of ψυχή in Orphic and Pythagorean contexts is pitifully small and easily subject to misinterpretation. A case in point is fragment B 7 of Xenophanes, a text containing one of the few possibly

---

11. Snell (1953), p. 17; (1969), p. 19; Regenbogen, p. 395; Gigon (1945), pp. 230–31; Kirk-Raven, p. 206; Reinhardt (1959), p. 201; cf. Vlastos (1955), p. 364.

12. Adkins (1970), p. 66.

13. Harrison, p. 77; Warden, p. 103.

14. Meissner, p. 64: "Indem dabei die ψυχή als das Wesentliche des lebenden Menschen angesehen wird, ist sie auch Träger seiner Eigenschaften. Dadurch wird ψυχή geeignet, einen zusammenfassenden Oberbegriff für eine Mehrzahl von Einzelbestimmungen dieses Bereiches zu bezeichnen."

15. Ibid., pp. 65–68. Meissner singles out the highly anomalous phrase at Pindar P. 4.122 ἂν περὶ ψυχὰν ἐπεὶ γάθησεν to document the early assimilation of ψυχή to organic status, and then proposes that ψυχή supplants other such organs of consciousness. He proposes further that the distinction between organic and non-organic words begins to break down in Euripides, with the result that ψυχή can be used almost interchangeably with καρδία. Although the role of ψυχή is largely limited, by this process, to emotional activities, instances of intellectual activity appear in the Orestes quotation, Troades 1171 (ἰδὼν μὲν γνούς τε σῇ ψυχῇ), and Bacchae 1268 (τὸ δὲ πτοηθὲν τόδ' ἔτι σῇ ψυχῇ πάρα;), and they show the development of ψυχή into a "psychischen Gesamtkomplex" (pp. 67–68).

authentic contemporary references to the use of the word ψυχή by the Pythagoreans. Someone, presumably Pythagoras, demands that a stop be put to the beating of a dog, since he has recognized that the voice of the dog belongs to the ψυχή of a friend: ἐπεὶ ἦ φίλου ἀνέρος ἐστιν / ψυχή, τὴν ἔγνων φθεγξαμένης ἀίων. These lines have been taken to show that for the Pythagoreans the ψυχή is personal and able to feel pain, and it must, therefore, "include all the functions of the personality." [16] But one can draw that conclusion only by making a deduction from the logic of metempsychosis, not from anything said explicitly in the text of Xenophanes. The fragment does show that Xenophanes knew about metempsychosis, but it is frankly absurd to imagine that we can penetrate its satirical style to find the actual substance or language of an underlying philosophical or religious doctrine. We cannot even know for a fact that an early Pythagorean initiate would himself refer to his transmigrating soul as a ψυχή. Whatever nomenclature the Pythagoreans adopted, the odds are that the ordinary Greeks to whom Xenophanes addressed himself in the fragment would think of the transmigrating soul as a version, however distorted, of the Homeric 'shade', the only entity that to their knowledge recurs after death as an identifiable remnant of its former self. They, and Xenophanes, could scarcely call this creation of Pythagoras anything other than a ψυχή. It follows, therefore, that although the fragment may depend on Pythagorean usage, it cannot be taken to prove such usage.

The secular explanations proposed for the development of ψυχή, on the other hand, are complicated more often by problems of meaning than by simple lack of evidence. The uses of ψυχή in Heraclitus and, occasionally, elsewhere in the Presocratics (I will pass over for the moment Democritus, whose treatment of ψυχή is perhaps different) regularly present difficult questions of interpretation. In the case of Heraclitus it is not enough simply to know that intelligence is in some way dependent on the condition of the soul; it is also important to understand what role, if any, the connection between ψυχή and the mental life has in Heraclitus' thought in general, and equally important, to know how to reconcile the psychological fragments on ψυχή with those that apparently have no such value but refer to physical animation. Since even Plato seems to avoid ambiguity between psychological and 'life' functions of soul until the middle dialogues, and since the same separation of meanings is observed in other texts of the Presocratics, this last point is by no means unimportant and calls for close scrutiny of the texts in question. Finally, the view that changes in

16. Furley, p. 11.

ψυχή took place in an ideological vacuum and can be traced to sheer linguistic analogy seems questionable for a word so charged with cultural significance. Such analogies, at any rate, must be tested for common sense as well as technical feasibility. A word like ψυχή obviously presents unusual problems for linguistic analysis, since it is certain to be sensitive to whatever ideologies, stated or not, exist in the mind of the speaker or writer about the soul.

As these studies make clear, any examination of the early use and meaning of ψυχή necessitates choosing among very different methods of analysis and types of evidence. No one approach will meet every argument. Certain omissions in the discussion that follows are, therefore, intentional. I have not attempted to place the study of ψυχή in an account of the development of Greek epistemological ideas, to provide anthropological or sociological comparisons and background materials, to discuss questions of religious belief in general, or, finally, to make my investigations an exercise in semantic theory. I have instead followed the plan of Burnet's famous essay on ψυχή, first published in 1916 under the somewhat optimistic title "The Socratic Doctrine of the Soul," [17] a work that was, in fact, the earliest response to the semantic problems raised by Rohde. With evidence drawn from a considerable misreading of Rohde, Burnet tried to show that no use of ψυχή before the end of the fifth century could be construed as having anything to do with rational knowledge or the conscious personality.[18] From the study of selected examples he was led to conclude that the designation of the ψυχή as self had come into being ex nihilo from the brain of Socrates—a result not unconnected, one suspects, to the high value placed on inventive genius in Burnet's own culture. But for all its flaws in execution this early essay remains a model for the study of ψυχή in its sensible appreciation of the questions to be probed and evidence to be consulted. How, Burnet asked, do the surviving uses of ψυχή in the documentary record accord with the belief that a gradual change in the Greek idea of the self, whatever its origins, occurred before Plato? The

17. Burnet (1916), pp. 235–59.
18. Whereas Rohde explicitly believed that ψυχή in the language of Greek philosophy and the poets expressed "the whole psychical content of the human individual ... from the fifth century onwards" and that only certain religious philosophers and poets "continued to use the word in its ancient and primitive sense," Burnet attempted to show that down to the end of the fifth century virtually all uses of ψυχή belonged to what he imagined to be the psychological life of the Doppelgänger. The activities of ψυχή thus have for him "affinity with the dream-consciousness"; it is the seat of "anxiety and depression," "strange, overmastering passion," but never "clear perception or knowledge, or even ... articulate emotion." He concludes, "it is still, therefore, the 'double' of primitive belief" (pp. 252–34).

directness of this plan has appealed to many of Burnet's readers over the years, and it accounts for the work undertaken here in the sense that I have tried to reexamine the meaning and development of ψυχή along the lines that Burnet set out but then pursued all too briefly.

In the following pages, then, my chief effort will be to categorize and discuss all important occurrences of ψυχή from Homer through the early dialogues of Plato. In addition, by comparing ψυχή with the seven other words that, along with it, denote human psychological agents of some kind in archaic Greek—θυμός, μένος, ἦτορ, κῆρ, κραδίη, φρήν/φρένες, and νόος— I will try to construct a general model of shared patterns of usage against which the meaning of ψυχή itself can be analyzed. How successful these comparisons are is for the reader to judge. They have led me on the whole to reject the orthodox analysis of these words by means of etymology and identification with specific physical organs and to doubt the widespread interpretation of human life in Homer as a field, so to speak, on which a variety of physical and mental organs compete with one another.[19] What is striking in both the archaic and classical periods, in my view, is the centrality and subtlety of those usages of ψυχή that focus on the notion of 'life-force'. I do not wish to imply, as Burnet does, that usages of ψυχή which might anticipate the qualities of the soul found in Plato never occurred earlier on. My point is, rather, that when ψυχή finally begins to appear in contexts giving it a new moral importance and suggesting that it is properly responsive to rationality, such occurrences are still intimately connected to the earlier connotations of ψυχή as 'life-force'.

One last point must be added by way of introduction. A measure of the difficulty encountered in defining the 'soul' words is the lack of appropriate language with which to describe usages we instinctively call "emotional" or "psychological"; such terms assume in themselves a natural separation of mind and body, if not the existence of a true dualism. When, for lack of better terms, I refer throughout to "psychological," "emotional," and "physical" meanings of these words, I am attempting to define, from a modern perspective, tensions that exist within the Greek words for 'soul'. To the archaic Greek speaker such distinctions are not possible, and it is that phenomenon, in essence, to which this study is addressed.

---

19. Snell (1953), chap. 1; Dodds, chap. 1; Harrison, pp. 63ff.; Fränkel (1962), pp. 85–89.

PART I:

The Homeric 'Soul' Words Other than ψυχή and Their Development

I

Patterns of Meaning Common to the Homeric 'Soul' Words

The problems of method and interpretation presented by the Homeric 'soul' words can be illustrated succinctly by the related word αἰών, even though αἰών is never itself a psychological agent. Since αἰών also offers some specific points of comparison to the other words, I shall begin with a brief account of its meanings.

The use of αἰών as 'life' can be shown by the following contexts. Its loss or destruction accounts for death in

> (1) λίπῃ ψυχή τε καὶ αἰών (Il. 16.453)
> (2) ἐκ δ' αἰὼν πέφαται—κατὰ δὲ χρόα πάντα σαπήῃ (Il. 19.27).[1]

It is 'life' in a seemingly more temporal sense in

> (3) μινυνθάδιος δέ οἱ αἰὼν / ἔπλετο (Il. 17.302)
> (4) ἐπὶ δηρὸν δέ μοι αἰὼν / ἔσσεται (Il. 9.415)
> (5) ἄνερ, ἀπ' αἰῶνος νέος ὤλεο (Il. 24.725).

It is used as 'life' in emotional contexts, although not as an emotional agent itself, in

> (6) κατείβετο δὲ γλυκὺς αἰὼν / νόστον ὀδυρομένῳ (Od. 5.152)
> (7) μηδέ τοι αἰὼν / φθινέτω (Od. 5.160).[2]

Finally, in the post-Homeric *Hymn to Hermes* (line 42) the phrase

> (8) αἰῶν' ἐξετόρησεν ... χελώνης[3]

---

1. Also Il. 22.58, 5.685; Od. 7.224.
2. Also Od. 18.204.
3. Also line 119 ἐγκλίνων δ'ἐκύλινδε δι' αἰῶνος τετορήσας.

has a specific physical denotation commonly taken to be 'marrow', on the basis of external evidence[4] and a gloss in Hesychius.[5] Only in post-Homeric usage is αἰών attested (appropriately enough in view of its etymological connection with αἰεί) with the meaning 'lifetime', as in line 6 in the *Hymn to Hephaestus* (αἰῶνα διάγουσιν) and *Eumenides* 315 (αἰῶνα διοιχνεῖ).

The issue raised by αἰών is clear enough. If we analyze its Homeric occurrences alone, we find that they suggest nothing more than 'life-force' in a not very precisely defined sense. 'Life-force' is wholly satisfactory in (1) and (2), even obligatory in the latter. Close inspection of (3), (4), and (5)—passages that seem to imply time—suggests a development along the lines of 'maturity' or 'period of maturity' in which the 'life-force' is strong, particularly since such statements seem limited to warriors in their prime.[6] Passages (6) and (7) can be either literal or metaphorical ways of linking this 'life-force' to emotional expressions, and there is no objective way to judge how literally they should be taken. Thus, although αἰών as it is used in (8) is obviously able to combine 'life' or 'life-force' in some sense with a specific bodily material or organ, an unbiased reading of the evidence should inhibit the natural tendency to treat the relatively abstract or intangible meaning as acquired and the explicit bodily reference of αἰών as original. On this evidence alone, the concrete manifestation of αἰών as 'marrow' appears to be secondary to the intangible sense of 'life-force' both chronologically and in importance.

That we should hesitate before treating 'life-force' as merely an inferred meaning of αἰών is confirmed by its etymology, since αἰών is derived from a root signifying 'vitality' or 'vital force of animated beings'.[7] The root meaning is clearly present in Homeric αἰόλος ('nimble' and 'changeful of hue') and αἰόλλειν ('to shift rapidly to and fro').[8] To state the problem simply, αἰών shows that Greek words centering on the idea of 'life' or 'life-force' cannot be predictably rationalized into early and relat-

---

4. Pi. fr. 111.5 and Hipp. *Epid.* VII.122.

5. αἰών· ὁ ἐν παντὶ τῷ σώματι μυελός.

6. Benveniste (1937), p. 108. The statement of Achilles at *Il.* 9.415 (that he will enjoy his αἰών in his old age in Phthia) weakens this argument. But the IE cognates (see following note)—Lat. *iuvenis*, Goth. *juggs*, Skt. *yuvan*—favor the notion of a period of vigor.

7. Ibid., pp. 104ff. "L'accord de l'Iranien et du Védique nous livre donc, dans *āyu (*yu) un terme chargé d'une signification concrète et humaine, la 'force de vie' qui se réalise dans l'accomplisse-ment de l'existence humaine mais qui est à l'origine independente de sa durée" (p. 107). These cognates ἀεί, *aevum*]. That the meaning 'marrow' or 'fluid' could arise out of a supposed primitive Degani objects (p. 40) to the separation of the temporal and nontemporal values on anthropological, but not linguistic, grounds. Cf. Treu, pp. 2–4.

8. Benveniste (1937), p. 107.

ively concrete meanings as opposed to late and relatively abstract meanings. Nevertheless, because *aἰών* is 'shed' in (6), Onians asserts that it
"connotes liquid in relation to the body," in this case tears but elsewhere
cerebrospinal fluid. The original meaning of *aἰών* is thus taken to have been
'life-fluid', from which, by gradual transition, it became that which the
fluid contains and represents, or 'life'.[9]

The difficulty with this apparently logical interpretation is not hard to
see. It is, of course, possible that for Homeric speakers *aἰών* brought to
mind vivid images of bodily fluid and marrow, but from the etymology
we must recognize that for a certain period in the history of Indo-European
or Proto-Greek it very likely did not, and that the time of transition to the
supposed Homeric meaning cannot be identified. Direct proof must be
supplied, therefore, by the Homeric texts themselves to show that *aἰών* has
in them a specific, consistent bodily identity and that it is not, as its uses
otherwise suggest, a term expressing 'life-force' as a self-sufficient idea.

The assumption of this study, accordingly, is that words like *aἰών* and
some or all of the traditional Greek 'soul' words—*ψυχή, θυμός, μένος, ἦτορ,
κῆρ, κραδίη, νόος, φρήν/φρένες*—are culturally idiosyncratic expressions
that cannot be understood apart from their historical setting. Such words,
like all religious, psychological, and moral terminology used in popular
speech, defy precise translation because we are in some measure bound to
be ignorant of the implicit attitudes and ideas that shape them.[10] In the case
of the 'soul' words, an "organic" model of the psychological life has
dominated efforts to interpret and translate from archaic Greek to modern
sensibilities. This has seemed natural enough, given the suggestiveness of
several of the etymologies, the Homeric and later use of *κραδίη/καρδία* as
the anatomical 'heart', and the unusually large number of words used in the
Homeric language to designate psychological agents, some of which do,
from time to time, appear to refer to a distinct physical organ or process.
That the apparent organic references must be taken as the underlying literal
value of these terms is in fact the explicit thesis of the two systematic studies
of the archaic 'soul' words published to date, that of Böhme in the late

9. Onians, pp. 208–09; "It fits the original sense of fluid for *aἰών* that unlike *ψυχή* and *θυμός* it is
not said to leave the body in a swoon or go to Hades. It flows away in tears. The unmistakable use of
aἰών for 'spinal marrow' has been regarded as later and derivative [i.e., arguing from the temporal
cognates *ἀεί, aevum*]. That the meaning 'marrow' or 'fluid' could arise out of a supposed primitive
meaning 'period of existence' is difficult to believe, and in fact, as we see, the earliest evidence lends no
support to the latter meaning. On the other hand it is not difficult to see how a word designating the life
'fluid' might come to mean the life which the fluid represents and so the life temporally considered, the
lifetime dependent upon it."

10. See the lucid and engaging discussion of this point in Evans-Pritchard, pp. 11–14.

1920s[11] and the more recent, massively documented work of Onians.[12] Less dogmatic positions have been taken by others, notably Snell, who evidently sees the 'soul' words as agents that function more by analogy to the visible organs of the body than as organs themselves. Nevertheless, it is fair to say that no objection to the "organic" model has been seriously or systematically put forward. Since this model of the mental and emotional life implies a largely disunified conception of personality, one vulnerable to transformation by almost any less concrete and atomistic representation, its accuracy is a matter of some importance.[13]

I see no compelling reason to accept this theory. At some earlier level in the development of the language, specific physical processes and organs may well have been identified as emotional or mental agents. Yet in the Homeric texts themselves there is little evidence for the active retention of

11. Böhme incorporated into his work, as Snell correctly pointed out in his review (Snell [1932], pp. 16ff.), a simplistic attempt to separate emotional and physical functions of the organs and agents that he examined, by assuming the Greeks themselves recognized such distinctions.

12. According to Onians (p. 49), if the φρένες are, as he believes, the lungs, the θυμός must be the breath, since consciousness is "naturally identified with the breath not only because to be conscious is to have breath, but also because the breathing is affected when there is violent emotion, and not only the breathing but the flow of blood. There is pulsation with flushing or pallor." This interpretation, however, is countered by more psychophysical language, e.g. (p. 51), "At the stage of thought when these beliefs emerged *there was difficulty in conceiving anything except material entities* [italics mine]. μένος is apparently not an abstraction or a mere state of something else, but conceived as itself something, either fluid or gaseous, which for convenience we may translate as 'energy' and which was inwardly felt much as we feel what we so name." See also pp. 52–53: "The association of the emotion with the breathing may seem strange to us, since we are in the habit of abstracting the emotion itself from its bodily expressions and thinking that the latter are *epiphenomena* or after-effects." But this awareness does not prevent constant reduction to concrete physical ideas, for example, the speculation on p. 81 that ἦτορ might mean the bronchial tubes and aorta, and the insistence (chap. 2) that the φρένες are the lungs; elsewhere, they too are the bronchial tubes. For an extensive and judicious criticism of Onians on more general grounds, see Bayet (1952).

13. Snell's argument (1953), p. 8, is especially pertinent: "There is, therefore, a gap in the Homeric terminology for soul comparable to the deficiency in physical terminology.... As before, the gap is filled with a number of words which do not possess the same centre of gravity as the modern terms, but which cover more or less the same area." In a sense this faults the Homeric terminology for failing to achieve a dualistic idea of the self at the same time that it interprets the language in terms of one. Snell's treatment of the 'soul' words as organs only in a metaphorical sense is judicious and avoids the specious rationalizations of Onians. But it leads nonetheless to a model of the person in which the physical significance of the 'soul' words is construed in so rudimentary a way that semantic development can be seen in any usage not compatible with the occupation of physical space. Thus (p. 17), he sees a clear development in the meaning of ψυχή in fragment B 45 of Heraclitus, since it is now "endowed with qualities which differ radically from those of the body and the physical organs," and to say "that someone has a deep hand or a deep ear is nonsensical." Snell's point that only in Heraclitus and the lyric poets is "intensity" of psychological experience described (p. 19: "intensity, the proper dimension of the spiritual, receives no attention in Homer") is at odds with the constant referral of the 'life-force' words in Homer to waxing and waning of energy.

consistent physical referents for these words, or for the differentiation of function suitable to bodily organs. In fact, the etymologies in question are often vague or impossible to interpret in the light of Homeric usage,[14] the physical referents are not, on the whole, either precise or self-consistent, and the mental and emotional functions in question are not easily distinguishable from word to word. It should also be a source of some caution that this organic model obviously satisfies the instinctive feeling, evident in the interpretation of *αἰών* given by Onians and pervasive in earlier anthropology, that any evolutionary pattern of this kind ought to move from simpler to more complicated ideas, from naive concreteness to sophisticated abstraction.

In order to make as empirical a study as possible of the meanings of these culturally bound words, it therefore seems reasonable to ask not what their antecedents might have been, or how we ought to identify them against a standing assumption that they are literal or figurative organs or processes of the body. We must ask, rather, what ideas best explain without preconception substantial numbers of unselected examples of the words as they are used in Homer. In contrast to the "organic" model, I propose to show that apart from *κραδίη* and *ψυχή* all Homeric 'soul' words can be explained as designating one of three things:

(1) a concrete, contextually determined 'thought' (or 'thoughts'), usually, but not always, immediate and temporary in nature;
(2) a force or energy on which the 'life' of a man depends;
(3) personifications of (1) and (2).

These categories are, of course, reductive in their way; but I believe they offer, on balance, a more satisfactory explanation of the Homeric evidence

---

14. *καρδία/κραδίη* is the only 'soul' word that has a common, specific anatomical value in the Indo-European languages (PIE *kērd/[kr̥d]; cf. Lat. *cordis*, Lith. *širdis*, OHG *herza*, etc., although it must be pointed out that many of the cognates have the meaning 'core', or 'marrow'). Even *καρδία* becomes vague or transformed in archaic and classical Greek, e.g., Thuc. 2.49, where it means 'stomach', and Archil. 114.4, *καρδίης πλέως*; but in light of its use as a tangible object at *Il.* 13.442 and the consistency with which its contexts suggest the palpable, beating 'heart', *καρδία* is properly regarded as a manifest organ of the body. Nevertheless, most usages are predominantly psychological and not physical per se. Etymologies for the other words give no obvious or precise physiological values. Since *καρδία* denominates the 'heart' as a physical object, *κῆρ* was able to acquire other connotations and, indeed, is likely to have survived in importance in Homeric usage by doing so. *θυμός* is cognate with Skt. *dhūma*-, Lat. *fumus*, (cf. Gr. *θυμιάω*), and presumes PIE *dhūmos*; it is customary (see Frisk) to assume a development from 'smoke' to 'breath' and the 'spirit'. (Chantraine Compares *θύω* on semantic grounds). *μένος* is cognate with Skt. mánas, 'spirit', from PIE *menos. Cognates of *ἦτορ* are OHG *ādara*, 'vein'; MHG *āder*, 'vein', pl. 'intestines'; OIr *inathar*, 'intestines' (references from Frisk).

as we have it than do any others. I must stress that I am not proposing that
these words exhibited similar meanings or a common pattern of development before Homer, or that they are precisely equivalent in meaning in
Homer. What I hope to show is that the chief emotional agents could not
be thought of in Homer apart from some feeling that the 'life' of a man was
dependent upon their activities, and that intellectual agents could not be
imagined without constant ambiguity with contextually determined
'thought'. These associations, further, largely determine the manner in
which the self can be imagined and expressed in early Greek, and they are
not accounted for by the "organic" model. Whatever the original differences in usage, and whatever the exact meanings of all these words in
pre-Homeric Greek, there has occurred, I suggest, by the time of the
composition of the Homeric texts, so much analogizing around these
implicit core meanings that it is the relationship of the words to those
meanings and only that relationship which determines their development
after Homer. In addition, the pattern identified by this hypothesis can be
used to account for the nature, development, and spread of ψυχή in popular
usage after Homer.

Of the 'soul' words that express the two types of underlying semantic
categories to be examined, those centering on contextual 'thought' or
'thoughts' are easier to deal with, and I shall treat them briefly before
turning to the 'life-force' words. Moreover, the 'thought' words—νόος
and φρήν/φρένες—are essential for the pattern of the group as a whole and
in any case have also been incorporated into the "organic" model of the
mental and emotional life in Homer—νόος only by analogy as an
imaginary organ of mental attention and intention,[15] but the φρένες
directly as 'lungs' or 'diaphragm'.

Von Fritz has correctly observed the strong tendency in Homer to use
φρήν/φρένες and, to a lesser extent, νόος when the results of the mental
activity in question are immediately discernible.[16] A more productive way
to put this point for our purposes is to say that it is often impossible to
decide whether either of these words denotes an autonomous psychological agent ('that which thinks') or the function of such an agent (the
'thought').[17] This ambiguity of agent and function and the correspond-
ingly close bonding to context can be seen in the case of φρήν/φρένες, for
example, when the singular φρήν is used to indicate a single manifest
thought or purpose. Thus, at *Iliad* 12.173 the φρένα Διός cannot be per-

15. Snell (1953), p. 13.
16. Von Fritz (1943), p. 229. The importance of φρήν/φρένες, like that of θυμός, is perhaps,
overestimated thanks to its frequency. See Harrison, pp. 74–75.
17. Examples discussed are from *Il.* 1–12 and *Od.* 1–12.

suaded once it has decided to give glory to Hector, and it becomes virtually synonymous with the concrete βουλή of Zeus in *Iliad* 1.5.[18] Unlike κατὰ θυμόν, which by itself (see below, p. 39) seems in certain contexts to designate imagination or silent knowledge as a form of personified exchange between the individual and his θυμός, κατὰ φρένα is used with verbs such as δείδειν, ὁρμαίνειν, and μερμηρίζειν (Achilles at *Iliad* 9.244 fears κατὰ φρένα lest the gods accomplish Hector's boast for him) to imply the process of looking ahead or failing to look ahead to the likely outcome of a given situation.[19] Close identification with an immediate and specific outcome also occurs in all but two instances[20] of κατὰ φρένα καὶ κατὰ θυμόν, since in every case there is an attempt to decide between two courses of action.[21]

As for plural uses, particularly the dative φρεσί by itself or with prepositions, it is equally hard to distinguish between result-oriented 'thought' or 'thoughts' and the subject or agent that can be supposed to contain or generate such thought. This ambiguity is evident in the use of φρεσί[22] in passages concerned with that by which or within which plans or contrivances for an immediate situation are to be discovered; at *Iliad* 9.423, for example, the ambassadors to Achilles are instructed to report his words to the other Achaeans so that they may devise in their φρένες a better plan to deal with their predicament (ἐνὶ φρεσὶ μῆτιν ἀμείνω). But examination of context suggests that the ambiguity of agent and function is present also where immediate purpose is less clearly at issue[23] and where thoughts of a moral character are intended, as when Athena complains to Zeus that a sceptered king should not know just things (*Od.* 5.9 φρεσὶν αἴσιμα εἰδώς), if his people are to be as forgetful of him as the Ithacans are of Odysseus.[24] Less clearly, 'thoughts' regularly directed toward a particular object may be felt as thoughts of a persistent nature (almost always in the nominative

---

18. Also, *Il.* 10.45, 46.

19. *Il.* 1.555, 2.3, 5.406, 9.244, 10.507, 538.

20. *Il.* 4.163 (= 6.447); *Od.* 4.813.

21. *Il.* 1.193, 297, 4.117, 120, 5.671, 8.169; *Od.* 4.117, 120, 5.365, 424, 6.118, 10.151.

22. *Il.* 1.55, 6.61 (= 7.120 [φρένας]), 8.218, 9.423, 434, 596, 11.793; *Od.* 1.42, 89, 427, 444, 2.363, 3.26, 132, 151, 4.632, 676, 739, 777, 843, 5.427, 8.273, 9.419, 11.146, 454, 474.

23. *Il.* 1.107, 297 (= 9.611), 4.39, 5.259, 8.366, 10.237, 11.89 ('thoughts' directed to action); 2.241, 3.45, 4.245 (same, but with ἀλκή or βίη); 2.33, 70, 301 ('thoughts' dwelt on for sustained motivation); 9.313, 10.4 (intention?); 1.333, 8.446 (recognition, not action); *Od.* 2.34, 4.729, 10.438, 557, 11.428 ('thoughts' directed to action); 6.180, 10.533 (same, but with the action undefined); 1.322, 3.76, 6.140 (same, with θάρσος and μένος); 4.825, 5.206 ('thoughts' dwelt on for sustained motivation); 1.328, 7.208 (recognition, not action); 1.115 (imagination [?], but perhaps 'thoughts' dwelt on' as above); 7.218, 219, 8.154, 11.195 (πένθος and κήδεα in 'thoughts' dwelt on').

24. *Il.* 1.342, 2.213, 5.326, 8.360 (specific, not general), 9.119; *Od.* 2.231, 3.266, 5.9, 8.240, 11.337, 367, 445.

and accusative plural)²⁵ and thus become the 'wits' of men that account for characteristic skill or craft²⁶ (*Od.* 2.117: Penelope knows fair handicrafts, cunning, and φρένας ἐσθλάς). Alternatively, the φρένες are 'thoughts' that account for the ability to act capably or reliably in general, and so account for foolish behavior by their absence²⁷ or removal (*Il.* 9.377 ἐκ γάρ εὖ φρένας εἵλετο μητίετα Ζεύς); and they are 'thoughts' that describe a man's power of reason as it becomes manifest²⁸ (*Od.* 10.493: the φρένες of Teiresias are still ἔμπεδοι, as Odysseus will be able to judge for himself when Teiresias speaks). Although these instances do not justify in themselves the view that the φρένες cannot be felt as persistent entities apart from the thoughts that they generate, the use of φρένες to designate characteristic skill or craft—a usage to which the last examples also seem related—can be compared directly with the doublet νοήματα καὶ φρένας in a context (*Od.* 8.559 ἀλλ' αὐταὶ ἴσασι νοήματα καὶ φρένας ἀνδρῶν, of the Phaeacian ships) in which there can be no doubt about the objective quality of νοήματα.

It is important, therefore, that of a sample of 147 instances of φρήν/φρένες (*Iliad* and *Odyssey* 1–12) only twenty-five are not ambiguous with 'thought', 'thoughts', or 'wits' as described. Of these exceptional occurrences four²⁹ are anatomical (three of these are imprecise and ambiguously emotional), four³⁰ place the θυμός or ἦτορ in the φρένες, one³¹ describes the return of consciousness to the φρήν after syncope, and four are anomalous.³² Of the remaining twelve uses of φρήν/φρένες only two are not in the singular,³³ and of the ten other passages six³⁴ describe dis-

----

25. The exception is *Od.* 8.556.

26. *Il.* 1.115; *Od.* 2.117, 4.264, 7.111, 8.168, 448, 556.

27. *Il.* 3.442, 6.237, 7.360.

28. *Il.* 4.104, 5.493 (ambiguous with 'thoughts' directed to action); 3.108, 6.352 (mental powers and intention?); 1.362, 6.355, 8.124, 316 (ἄχος, πόνος, πένθος affect the φρένες); *Od.* 10.493 (mental powers), 8.541 (ἄχος).

29. *Il.* 1.103, 10.10; *Od.* 4.661, 9.301.

30. *Il.* 8.202, 413, 9.232, 458.

31. *Od.* 5.458.

32. *Il.* 9.184: Odysseus and the others hope to persuade the μεγάλας φρένας of Achilles; *Il.* 10.139: the voice of Nestor reaches περὶ φρένας of Odysseus as he awakens; *Od.* 6.65: Nausicaa says that the provision of clothing is a care ἐμῇ φρενί, a passage that may simply indicate 'intention' but tends to characterize φρήν as a general psychological entity without a specific function; *Od.* 7.327: Odysseus will know ἐνὶ φρεσί that the ships of Alcinous are the best.

33. φρένες. *Od.* 1.328: Penelope in her chamber hears φρεσί the song of the minstrel; 11.337: Arete asks the Phaeacians how Odysseus seems to them εἶδός τε μέγεθός τε ἰδὲ φρένας ἔνδον ἐίσας; φρήν: *Il.* 1.474, 6.285, 481, 8.559, 9.186, 11.683; *Od.* 4.102, 6.106, 147, 8.131.

34. Those which do not do so are *Il.* 6.285: the φρήν of Hector would forget its sorrow if Paris died; 6.481: the mother rejoices φρένα when a victorious son comes home; *Od.* 4.102: Menelaus delights (τέρπομαι) his φρήν with weeping; 6.147: Odysseus fears that Penelope will be angry φρένα if he embraces her.

passionate pleasure of the sort that may be derived, for example, from music—a usage which significantly distinguishes φρήν from the 'life-force' words when it acts as an emotional agent not readily connected with 'thoughts'. Of the 122 instances that can be regarded as ambiguous with 'thought', fifteen[35] clearly tend to characterize φρήν/φρένες as a persistent entity by the generality of their contexts or by making φρήν/φρένες the subject of emotional states like πόνος and ἄχος, but even these are interpretable as 'thoughts'. This strong ambiguity between agent and function must be seen, therefore, as decisively weakening the ability of φρήν/φρένες to be perceived as an autonomous *source* of thought and emotion, and thus as something denoting the self of the man as a whole. As a result, it is understandable that the words φρήν and φρένες occupy the strongly personifying subject position only nine times in the twenty-four books of Homer taken as a sample (φρήν once, the rest φρένες), a position typical for most of the other 'soul' words.

The usages of νόος are almost identical in scope to those of φρήν/φρένες and are comparable in detail. Like φρήν/φρένες, νόος can regularly be that in which a thought is conceived or the 'thought' itself, as von Fritz[36] observes. It can be a distinct plan or intent, as exhibited by its frequent doubleting with βουλή and by its attribution to Zeus (cf. φρένα Διός).[37] It can be used, like φρένες, with ἔμπεδος to describe the persistence of simple mental activity.[38] It can be that aspect of men 'known' by the traveler.[39] It diverges significantly from φρήν/φρένες only when, as a pure function devoid of all ambiguity with its role as a psychological agent, it undergoes specialization into something akin to 'reason' (*Il.* 20.133 Ἥρη, μὴ χαλέπαινε παρὲκ νόον: Hera is told by Poseidon not to be angry beyond reason).

With this exception, there is virtually no contextual usage of νόος not available to φρήν/φρένες, nor are there any of φρήν/φρένες, other than those of an anatomical character (whether actual or metaphorical), from which νόος is excluded. But the impressions conveyed by the two words are very different. Unlike φρήν/φρένες, νόος regularly takes a subject position in the manner of θυμός, κῆρ, and ἦτορ, and this accounts for approximately half its

35. *Il.* 1.333, 362, 4.163 (= 6.447), 6.355, 8.124, 316, 446; *Od.* 1.151, 4.813, 5.74, 7.208, 8.368, 556, 10.48.

36. Von Fritz (1943), pp. 81ff.

37. Doublet with βουλή: *Od.* 2.281, 3.128, 4.267, 11.177, 12.211, 13.305, 16.374; with μῆτις: *Il.* 7.447, 15.509, *Od.* 19.326; νόος Διός: *Il.* 8.143, 14.160, 15.242, 461, 16.103, 688, 17.176, 546; *Od.* 5.103, 137, 24.164.

38. *Il.* 11.813, *Od.* 10.240; cf. ἐναίσιμος at *Od.* 5.190.

39. *Od.* 1.3; cf. 4.493, 21.205; also 6.121, 8.576, 9.176, 13.20.

occurrences,[40] most of which cannot easily be seen as ambiguous with contextually defined 'thought' of the kind just described (e.g., *Od.* 2.92 *νόος μενοινᾷ*; *Od.* 1.347 *νόος ὄρνυται*). It is also, perhaps, more easily characterized as a long-lasting disposition (e.g., *Od.* 18.392, where it is used with *αἰεί*) than is *φρήν/φρένες*. In a spectrum of uses extending from contextually limited function (again, 'thought') to autonomous agent ('mind'), *νόος* is thus more closely identified with the qualities of autonomy and self-containment essential to the latter.

The higher frequency of 'agent' uses for *νόος*, as opposed to *φρήν/φρένες*, raises a problem fundamental to all Homeric 'soul' words. An assumption of the "organic" model of the psychological life, as I have said, is that the ability of *φρήν/φρένες* to act as a psychological agent stems from its supposed anatomical identity, and from the analogy of *αὐχήν* and *σπλήν* it cannot be doubted that in origin *φρήν* was indeed a bodily part.[41] *Νόος*, on the other hand, must be treated etymologically as a *nomen actionis* of the same type as *λόγος* and cannot possibly have its Homeric character accounted for by reference to some original physical identity. However generous an "organic" treatment of these words we assume historically— that thought, perhaps, was once attributed directly by Proto-Greek speakers to the lungs or diaphragm and that *νόος* too became a psychological agent within the context of such ideas—it still follows from the disparity in usage just noted that no correlation exists in Homer between the tendency of the two words to be felt directly or etymologically as bodily organs and their ability to function as psychological agents independent of a limiting context and ambiguity with 'thought' directed to that context. Indeed, if there is a correlation it is the opposite of what the "organic" model leads us to expect. This difference should make us reconsider what it is, not in etymology but in the Homeric mind, that

40. Apart from the usages listed in nn. 37–39, which may perhaps be taken as making it something objective, the occurrences of *νόος* can be broken down as follows. 'Attention' or 'perception of a given situation': *Il.* 15.699, *Od.* 19.42, 479; 'reason' or 'sense': *Il.* 10.391, 20.133 (not ambiguous with agent uses), *Il.* 9.108, 23.604; 'plan' or 'intent': *Il.* 4.309, 9.104, 22.382, 23.149, 24.367, *Od.* 2.124, 4.256, 5.23, 13.255, 14.490, 22.215, 24.479; 'plan', 'intent', or 'seat of intent': *Il.* 15.52, *Od.* 3.147, 7.263, 24.474; 'thought' (moral, judgmental, or contextually limited in some way) or 'seat of thought': *Il.* 1.132, 2.192, 9.514, 10.226?, 12.255, 18.419, 20.25, 22.185, 23.590?, 24.354, *Od.* 1.66, 2.236, 6.320, 10.494, 11.272, 13.229, 16.197, 18.136, 23.77; 'seat of mental activity' or 'wits': *Il.* 11.813, 14.217, 15.129, *Od.* 10.240; 'seat of intelligence or general thought': *Il.* 10.122, 13.732, 14.62, 15.80, 643, 24.358, 377, *Od.* 2.346, 7.73, 8.177, 10.329, 18.332, 392, 20.366; general mental and emotional agent: *Il.* 1.363 (= 16.19), 3.63, 9.554, 16.35, 23.484, *Od.* 1.347, 2.92 (= 13.381), 5.190, 8.7, 18.283, 381. If the last two categories are considered representative of *νόος* as an autonomous agent, more than one in four occurrences of *νόος* falls into this category, as against, roughly, half as many for *φρήν/φρένες*.

41. Chantraine (1933), p. 166.

determines the ability of such words to act as mental agents. Against the view that νόος and φρήν/φρένες are portrayed as they are because of the feeling that they are something inherently tangible and autonomous in the man—actual or analogical organs with a distinctive identity—it can be suggested that they are so treated because something not originally concrete in nature has undergone personification. That the decidedly more intangible νόος is more frequently and freely an autonomous agent in Homeric psychology must raise the possibility that in Homer, at least, it is only as personifications of their psychological functions that νόος and φρήν/φρένες begin to be felt as inner beings of some kind.

If we try not to rationalize naively the history of these words, therefore, but to base our conclusions only on the observed Homeric usages, it is scarcely possible to take φρήν/φρένες as indicating a well-defined interior self still strongly characterized by its anatomical identity—in Böhme's words, as something able to encompass "das Erlebnis der ganzen Menschen, Körper und Seele."[42] The close parallelism with νόος, complete in all respects except the anatomical, and the greater success of νόος as a psychological agent, argue that an idiosyncratic pattern of meaning, independent of any earlier organic roles, has absorbed both words. It is not essential that we describe this pattern as contextual 'thought' and its personification—although that seems to me a reasonable statement of what is observed. But it is essential, surely, that the existence of a shared idiosyncratic pattern be given proper weight in deciding whether Homeric speakers actually assign thought to the lungs and diaphragm when they use φρήν/φρένες in connection with psychological activity.

In addition to ψυχή, four of the Homeric 'soul' words—θυμός, μένος, ἦτορ, κῆρ—can be translated as 'life' in certain contexts, either as 'life destroyed at death' (θυμός, μένος, ἦτορ) or as the 'life' component in a-privative adjectives meaning 'lifeless' (μένος, κῆρ). What I shall attempt to show first is that the pattern of nonpsychological, or physical, 'life' usages established for αἰών (apart from those implying temporality) also applies, with modifications and extensions, to θυμός and the other words and suggests again decidedly idiosyncratic ideas of the physical 'life' that are closely linked to one another. Second, I will argue that the psychological uses of these words can be most successfully explained as direct extensions of these 'life' or 'life-force' contexts.

The centrality of the meaning 'life-force' in a sense comparable to

42. Böhme, p. 9, n. 2.

αἰών can be demonstrated by a survey of uses of the words not instinctively seen by us as psychological. Like αἰών, θυμός regularly 'leaves' the body, with no implication of afterlife survival (*Il.* 4.470), and in so doing may be 'breathed out' (*Il.* 13.654 θυμὸν ἀποπνείων and *Il.* 20.403 θυμὸν ἄϊσθε) or simply cease to animate, without any implication about breath (*Od.* 3.455 λίπε δ᾽ ὀστέα θυμός). It is used with ὀλλύναι (*Il.* 1.205) and is therefore something that may be 'destroyed', if we extend the root meaning of ὀλλύναι to such contexts, but it is not used with λύειν or with more metaphorical notions of destruction like that of the phrase ἐκ δ᾽ αἰὼν πέφαται. Like αἰών, θυμός is frequently used with endearments or with φίλος in the reflexive sense (*Il.* 11.407 φίλος; *Il.* 17.17 μελιηδύς), and in all but one instance (*Od.* 13.40) such uses apply to 'life' as it is found in death contexts, not emotional ones. The notion of 'wasting' or 'waning' in an emotional context occurs at *Odyssey* 19.263 (θυμὸν τῆκε) and *Iliad* 22.242 (ἔνδοθι θυμὸς ἐτείρετο πένθεϊ λυγρῷ). When the θυμός is diminished in quantity, the physical state is directly threatened. Thus, at *Iliad* 1.593 (ὀλίγος ἔτι θυμὸς ἐνῆεν) Hephaestus is either exhausted, nearly dead, or in a faint after his fall from Olympus. Similarly, the θυμός of men who have to row without a wind is worn out (*Od.* 10.78 τείρετο δ᾽ ἀνδρῶν θυμὸς ὑπ᾽ εἰρεσίης ἀλεγεινῆς), as is that of mules straining to move great timbers (*Il.* 17.744). In these cases θυμός obviously implies 'strength', a value contiguous with that of the word in contexts of eating and drinking (*Od.* 5.95 ἤραρε θυμὸν ἐδωδῇ) and in the recovery of consciousness after syncope (*Il.* 22.475 ἐς φρένα θυμὸς ἀγέρθη). The use of θυμός at *Iliad* 16.540, where Hector is accused of being forgetful of his allies, who are wasting their θυμός(θυμὸν ἀποφθινύθουσι), offers a direct parallel to the use of αἰών at *Odyssey* 5.160, quoted above, and shows fruitful ambiguity between the emotional θυμός and the meanings 'strength' and 'life'. Certain evidence of this ambiguity is provided by the compound θυμοφθόρος, which entails either 'death' (*Od.* 2.329 φάρμακα θυμοφθόρα) or suffering (*Od.* 4.716 ἄχος θυμοφθόρον: Penelope on the departure of Telemachus). When described as a concrete physical entity or substance, θυμός is 'breath'-like (*Il.* 21.386 δίχα δέ σφιν ἐνὶ φρεσὶ θυμὸς ἄητο), 'blood'-like, and even 'heart'-like (*Il.* 7.216 θυμὸς ἐνὶ στήθεσσι πάτασσεν). It is located, as these quotations show, in the φρένες and the στήθεα and nowhere else, except for what may be imagined from the phrase λίπε δ᾽ ὀστέα θυμός and the use of the word in a death context with ῥέθη.

The word κῆρ designates physical 'life' only in the compound ἀκήριος (*Il.* 11.392 ὀξὺ βέλος πέλεται καὶ ἀκήριον αἶψα τίθησι: Meriones boasting of his spear). 'Lifelessness' is probably the implication of *Iliad* 21.466, where Apollo speaks of the general fate of mortals as that of 'wasting away' (ἄλλοτε δὲ φθινύθουσιν ἀκήριοι), but other instances of ἀκήριος do not involve mortality, for example, *Iliad* 5.812, where fear makes a man ἀκήριος. κῆρ is also used with φίλος, this time in emotional contexts as opposed to 'life' contexts for θυμός (e.g., *Il.* 14.139 above). It undergoes 'waning' in emotional contexts (*Il.* 1.491 φθινύθεσκε φίλον κῆρ: of Achilles remaining by the ships when he wants to fight), is the seat of desire for food and drink, like θυμός (*Il.* 19.319), and is probably involved in the onset of syncope (*Od.* 5.454 ἀλὶ γὰρ δέδμητο φίλον κῆρ ... ὁ δ' ἄρ' ἄπνευστος καὶ ἄναυδος / κεῖτ' ὀλιγηπελέων, κάματος δέ μιν αἰνὸς ἵκανεν. / ἀλλ' ὅτε δή ῥ' ἔμπνυτο καὶ ἐς φρένα θυμὸς ἀγέρθη: the κῆρ of Odysseus is overcome and his θυμός is restored in the context of exhaustion after swimming to Phaeacia). This instance of syncope caused by physical exhaustion can be compared with ἀχνυμένῳ κῆρ used of a pair of exhausted horses at *Iliad* 23.443, a formula that is psychological in every other context. The κῆρ is located in the φρένες, the στήθεα, and once in the θυμός (*Il.* 6.523), and is usually 'heart'-like. Thus Penelope has sharp cares ἀμφ' ἀδινὸν κῆρ (*Od.* 19.516) and, in an unusually physical passage, Patroclus wounds Sarpedon where the φρένες lie ἀμφ' ἀδινον κῆρ (*Il.* 16.481). An additional nonpsychological usage of κῆρ—shared with μένος and, later, ψυχή—is in periphrasis for the man (*Il.* 14.139 Ἀχιλλῆος ὀλοὸν κῆρ; *Od.* 4.270 Ὀδυσσῆος ... φίλον κῆρ; *Il.* 2.851 Πυλαιμένεος λάσιον κῆρ).

A slightly more comprehensive pattern is exhibited by ἦτορ. It is said to leave the body at death, not with λείπω but ἀΐω[43] (*Il.* 15.252 ἐπεὶ φίλον ἄϊον ἦτορ). Like θυμός and μένος it is used with ὀλλύναι to describe death (*Il.* 5.250 μή πως φίλον ἦτορ ὀλέσσῃς). Usages with λύειν, on the other hand, always signify emotional duress rather than death. The formula λύτο γούνατα καὶ φίλον ἦτορ describes great fear or joy at a moment of extreme crisis (*Od.* 4.703: Penelope hears that Telemachus has gone; *Od.* 23.205: Penelope recognizes the tokens; *Od.* 5.406: Odysseus realizes that he is about to crash on the reef; *Il.* 21.114: Lycaon realizes that Achilles is about to kill him). The absence of λύειν in death contexts is offset somewhat by the use of ἦτορ with δαΐζειν in the phrase δεδαϊγμένον ἦτορ (*Il.* 17.535), if this expression is not entirely metaphorical. As the quotations above show, ἦτορ is frequently used, like θυμός and κῆρ, with φίλος, although in contrast to the usage of θυμός this phrase always occurs in emotional rather than explicit 'life' contexts. Like the other words, ἦτορ is thought to 'wane' or 'decline' under emotional duress. Thus Penelope wastes away in her ἦτορ for Odysseus (*Od.* 19.136 φίλον κατατήκομαι ἦτορ). In the same context in

---

43. On ἀΐω Chantraine follows Eustathius' ἄϊον· τὸ ἀπέπνεον.

which the supplies and μένος of Menelaus and his companions are exhausted by the experience of being marooned, the ἦτορ is also affected and the same ambiguity results: Eidothea tells Menelaus he has been trapped on the island so long that the ἦτορ of his comrades is in decline (Od. 4.374 μινύθει δέ τοι ἦτορ ἑταίρων), and it is not possible to know whether this implies emotional despair or physical weakness resulting from lack of food and sustenance. A less ambiguous physical context is found at Iliad 10.575, where Odysseus and Diomedes refresh the ἦτορ (ἀναψύχειν) by bathing in the sea. Similarly, responsiveness of the ἦτορ to food and drink is indicated at Iliad 19.169, where the ἦτορ of a well-fed man is θαρσαλέον even if he must fight all day, and at Iliad 9.705, where Diomedes instructs the Achaeans to rest after eating (τεταρπόμενοι φίλον ἦτορ / σίτου καὶ οἴνοιο· τὸ γὰρ μένος ἐστὶ καὶ ἀλκή). The ἦτορ is located, like the other words, in the στῆθος at Iliad 22.452 (ἐν δ' ἐμοὶ αὐτῇ / στήθεσι πάλλεται ἦτορ ἀνὰ στόμα), a line in which πάλλεται possibly suggests the 'heart', and this usage may be contrasted with the 'breath' implications of ἀΐω above; the ἦτορ is situated also in the φρένες (Il. 17.111 τοῦ δ' ἐν φρεσὶν ἄλκιμον ἦτορ / παχνοῦται) and, surprisingly, in the κραδίη itself (Il. 20.169 ἐν δέ τέ οἱ κραδίη στένει ἄλκιμον ἦτορ).

Although μένος differs conspicuously from this pattern in one respect, it is paradoxically the easiest of the words to identify as a 'life-force'. This identification is due to its use, unique among the 'soul' words, in nonhuman contexts—a quivering spear whose movement must be stopped by Ares (Il. 13.444), rivers (Il. 12.18), the sun (Il. 23.190), and fire (Il. 6.182). Unless all such usages are taken metaphorically, μένος can scarcely be an explicit part or process of the body. The resulting sense of impersonality explains why μένος is described not with personalizing terms like φίλος but with modifiers appropriate to the notion of an impersonal force (Il. 5.892 ἀάσχετον οὐκ ἐπιεικτόν; Od. 19.493 ἔμπεδον; Il. 17.456 ἠΰ; Il. 17.742 κρατερόν; Il. 17.565 αἰνόν; Il. 23.177 σιδήρεον; h. Dem. 361 ἤπιον; Od. 24.319 δριμύ). Despite the deviation of μένος from the pattern, the parallels with the other words are impressive. Although μένος lacks any death contexts in which it 'departs' from the body, it is used in doublets with θυμός and ψυχή with, respectively, ὀλλύναι and λύειν (Il. 8.358 μένος θυμὸν τ' ὀλέσειε, and Il. 8.315 λύθη ψυχή τε μένος τε). When used with φθίω is meaning is ambiguously 'life', 'strength', or 'spirit' (Od. 4.363 καί νύ κεν ἤϊα πάντα κατέφθιτο καὶ μένε' ἀνδρῶν: Menelaus on the consequences of being marooned). When μένος wanes, however, the contexts are not ones of fainting or emotional strain; since infusions of it lead primarily to physical stamina and readiness for battle (cf. Il. 6.261: the μένος of a tired man is increased by wine), its absence or decline simply makes one weak and unfit for bold undertakings (*Il.* 5.472). None of its usages is sufficiently specific to identify it as a concrete physical entity or process, although phrases like *Odyssey* 4.661 (μένεος ... φρένες ἀμφιμέλαιναι πίμπλαντ᾽) have been taken by Onians to suggest the "flow of blood to the lungs in crisis," and *Il.* 10.482 (ἔμπνευσε μένος), the idea of an infusion of 'breath'.[44] It is located in the φρένες (*Il.* 1.103), in the στήθεα (*Il.* 5.513), it may be put into the knees (*Il.* 17.451) and, most important, I believe, for the thesis argued here, into the θυμός itself (*Il.* 16.529 μένος ἔμβαλε θυμῷ). Like κῆρ, however, μένος is found also in the periphrasis of proper names (*Il.* 11.268 μένος Ἀτρεΐδαο, and *Od.* 7.167 ἱερὸν μένος Ἀλκινόοιο), a usage regularly ambiguous with μένος as 'strength' (*Il.* 7.38 Ἕκτορος ὄρσωμεν κρατερὸν μένος). Last, it is worth noting in this context that the compounds of μένος—most of which, like ὑπερμενής, δυσμενής, εὐμενής, have to do with disposition or power—include ἀμενηνός, which later means 'feeble' or 'weak' and in Homer is associated with 'shades' (*Od.* 10.521 νεκύων ἀμενηνὰ κάρηνα), dreams (*Od.* 19.562), and the wounded (*Il.* 5.887 ἤ κε ζὼς ἀμενηνὸς ἔα χαλκοῖο τυπῇσι: Ares speaking of himself says that had he not escaped Diomedes he would now be left among the dead or "live ἀμενηνός from the blows of the bronze"). The phrase ζὼς ἀμενηνός is a particularly clear indication that to be 'without μένος' is to be 'without life-force', not 'without life', although the second interpretation is a natural inference from the use of the word to describe the dead.

The comparisons so far made not only point out important connections between these words and the usages of αἰών but also show that in the case of meanings related directly to 'life', shared usages are more common than unshared. The attribution of μένος to inanimate objects constitutes an important exception, but on the whole it is only by the frequency of use within given contexts, rather than the range of contexts, that the words can be distinguished. The congruence of these 'life' contexts and the lack of consistent physical identification again imply that the terms in question have been sufficiently analogized in the diction of Homer to be seen as manifestations of a common underlying idea or belief.[45] A reasonable conclusion, therefore, is that if they mean 'life' they do so, like αἰών, not by

---

44. Onians, p. 51.

45. A middle ground between the concrete-to-abstract reasoning of Onians and the position taken here, that 'life-force' can be regarded in itself as a discernible semantic category in archaic Greek, is that of Nilsson (1955), vol. 1, pp. 40–43 (this material was first published by him in *Revue d'Histoire et de Philosophie Religieuses* 10 (1930): 113–25). Nilsson's premise is that in primitive languages 'life' cannot be expressed except in concrete representations, e.g., blood, breath, and other bodily parts or external entities such as soul-animals, portraits, and the shadow. This insistence on the systematic concreteness of Homeric language, however, is incompatible with the inconsistent and often vague physical characterizations implied by the soul words.

inferences drawn from the imagined behavior of a part or process of the body with which they are identified. Taken together, they suggest instead that 'life' in the sense of a 'life-force' inseparable from the body and an entailment of bodily existence—yet something without precise or consistent organic identity—was in Homeric speech a self-contained category of thought about the person, able to unify inherently all physical, psychological, and 'life' uses of these words. It is clear that μένος originates in or embraces a less personal idea of 'life-force' than do the other words, but that it is drawn some distance into the more personal pattern by its participation in death and emotional contexts seems self-evident. Whether the periphrastic instances of μένος and κῆρ belong to this pattern is unclear, since the same periphrasis is used with βίη and ἴς, where it must imply a less human and personal sense of 'force'. On the other hand, the shared usage of βίη, ἴς, μένος, and κῆρ in periphrasis shows that κῆρ is semantically linked to the notion of 'force', and hence 'life-force', not 'heart', as it is usually taken.

If the nonpsychological uses of θυμός, μένος, ἦτορ, and κῆρ are characterized by a pervasive tendency to perceive all such agents in terms of a common set of 'life-force' characteristics, one would expect the use of these words as psychological agents to have a similar explanation. To explore this hypothesis, and to provide some comparison with the earlier study of Böhme, it is easiest to deal in detail with κῆρ—a word that occurs less frequently than θυμός or μένος—and then to summarize the patterns exhibited by other words.

A useful point of departure is the list of emotions that Böhme assigns to κῆρ.[46] On the assumption that the described emotions belong to the 'heart' itself, he designates the κῆρ as the seat of joy, pain, fear, courage, hate, honor, love, harshness, anger, endurance, and desire. To document this comprehensive, though uneven, list of emotions twenty-seven examples of κῆρ are adduced.[47]

---

46. Böhme, p. 64.

47. (1) Joy. Il. 4.272: Idomeneus promises to fight, predicting death and woe for the Trojans, with the result that Agamemnon passes on γηθόσυνος κῆρ; Od. 9.413 ἐμὸν δ᾽ ἐγέλασσε φίλον κῆρ / ὡς ὄνομ᾽ ἐξαπάτησεν: Odysseus laughs after the οὖτις trick succeeds in eliminating the other Cyclopes. (2) Pain. Il. 7.428: the Trojans burn their corpses in silence ἀχνύμενοι κῆρ; Il. 5.399: Hades struck with an arrow goes to Olympus κῆρ ἀχέων; Il. 11.274 ἤχθετο γὰρ κῆρ: the wounded Agamemnon, with pains like those of childbirth, goes off in his chariot: Il. 18.33 ὁ δ᾽ ἔστενε κυδάλιμον κῆρ: Antilochus holds back the hands of Achilles lest he kill himself. (3) Fear, Shame. Il. 12.45 σθένεϊ βλεμεαίνων ... τοῦ δ᾽ οὔ ποτε κυδάλιμον κῆρ ταρβεῖ οὐδὲ φοβεῖται: a cornered lion or boar wheels to fight; Il. 24.435: Hermes is ashamed περὶ κῆρι to defraud Achilles by accepting a gift from Priam without Achilles' knowledge. (4) Anger. Il. 1.44: Apollo comes down from Olympus χωόμενος κῆρ. (5) Hate. Il. 4.53: Hera will allow Zeus to sack her

There are two major problems with this analysis. First, it ignores, as all studies of these words have done, the ability of certain uses of case or formulae to acquire an idiomatic value. Seven of Böhme's psychological examples of κῆρ belong to the formula περὶ κῆρι, and all of them are used in contexts that have no apparent connection with the notion of 'life-force'. I will suggest that the phrase περὶ κῆρι, like certain uses of θυμός and ψυχή to be examined later, has an idiomatic quality that deprives it of a significant semantic relationship to κῆρ itself. (An appropriate modern example, if I may offer it without prejudice to the concrete identity of κῆρ, is English "heart"/"heartily".) Briefly, περὶ κῆρι is found fourteen times in Homer: four of these occurrences offer variant expressions of the idea that one is loved περὶ κῆρι by Zeus, the gods, or one's parents (*Od.* 15.245, *Il.* 13.430, 24.61, 24.423); five express the idea of being honored περὶ κῆρι by Zeus, one's family, or the people (*Il.* 4.46, *Od.* 5.36, 7.69, 19.280, 23.339); and three appear in contexts of destructive wrath or hatred (*Il.* 4.53, 13.119, 13.206). The last two occurrences of περὶ κῆρι are at *Iliad* 24.435, where Hermes is ashamed περὶ κῆρι to defraud Achilles, and *Odyssey* 6.158, where Odysseus tells Nausicaa that the man she marries will be blessed above all others (κεῖνος δ᾽ αὖ περὶ κῆρι μακάρτατος ἔξοχον ἄλλων). In the last passage we may doubt that the κῆρ belongs to a specific human being, since the predictable idea that one is beloved 'at heart' of another—assuming that κῆρ connotes the 'heart' in some way—must be altered to say that the beloved is blessed 'in his own heart'. This interpretation is certainly not impossible, but it shows a casualness toward the attribution of περὶ κῆρι indicative of great idiomatic freedom. More important, every instance of περὶ κῆρι can be translated, as in this line, as simply 'exceedingly'—an improbable standardization if κῆρ does indeed function as a psychological

---

cities whenever they are hateful to him περὶ κῆρι. (6) Honor. *Il.* 4.46: Troy was most honored of the cities of the earth to Zeus περὶ κῆρι. (7) Love. *Il.* 9.117: Agamemnon tells Hector that the man whom Zeus loves κῆρι is worth many hosts; *Il.* 13.430: Hippodamia is loved by her father and mother περὶ κῆρι; *Il.* 24.61: Achilles is beloved by the gods περὶ κῆρι; *Ol.* 24.423: the corpse of Hector is loved περὶ κῆρι; *Od.* 15.245: Amphiarus is loved by Zeus and Apollo περὶ κῆρι. (8) Harshness. *Od.* 23.167: Odysseus tells Penelope that the gods have given her a κῆρ ἀτέραμνον beyond that of any other woman. (9) Courage. *Il.* 7.100: unwilling to fight, the Greeks sit ἀκήριοι; *Il.* 5.812, 5.817, 13.224: fear is described as making one ἀκήριος. (10) Mastery. *Il.* 1.569: Hera, rebuked by Zeus, sits down ἐπιγνάμψασα φίλον κῆρ. (11) Endurance. *Il.* 13.713 οὐ γάρ σφι σταδίη ὑσμίνη μίμνε φίλον κῆρ: the Locrians are reproached; *Od.* 16.274 σὸν δὲ φίλον κῆρ τετλάτω ἐν στήθεσσι: Telemachus is told how to act if Odysseus is reviled in the house. (12) Desire. *Il.* 15.52 μεταστρέψειε νόον μετὰ σὸν καὶ ἐμὸν κῆρ: Zeus tells Hera that if she joins her thoughts to his, Poseidon will bend his mind to their desire; *Od.* 4.539 οὐδέ νύ μοι κῆρ | ἤθελ᾽ ἔτι ζώειν: Menelaus, after hearing of the death of Agamemnon, no longer wished to go on living; *Od.* 12.192: the κῆρ of Odysseus wishes to listen to the Sirens. I omit the category described as "allgemeine Erregung," for which is cited, e.g., παλλομένη κραδίην at *Il.* 22.461.

agent. This pattern must imply that κῆρ has lost its original force in the phrase περὶ κῆρι, and indeed a mechanism for this change in meaning can be shown through κῆρι by itself (Il. 9.117, quoted above) and the regular use of κηρόθι (e.g., Od. 5.284 ὁ δ᾽ ἐχώσατο κηρόθι μᾶλλον: Poseidon sees Odysseus on the raft); in every instance κῆρι and κηρόθι alone can be translated, like περὶ κῆρι, as simple assertions of excess or high degree. Such restriction of κῆρι and κηρόθι to contexts of excess allows περὶ κῆρι to be interpreted as a redundant expression combining previously independent usages of κῆρι and περί, a phenomenon that could not have occurred unless κῆρι had first weakened idiomatically to a meaning comparable to ad-verbial περί. Thus Τυδεΐδη, περὶ μέν σε τίον Δαναοί at Iliad 8.161 is indis-tinguishable in meaning from ὅν τε Ζεὺς κῆρι φιλήσῃ at Iliad 9.117 and ὣς κείνη περὶ κῆρι τετίμηται at Odyssey 7.69. The use of περὶ κῆρι, perhaps reinterpreted as a prepositional phrase but still a formula meaning 'exceed-ingly', is therefore unacceptable evidence for the intentional placement of such things as dispassionate love, honor, and shame in the κῆρ.

The second, equally important criticism that must be directed to Böhme's analysis of κῆρ is that its catalogue of the emotions dependent on κῆρ focuses on ones superficially named in the text. Since the distinctions made at this level inevitably determine the larger conclusions that are reached, this uncritical treatment of context leaves much to be desired. In contrast, a more systematic patterning of psychological uses can be built on the 'life-force' ideas discussed in the preceding section. As before, no criteria of proof beyond those of economy, adequacy, and internal con-sistency are alleged. What I propose, simply, is that the psychological uses of κῆρ can be described by a model, or grouping of categories, in which both the concrete activity of the κῆρ and the contextual settings of its activity are brought into a spectrum that allows ostensibly random psycho-logical usages to be interpreted as extensions of usages more directly tied to the physical 'life-force':

    I. The 'life-force' that is
        (1) diminished or slain by wounds to the body
        (2) 'worn out' by physical exertion
        (3) restored or satisfied by food and drink
        (4) refreshed by coolness, bathing, and the like
    II. The 'life-force' that is the seat of
        (5) physical readiness and strength for fighting
        (5a) courage and daring
        (6) desire or fear of battle or physical crisis

    (6a)   extreme wrath, anger, or anger ambiguous with grief of a kind usually vented by violence

III. The 'life-force' or 'life-force' personified that

    (7)   waxes and wanes in emotional contexts

    (8)   brings syncope or near death when lost or diminished in this way

    (9)   is threatened (in the sense of willingness or ability to live) by extreme sorrow

    (9a)   is thus the seat of extreme 'life'-affecting joy, grief, or despair not ambiguous with anger

The major categories of this model (groups I–III) are intended to embrace loosely a progression from uses that we would probably call physical to ones we would consider psychological, and this progression is repeated independently by each set of subdivisions (1–4, 5–6a, 7–9a). These are not, of course, categories by which the observed usages of κῆρ can be neatly separated from one another. What I offer is merely a model intended to explain and illustrate by its structure—however rough and arbitrary the distinctions that must be made in certain instances (hence the lettered categories)—a body of usages that were perceived by the Homeric speaker as expressions possessing unity of some kind.

    If we now turn back to Böhme's twenty-seven examples of κῆρ in light of this model and of the idiomatic use of περὶ κῆρι, rather than named emotions, a very different picture of κῆρ emerges. Seven of these examples must be omitted from an accounting of κῆρ because they occur as περὶ κῆρι and are therefore not trustworthy evidence for κῆρ itself. Nine others, all from the *Iliad* (1.44, 4.272, 5.812, 5.817, 7.100, 11.274, 12.45, 13.274, and 13.713), refer directly to the κῆρ as emotion, or the seat of emotion, directed toward fighting: rage, eagerness to fight, and courage. Three (*Il.* 7.428, 18.33, *Od.* 4.539) are used in situations of extreme grief for the dead. Two are used in expressing the feelings that arise when a man is wounded (*Il.* 5.399, 11.274). Since all are readily accounted for by the 'life-force' model, only five uses of κῆρ from Böhme's original list remain to be analyzed. Of these, three—Hera's repression of her κῆρ at *Iliad* 1.569, Odysseus' joyful κῆρ at the departure of the Cyclopes at *Odyssey* 9.413, and the κῆρ ἀτέραμνον that enables Penelope to hold out against her desire to grant recognition to Odysseus at *Odyssey* 23.167—are not difficult to see as extensions of the κῆρ that gives one the strength or courage to fight in battle or that undergoes metamorphosis into violent anger. The phrase μετὰ ἐμὸν κῆρ at *Iliad* 15.52 provides the only instance in Homer of κῆρ used

as an emotion per se, and not as a seat of emotion, and its usefulness as a
witness to the meaning of κῆρ itself as a psychological agent is therefore
questionable. Thus, of Böhme's examples, only the κῆρ of Odysseus that
desires to hear the Sirens (Od. 12.192) offers a use of the word that is directly
incompatible with 'life-force' ambiguously perceived as physical and psychological in situations of readiness to fight, extreme grief, and direct invigora-
tion or deterioration of bodily strength and energy.

To provide a fuller picture, κῆρ is used, in all, sixty times in the
Homeric poems, excluding κῆρι and κηρόθι for the reasons I have already
given. A full and unselected accounting of the use of κῆρ with regard to
contextual situation as suggested by the model, rather than type of emotion, follows.

Periphrasis Alone. Twice in the *Iliad* and once in the *Odyssey*.[48] Here
should be noted also *Iliad* 14.139, where the expression Ἀχιλλῆος ὀλοὸν κῆρ
is used to name Achilles but is ambiguously emotional.

Group I Uses. Six times in the *Iliad* and two in the *Odyssey*. These
require further subdivision. *Iliad* 16.481: heart per se; *Iliad* 23.443: physical
exhaustion alone; *Odyssey* 5.454: exhaustion with syncope; *Iliad* 19.319:
restoration by food and drink but ambiguous with κῆρ as the seat of grief
and anger, as Achilles refuses to eat out of grief for Patroclus; *Odyssey* 1.310:
refreshment by bathing and hospitality; *Iliad* 5.399, 11.274, 11.400: center
of suffering induced by a physical wound.

Group II Uses.

DISPOSITION TO FIGHT: nine times in the *Iliad* and seven in the
Odyssey.[49] By this I mean the complex of emotions surrounding the
impulse to do battle, such as extreme anger leading directly to acts of
violence, vengeance, and the like. These occurrences are all self-evident on
examination of context and need no comment.[50]

GRIEF AND/OR ANGER: four times in the *Iliad*.[51] *Iliad* 19.57 (cited in the
preceding group: Achilles asks Agamemnon whether they were better off
when they contended ἀχνυμένω κῆρ | θυμοβόρῳ ἔριδι) shows explicitly that
'grieving' can automatically imply a state of anger. In contexts of grieving
for the dead (all four passages) such anger is a regular means of relieving
grief, and hence unites contexts of violence or battlefield frenzy involving

48. *Il.* 2.851, 16.554; *Od.* 4.270.
49. *Il.* 1.44, 569, 4.272, 326, 12.45, 13.713, 14.139, 19.57, 21.542; *Od.* 9.413, 10.376, 16.274,
17.216, 18.344, 22.58, 188.
50. Possibly includable here are four uses of ἀκήριος: *Il.* 5.812, 817, 7.100, 13.224.
51. *Il.* 16.585, 17.539, 18.33, 23.37.

κῆρ with contexts of grief. At *Iliad* 17.538 Automedon says this directly: ἦ δὴ μὰν ὀλίγον γε Μενοιτιάδαο θανόντος / κῆρ ἄχεος μεθέηκα χερείονά περ καταπεφνών.

Group III Uses.

GRIEF AS 'LIFE'-WASTING DESPAIR: once in the *Iliad* and three times in the *Odyssey*. Instances are *Iliad* 1.491: the κῆρ of Achilles wastes away beside the ships; *Odyssey* 10.485: the κῆρ of Odysseus wastes away at Circe's; *Odyssey* 1.341: Penelope's κῆρ is worn away by grief; *Odyssey* 19.516: she is afflicted with sharp pains for Odysseus.

EXTREME GRIEF NOT DIRECTLY AMBIGUOUS WITH THE PHYSICAL 'LIFE'. (a) GRIEF FOR THE DEAD: five times in the *Iliad* and twice in the *Odyssey*.[52] (b) NONSPECIFIC GRIEF: twice in the *Iliad* and five times in the *Odyssey*. Five of these suggest simply 'grief' as crucial despair. *Odyssey* 12.250: Odysseus' men grieve as they are attacked by Scylla; *Odyssey* 12.153: Odysseus suffers as he warns his men of their coming trials; *Odyssey* 21.247: Eurymachus fails to string the bow; *Odyssey* 10.247: Eurylochus relates what has happened at Circe's; *Iliad* 10.16: Agamemnon is at a loss what to do. The remaining two imply shame. *Iliad* 6.523: Hector's κῆρ grieves when he hears about Paris from the Trojans (ἄχνυται ἐν θυμῷ); *Odyssey* 10.67: Odysseus recounts to Aeolus why he has returned ἀχνύμενος κῆρ.

Other Uses. The remaining eleven passages are extensions of the contexts described above or fall outside them. Straightforward extensions, I think, are *Odyssey* 4.259 (the κῆρ of Helen rejoices at the success of Odysseus in invading Troy because her κραδίη wished to return home—a usage that may be compared with the κῆρ of Odysseus, which wanes as he wants to return home at *Odyssey* 10.485), the κῆρ ἀτέραμνον of Penelope at *Odyssey* 23.167 (discussed above), and *Odyssey* 7.309 (in a phrase stemming from the involvement of the κῆρ with violence and fighting, Alcinous states that his κῆρ is not one to grow rashly violent). Passages falling outside these categories, at least on first examination, are *Iliad* 15.52 (μετὰ σὸν καὶ ἐμὸν κῆρ: κῆρ is used as the emotion 'desire'), *Iliad* 14.208 (Hera asks Aphrodite for the girdle so that she may unite Oceanus and Tethys, who no longer sleep together, by persuading their φίλον κῆρ), *Iliad* 15.10 (ὁ δ' ἀργαλέῳ ἔχετ' ἄσθματι κῆρ ἀπινύσσων: after being hit by a stone Hector is found lying senseless on the plain), *Iliad* 18.557 (a king sees his subjects at harvest γηθόσυνος κῆρ), *Iliad* 22.504 (Astyanax, after play, sleeps in the arms of his nurse θαλέων ἐμπλησάμενος κῆρ), *Odyssey* 7.82 (πολλὰ δέ οἱ

52. *Il.* 7.428, 431, 23.165, 284, 773; *Od.* 4.539, 24.420.

κῆρ / ὅρμαιν' ἱσταμένῳ: Odysseus reacts to seeing the palace of Alcinous),
Odyssey 12.192 (the κῆρ of Odysseus wishes to listen to the Sirens), and
Odyssey 23.85 (πολλὰ δέ οἱ κῆρ / ὅρμαιν', ἢ ἀπάνευθε φίλον πόσιν ἐξερεείνοι, / ἢ
παρστᾶσα κύσειε κάρη καὶ χεῖρε λαβοῦσα: Penelope reacts after Odysseus is
first revealed to her by Eurycleia).

A clear difference exists between this analysis of κῆρ and that of
Böhme and others who treat κῆρ as, say, the 'heart as seat of emotions'.
Böhme's list of "emotions" suggests that although the κῆρ leans toward
emotional activity, it regularly experiences everything that the man himself experiences, and hence, although Böhme does not make this clear,
approaches the status of a microcosm or duplicate of the man himself as he
feels anger, love, hate, and so forth. The analysis offered here shows, on the
contrary, that in the great majority of instances (more than fifty out of
sixty) the uses of κῆρ conform to the thesis that it can be one of two things:
(1) a man's 'life-force' itself, directly acting in contexts where palpable
waxing and waning of physical strength, consciousness, energy, endurance, and the like replace what we would call emotions in such contexts as
grief for the dead, syncope, excitement in battle, and the like; (2) the 'life-
force' personified—for example, ἐμὸν κῆρ οὐδ' ἤθελε ζώειν—but still generally restricted to contexts appropriate to the 'life-force'. In only the last
seven cases cited is the κῆρ treated in such a way as to eliminate direct
connotations of 'life-force', but in at least two of these some involvement
with the notion of 'life-force' may persist. Thus Hector's κῆρ in the phrase
κῆρ ἀπινύσσων can be thought of as the κῆρ with which one fights, which—
personified—is in this instance unable to perform its function of giving
him energy and courage to fight. It is not a general seat of intelligence,
as a superficial assessment of its use with ἀπινύσσω suggests. Similarly, the
κῆρ of Penelope may debate her course of action, not because the κῆρ is
at any point regarded as a seat of rational choice, but because her κῆρ,
personified as the seat of her deep feeling for Odysseus,[53] has a kind of
intelligence attributed to it in those contexts in which it must act. Although
such personification seems to erode the elemental connotations of 'life-
force', it can scarcely make reflective intellectual activity a persistent or
autonomous quality of the κῆρ or drastically extend the ability of κῆρ to
describe the psychological life. The other instances (Il. 14.208, 18.557,
22.504, Od. 7.82, 12.192) are, from the point of view I have proposed,
genuinely anomalous. A suggestion for dealing with these passages can be
made more easily after discussing θυμός.

---

53. A passage Böhme (p. 65, n. 2) takes to show the connection of heart and thought.

$$\kappa\tilde{\eta}\rho^{54}$$

		Iliad	Odyssey
'Life'			
Periphrasis		2	1
Anatomical part		1	
I	(1)	4[a]	
	(2)	1	1
	(3)	1	
	(4)		1
II	(5)		
	(5a)		1[c]
	(6)	9	8[d]
	(6a)	4	
III	(7)	1	3
	(8)		
	(9)	7	7
	(9a)		2[e]
Emotion per se		1	
Other		3[b]	2[f]

[a] Including *Il.* 15.10
[b] 18.557, 22.504, 14.208
[c] *Od.* 23.167
[d] Including 7.309
[e] Including 23.85, 4.259
[f] 7.82, 12.192

The uses I have just considered in detail, with the anomalous instances now redistributed, are summarized statistically in the table above—a procedure on which I shall have to rely more extensively, for obvious reasons, in discussing the psychological uses of the other words.

The word exhibiting the pattern closest to that of *κῆρ* is *ἦτορ*, which in both poems is strongly represented in groups II and III, as is shown in the table below. The 'life and death' quality is perhaps stronger in usages of

54. Periphrasis: *Il.* 2.851, 16.554; *Od.* 4.270. Anatomical: *Il.* 16.481 (1) *Il.* 5.399, 11.274, 400, 15.10 (2) *Il.* 24.443, *Od.* 5.454 (3) *Il.* 19.319 (4) *Od.* 1.310 (5a) *Od.* 23.167 (metaphorically) (6) *Il.* 1.44, 569, 4.272, 326, 12.45, 13.713, 14.139, 19.57, 21.542; *Od.* 7.309, 9.413, 10.376, 16.274, 17.216, 18.344, 22.58, 188 (6a) *Il.* 16.585, 17.539, 18.33, 23.37 (7) *Il.* 1.491, *Od.* 1.341, 10.485, 19.516 (9) *Il.* 6.523, 7.428, 431, 10.16, 23.165, 284, 773; *Od.* 4.539, 10.67, 247, 12.153, 250, 21.247, 24.420 (9a) *Od.* 4.259, 23.85. Emotion per se: *Il.* 15.52. Other: see notes to table.

ἦτορ[55]

		Iliad	Odyssey
'Life'		4	1
Periphrasis			
Anatomical part		1[a]	
	(1)	4	
I	(2)	1	1
	(3)	3	1
	(4)	3	
	(5)		
II	(5a)	4	
	(6)	5	5
	(6a)	10	2
	(7)		2
III	(8)	3	1
	(9)	4	20
	(9a)		5
Emotion per se			
Other		3	5

[a] Il. 22.452.

ἦτορ under (9) and (9a) in the *Odyssey* than it is in usages of·κῆρ listed under the same categories. In addition to the feelings of Athena at 1.48, the emotions included under (9) are those of Penelope for the absent Telemachus and Odysseus (three times); of Telemachus for the absent Odysseus; of a person deserted at sea (13.286, 15.481); of Amphinomos after he is warned by Odysseus and has forebodings in his ἦτορ of the coming evil (18.153); of Odysseus and his men at moments when they have escaped disasters involving the death of their companions, and when they encounter the need to face a new challenge (ten times); of Menelaus at the moment he hears of Agamemnon's death, and when he is told he must

55. 'Life': *Il.* 5.250, 11.115, 21.201, 24.50; *Od.* 16.428; Anatomical: *Il.* 16.660? (1) *Il.* 5.364, 17.535, 20.169, 21.425 (2) *Il.* 2.490, *Od.* 7.287 (3) *Il.* 9.701, 19.169, 307; *Od.* 4.374 (4) *Il.* 10.575, 13.77, 84 (5a) *Il.* 5.529, 15.166, 16.209, 242 (6) *Il.* 3.31, 8.9, 413, 17.111, 21.571; *Od.* 5.297, 406, 9.256, 22.68, 147 (6a) *Il.* 1.88, 5.570, 8.437, 9.568, 10.107, 14.367, 15.554, 16.509, 19.366, 24.585; *Od.* 8.303, 16.92 (7) *Od.* 4.840, 19.136 (8) *Il.* 15.252, 21.114, 22.452; *Od.* 24.345? (9) *Il.* 16.450, 22.169, 24.205, 521; *Od.* 1.48, 114, 4.481, 538, 703, 804, 9.62, 105, 10.77, 133, 198, 313, 496, 566, 12.277, 13.286, 15.481, 17.46, 18.153, 23.205 (9a) *Od.* 7.269, 13.320, 20.84, 23.53, 93.

return to Egypt before going home (4.538 and 481). Under (9a) are included feelings that are perhaps metaphorically 'life'-enhancing, for example, those of Penelope as she begins to recognize Odysseus (23.93), of Odysseus and Penelope when reunited, and of Odysseus at sea when Phaeacia finally appears to him. Less vital emotions are those of the wanderer after Troy (13.320) and those of a distressed man before sleep overtakes him (20.84).

Anomalous usages included under the category "other" are for the *Iliad* 9.497 (Phoenix tells Achilles to overcome his great θυμός, since he should not have a pitiless ἦτορ), 21.389 (Zeus laughs in his ἦτορ when he sees the gods fighting), and 23.647 (Nestor rejoices in his ἦτορ when Achilles gives him a gratuitous present). For the *Odyssey* they are 1.60 (Zeus' ἦτορ is not concerned with Odysseus), 1.316 (Telemachus is to give Athena whatever gift his ἦτορ wants), 2.298 (Telemachus goes into the house after receiving instructions from Athena φίλον τετιμένος ἦτορ), 17.514 (Odysseus will speak such words as will charm the ἦτορ of Penelope), and 19.224 (Odysseus in a false tale will describe the 'absent' Odysseus ὥς μοι ἰνδάλλεται ἦτορ).

In contrast to the comprehensive pattern of ἦτορ, μένος, as might be expected is confined largely to group II uses. But for μένος the contexts are so undifferentiated among 'strength', 'readiness for battle', 'battle rage', 'courage', and the like that on the whole attempts to classify at the level of subcategories are of little value. It is also impossible to distinguish μένος as predominantly a psychological agent from μένος as an emotion per se,[56] and no attempt to do so is made in the table below except for *Odyssey* 24.319. It is clear that the basic function of μένος in Homer is to provide the fundamental energy and strength needed for bold enterprises or extraordinary feats. In the *Iliad* nearly all contexts are of this type, and of course, the narrative constantly needs such usages. A fundamental distinction of μένος as against κῆρ and ἦτορ is the lack of the characteristic sense of 'wrath', and particularly 'grief' ambiguously felt with 'wrath', which belongs to the other words and surrounds the impulses and drives of the battlefield. Thus, while the character of ἦτορ and κῆρ is unchanged between the *Iliad* and *Odyssey*—both characterize emotions as direct and vital expressions of a man's 'life'—the comparatively impersonal role of μένος perhaps accounts for the more relaxed contexts that it acquires in the later poem. The violent emotion of the battlefield becomes merely 'courage' of any

56. Cf., e.g., *Il.* 1.282: σὺ δὲ παῦε τεὸν μένος.

$$\mu\acute{\varepsilon}\nu o\varsigma^{57}$$

		Iliad	Odyssey
'Life'		9	1
Periphrasis		6[a]	16
Force in nonhuman context		12	2
	(1)		
I	(2)	8[b]	4[d]
	(3)	3	
	(4)		
	(5)	57	8
II	(5a)		6
	(6)	9[c]	
	(6a)	7[c]	1
	(7)		
III	(8)		
	(9)		
	(9a)	1	
Emotion per se			1
Other		3	1

[a] All uses are ambiguous with (5). Cf. esp. Πατρόκλου ποθέων ἀνδροτῆτά τε καὶ μένος ἠΰ for the flexibility of this usage.
[b] All of animal 'strength'.
[c] The distinction of these uses over (5) is largely arbitrary.
[d] One of animal, three of human strength.

nature when applied, for example, to Telemachus as he faces the suitors in the assembly (Od. 1.89). The occurrences of μένος categorized as "other" describe the 'impulse' to act in random situations (Od. 8.15: Athena rouses the Phaeacians to assemble; Il. 24.198: the μένος of Priam urges him to go to the ships) and the impulse to flight and panic, not attack (Il. 20.93, 23.468).

57. 'Life': Il. 3.294, 5.296, 6.27, 8.123, 315, 358, 16.332, 17.29, 298; Od. 3.450. Periphrasis: Il. 7.38, 14.418, 16.189, 17.638, 18.264, 23.837, Od. 7.167, 178, 8.2, 4, 359, 385, 421, 423, 10.160, 11.220, 13.20, 24, 49, 64, 16.269, 18.34. Nonhuman Force: Il. 5.506, 524, 6.182, 12.18, 13.444, 16.613, 17.529, 565, 23.177, 190, 238, 24.792, Od. 5.478, 19.439 (2) Il. 17.451, 456, 476, 742, 23.390, 400, 524, 24.442, Od. 7.2, 11.270, 12.279, 21.426 (3) Il. 6.261, 9.702, 19.161 (5) Il. 2.387, 5.2, 125, 136, 254, 470, 513, 516, 563, 792, 892, 6.72, 101, 502, 7.309, 457, 8.178, 335, 450, 10.366, 479, 482, 11.291, 12.166, 13.105, 155, 287, 318, 634, 14.73, 15.60, 493, 500, 510, 514, 594, 667, 16.210, 275, 529, 602, 621, 17.20, 156, 423, 19.37, 159, 20.80, 372, 374, 21.145, 383, 411, 482, 488, 22.204, 459, Od. 3.104, 9.457, 11.502, 515, 20.19, 22.203, 226, 24.520 (5a) Od. 1.89, 2.85, 271, 303, 17.406, 19.493 (6) Il. 5.472, 6.407, 12.266, 13.78, 15.232, 262, 20.110, 174, 22.96 (6a) Il. 1.207, 282, 13.424, 19.202, 21.305, 340, 22.346, Od. 11.562. (9a) Il. 11.268. Emotion per se: Od. 24.319

The last two passages are important because they show again the imperson-ality of μένος compared with the other words, all of which regularly act to accomplish an assertion of self in some way when they increase in strength. Finally, an extreme pain is found once in the μένος of Agamemnon (*Il.* 11.268 ὀξεῖαι ὀδύναι δῦνον μένος ’Ατρεΐδαο), but this deviation from the pattern is almost certainly dependent on the periphrasis of Agamemnon and describes in any case the physical agony of wounds. A single occur-rence of μένος as an emotion and only that is found at *Odyssey* 24.319 (when Odysseus sees Laertes a sharp feeling goes through his nostrils: ἀνὰ ῥῖνας δέ οἱ ἤδη | δριμὺ μένος προΰτυψε); this is, perhaps, the physical sensation that immediately precedes tears.

Despite the frequent use of θυμός in psychological contexts, it too can be shown to be a part of this pattern rather than a more general psycholo-gical agent responsible for cognition, feeling, judgment, and the like, as surveys like those of Böhme[58] and, more recently, Harrison[59] imply. An important omission from these studies is the correlation of certain mean-ings with the dative θυμῷ, a pattern that must suggest the same conclusion as that reached for περὶ κῆρι. Like περὶ κῆρι, almost every instance of θυμῷ can be translated as 'exceedingly' or 'very much'. Equally, most of the uses of θυμός that cannot be explained by the 'life-force' model or otherwise occur as θυμῷ.[60] Such experiences as the awe of killing a guest or stripping armor (*Il.* 6.167 σεβάσσατο γὰρ τό γε θυμῷ [= 6.417]), the persistent desire of Athena and Hera to sack Troy (*Il.* 7.31), the feeling of foolishness at being caught apart from one's chariot or of forgetting to make a sacrifice (*Il.* 11.340 ἀάσατο δὲ μέγα θυμῷ [= 9.537]), disdain at doing menial work (*Il.* 10.69 μηδὲ μεγαλίζεο θυμῷ: Agamemnon to Menelaus not to spare himself from the task of gathering the leaders), Odysseus' pity for Elpenor when he firsts sees him in the underworld (*Od.* 11.55 τὸν μὲν ... ἐλέησά τε θυμῷ), Odysseus seeing the baths at Circe's (*Od.* 8.450 ἀσπασίως ἴδε θυμῷ), and his amazement at the skill of the Phaeacian dancers (*Od.* 8.265 θαύμαζε δὲ θυμῷ) are all implausibly segregated by the use of θυμῷ as opposed to θυμός or θυμόν. As in the case of κῆρι it seems logical to argue that although θυμός may be felt as a psychological agent in some usages (e.g., *Il.* 9.321 ἐπεὶ πάθον ἄλγεα θυμῷ [cf. *Il.* 6.157]), unusual contexts for θυμός cannot be accepted as proven if they are found only with θυμῷ. The observation that if phrases with θυμῷ are excluded, the remaining psychological occur-rences of θυμός can be brought into agreement with the pattern of the 'life'

58. Böhme, p. 69ff.
59. Harrison, p. 71.
60. This accounts for 43 occurrences of θυμός in *Iliad* and *Odyssey* 1–12.

words established above seems to confirm the problematical quality of these uses. (The sample for the table below is *Iliad* and *Odyssey* 1–12.)

θυμός[61]

		Iliad	*Odyssey*
'Life'		25[a]	5[e]
Periphrasis			
	(1)	5	
I	(2)	1	4
	(3)	9[b]	10[f]
	(4)		1
	(5)	11	2
II	(5a)	12	9
	(6)	21	
	(6a)	19	12
	(7)	2[c]	3[c]
III	(8)	2	4
	(9)	8[d]	8
	(9a)		
Emotion per se		2	2
Other		See following discussion	

[a] Does not include the anomalous θυμὸν ἀπὸ μελέων δῦναι δόμον Ἄϊδος εἴσω (7.131).

[b] 11.555 and 12.300 may be ambiguous with group II and III usages; 8.189, 4.263, and 9.177 may simply indicate uncharacterized impulse (see discussion). The rest are repetitions of the formula οὐδέ τι θυμὸς ἐδεύετο δαιτὸς ἐΐσης.

[c] 1.243 and 6.202 (both metaphorical—the θυμός is 'eaten' in anguish); *Od.* 9.75, 10.143, 379 (same).

[d] 3.412 may indicate wrath; 2.171, 6.524, 8.147 are combined with κραδίη or κῆρ. 3.98, 12.179, 8.138, 9.8 are unambiguous.

[e] Includes ἀπὸ δ' ἔπτατο θυμός (10.163 [= 19.454]).

[f] 10.374 may be ambiguous with a group II usage. 3.342 (= 3.395, 7.184, 7.228) and 8.70 may be uncharacterized impulses; 5.95, 8.98, 10.461, and 10.217 are unambiguous.

61. 'Life': *Il.* 1.205, 4.470, 524, 531, 5.155, 317, 346, 673, 691, 848, 852, 6.17, 8.90, 270, 358, 10.452, 495, 506, 11.334, 342, 381, 433, 12.150, 250, 386, *Od.* 3.455, 10.163, 11.221, 12.350, 414 (1) *Il.* 1.593, 3.294, 5.400, 869, 11.458 (2) *Il.* 11.88, *Od.* 5.83, 157, 468, 10.78 (3) *Il.* 1.468, 602, 2.431, 4.263, 7.320, 8.189, 9.177, 11.555, 12.300, *Od.* 3.342, 395, 5.95, 7.184, 228, 8.70, 98, 10.217, 374, 461 (4) *Od.* 1.311 (5) *Il.* 3.9, 438, 4.208, 309, 5.806, 9.42, 595, 10.220, 319, 389, 11.804, *Od.* 5.222, 9.295 (5a) *Il.* 1.173, 228, 4.289, 313, 5.643, 6.361, 444, 7.152, 10.205, 232, 244, 447, *Od.* 1.320, 353, 4.158, 447, 459, 8.204, 9.435, 500, 11.105 (6) *Il.* 2.276, 5.470, 510, 671, 676, 792, 6.72, 7.2, 7.25, 74, 173, 216, 8.301, 310, 322, 9.598, 699, 11.291, 792, 12.307, 407 (6a) *Il.* 1.192, 2.196, 223, 3.395, 4.494, 5.29, 6.51, 9.109, 255, 386, 436, 496, 587, 608, 629, 631, 637, 639, 675, *Od.* 1.119, 2.138, 192, 248, 4.658, 5.191, 7.306, 9.272, 287, 368, 501, 11.562 (7) see notes to table (8) *Il.* 4.152, 5.698, *Od.* 4.548, 5.459, 11.201, 203 (9) *Il.* 2.171, 3.98, 412, 6.524, 8.138, 147, 9.8, 12.179, *Od.* 1.4, 2.79, 8.149, 577, 10.248, 11.39, 12.266, 427. Emotion per se: *Il.* 1.136, 9.645?, *Od.* 3.128, 9.302.

Although there are in total 117 occurrences that I catalogue as "other," they are found in surprisingly few categories. (1) θυμός is the seat of affection,[62] as when Achilles describes Briseis and Phoenix describes Achilles (9.343, 486) as persons loved ἐκ θυμοῦ. (2) it is used to explain a mental event which, through circumstance, cannot be treated as an exchange between persons.[63] Here the situation of the hero isolated in battle, who has no one else to talk to and must make a decision, is typical (e.g., *Il.* 11.403 ὀχθήσας δ᾽ ἄρα εἶπε πρὸς ὃν μεγαλήτορα θυμόν: Odysseus is cut off and ponders retreat). Such exchanges may also, I believe, be epitomized by the use of θυμός alone with a preposition. The observation of Russo and Simon[64] that almost all forms of activity in Homer, not just shameful or bold acts, require personified exchange bears importantly on this point. Such compression can best be illustrated from *Iliad* 2.409, where Menelaus is said to have come unbidden to the feast, knowing κατὰ θυμόν what his brother was doing. No significant mental or emotional characterization seems intended or discernible in this passage, and κατὰ θυμόν simply explains, perhaps, the fact of Menelaus' action, because the poet is reluctant to leave any act unmotivated. No one has told Menelaus of the feast, and the poet says, therefore, that it is his θυμός that has done so. With the exception of two uses of κατὰ θυμόν in which θυμός is desire per se (*Il.* 1.136: the Achaeans must give Agamemnon a prize ἄρσαντες κατὰ θυμόν [cf. 9.645]), every occurrence of κατὰ θυμόν and ἀνὰ θυμόν in Homer is of this type; that is, the person involved is by accident or design unable to speak to others in the normal fashion of Homeric exchange.[65] Additional evidence for this interpretation is the use of κατὰ θυμόν, in contrast to κατὰ φρένα by itself, only by the poet of his characters, not by characters of themselves

---

62. *Il.* 1.562, 3.139, 4.43, 360, 5.243 (= 5.826, 10.234), 8.202, 430, 9.343, 482, 11.608, 12.174, *Od.* 4.71, 366, 5.126, 6.155, 313, 7.42, 55.

63. *Il.* 11.403, 407 (cf. 17.90, 97, 18.5, 20.343, 21.53, 552, 562, 22.98, 122, 385); *Od.* 5.285, 298, 355, 376, 407, 464.

64. Russo and Simon, p. 498. Cf. *Od.* 3.128 and 9.302 for emotion per se uses not in prepositional constructions.

65. *Il.* 1.429 (Achilles sits alone by the shore), 2.5 (Zeus planning alone to deceive Agamemnon; cf. 14.161: Hera planning alone to deceive Zeus), 2.36 (Agamemnon alone), 2.409, 10.17 (Agamemnon alone), 10.355 (Dolon alone), 10.491 (Odysseus acting in silence in the Trojan camp); *Od.* 1.29 (Zeus has been thinking of Aegisthus, before addressing the other gods), 1.33 (Telemachus seeing the bird epiphany of Athena), 2.116 (Penelope deceiving the suitors), 2.156 (the suitors pondering the omen), 4.187 (Peisistratos remembers Antilochus), 4.638 (the suitors learn about the voyage of Telemachus but must conceal their immediate response), 5.444 (Odysseus praying to the god of the river), 9.318, 424 (Odysseus making plans against Cyclops), 10.50 (Odysseus contemplates suicide after the winds are let loose), 10.317 (Circe plots evils ἐνὶ θυμῷ), 11.230 (Odysseus draws his sword in the underworld). The exception is amazement ἀνὰ θυμόν in Aeolus when he sees Odysseus return.

while talking to others. The difference is plausibly that the φρήν never participates in a personal exchange of the type found with θυμός (e.g., Il. 11.407 ἀλλά τίη μοι ταῦτα φίλος διελέξατο θυμός) or κραδίη (e.g., Od. 20.18 τέτλαθι δή, κραδίη ...), and it can therefore be used by a speaker in conversation with others without allusion to such poetically stylized events. The poet's treatment of the appearance to Achilles of Athena, invisible to others, might aptly be compared. (3) An equally limited prepositional usage is the familiar κατὰ φρένα καὶ κατὰ θυμόν,[66] where, as in the other doublets with θυμός, θυμός seems the weaker partner and may serve, like most occurrences of θυμός except those in the dative θυμῷ, to indicate that the context is one of imminent action. The presence of φρήν in these phrases, in any case, makes a clear definition of θυμός difficult. Possibly κατὰ θυμόν supplements κατὰ φρένα through its quality of energy and activity and does not reinforce the intellectual connotations of φρήν. (4) Like μένος, θυμός appears regularly as an undifferentiated energy or impulse that accounts for a wide range of major or minor actions, and as such it may signify nothing more than a general readiness to act—for example, Iliad 4.208 (Talthybius sends Machaon to tend Menelaus), 6.256 (Hecuba says that the θυμός of Hector sent him to the city to pray), 9.462 (the θυμός of Phoenix could no longer be restrained to stay in the halls of his father), 10.534 (the θυμός of Nestor bids him speak as he hears the approaching horses). When θυμός is used in this sense with regard to speech it implies that the speaker is saying what he really means (e.g., Zeus at Il. 8.6; cf. 10.534 and Od. 4.140).[67] Many of these occurrences may be ambiguous with other characteristic usages of θυμός,[68] as in Iliad 9.398 (the θυμός of Achilles urged him to stay in Phthia) and Odyssey 10.406 (the θυμὸς ἀγήνωρ of Odysseus is persuaded by Circe to get his men), both of which suggest strong desire. But the repeated use of θυμός in relatively relaxed contexts of this type (e.g., Od. 9.139: the harbor is one where sailors can beach a ship

66. Il. 1.193, 4.163 (= 6.447), 5.671, 8.169, 11.411, Od. 1.294, 4.117, 120, 813, 5.365, 424, 6.118, 10.151.

67. Il. 2.142, 4.208, 6.256, 439, 7.68, 349, 8.6, 39 (Zeus speaks without θυμῷ πρόφρονι), 9.101, 398 (hypothetical action), 9.462, 10.534, Od. 1.275, 2.90 (Penelope has deceived the θυμός of the suitors for three years—that is, they have not done what they came for), 2.103 (same, = 10.466, 12.28), 4.140, 713, 5.89, 7.187 (= 8.27), 7.258, 8.15, 45, 9.12, 139, 278, 10.406 (doubtful, since characterized by ἀγήνωρ), 10.373, 484, 550 (= 12.324), 11.206, 566. Extensions of the notion of sincerity of speech are passages that suggest genuine understanding: Od. 1.361 (Penelope takes what Telemachus has said into her θυμός), 2.112 (Telemachus should know the suitors' instructions in his θυμός), 12.217 (Odysseus' instructions to the steersman).

68. E.g., Il. 9.462, with 'anger'.

and wait until the θυμός bids them put out to sea) is unmistakable and seems dependent not on the reflective or psychological quality of the motivation but on the Homeric tendency to explain every human activity as a personified exchange of some kind.

The table below offers a numerical breakdown of the uses of θυμός categorized as "other" above. Of the twelve anomalous occurrences of θυμός, three designate prophetic knowledge of some kind (e.g., *Od.* 9.213: Odysseus takes wine along because of the foreboding of his θυμός [cf. *Od.* 1.200, *Il.* 7.44]). A possible extension of this usage is found at *Odyssey* 4.452, where Proteus fails to know in his θυμός the trick being played on him.[70] Four times the θυμός is dispassionately attracted to or pleased by such pleasures as gifts (*Il.* 10.401 [ambiguous with 'seat of courage'?] and *Od.* 8.395), the lyre (*Il.* 9.189), and games (*Od.* 1.107). Finally, three Odyssean occurrences are elsewhere unexampled. At 10.415 θυμός is the seat of imagination when the θυμός of Odysseus' men imagines that they have already reached home. At 12.58 Circe tells Odysseus to decide in his θυμός which course to follow after passing the Sirens, a usage that may be dependent on his isolation at the time of decision. At *Odyssey* 4.694 Penelope tells Medon that his θυμός and shameful deeds are clear to her. She means, presumably, something like his overall 'disposition'.

θυμός[69]

	Seat of Affection	Address to θυμός	κατὰ θυμόν, etc.	κατὰ φρένα καὶ κατὰ θυμὸν	Immediate Impulse or Will to Act	Anomalous
Iliad	13	2[a]	7	5	12[b]	3
Odyssey	7	6	13	8	26[b]	9

[a] Distorted somewhat by dividing the poem, since there are nine occurrences of these formulae in the untabulated books 13–24.

[b] Includes *Od.* 1.361, 2.112, 12.217 and *Il.* 8.39 (cf. 22.183 and 24.140), which I regard as extensions of the sincerity motif. These could be set off as a separate category.

69. Seat of Affection: see n. 62; Address to θυμός: *Il.* 11.403, 407, *Od.* 5.285, 298, 355, 376, 407, 464; κατὰ θυμόν, etc.: *Il.* 1.429, 2.5, 36, 409, 10.17, 355, 491, *Od.* 1.29, 323, 2.116, 156, 4.187, 638, 5.444, 9.318, 424, 10.50, 63, 317, 11.230; κατὰ φρένα καὶ κατὰ θυμόν: 1.193, 4.163, 5.671, 8.169, 11.411, *Od.* 1.294, 4.117, 120, 813, 5.365, 424, 6.118, 10.151; Impulse, etc.: 2.142, 4.208, 6.256, 439, 7.68, 349, 369, 8.6, 9.101, 398, 462, 10.534, *Od.* 1.275, 361, 2.90, 103, 112, 4.140, 713, 5.89, 7.187, 258, 8.15, 27, 45, 9.12, 139, 278, 10.373, 406, 466, 484, 550, 11.206 (?), 566, 12.28, 217, 324.

70. This and *Od.* 12.58 are the only examples of θυμῷ from the passages examined that are not translatable as 'exceedingly'. I have no explanation for this deviation.

If we recognize the idiomatic quality of θυμῷ and the apparent use of κατὰ θυμόν and other expressions to satisfy a fairly mechanical need for personified exchange, it can be seen that 'affection' is the only really important category added by θυμός to the 'life' uses of the other words. In fact, θυμός tends to be slightly less balanced and comprehensive in use than κῆρ or ἦτορ. The usages described under 'impulse' are reminiscent of μένος (cf. Od. 8.15, where Athena stirs the μένος and θυμός of the Phaeacians simply to assemble) and show, perhaps, a tendency for θυμός to acquire an impersonal use as against κῆρ and ἦτορ, which are always of vital importance to the individual in their influence over him.

Finally, the anomalous usages—for example, imagination (cf. ἰνδάλλεται ἦτορ at Od. 19.224)—may reflect only the need to represent certain inevitable but, in Homer, rarely described mental occurrences as they are occasioned by the text, rather than to characterize the θυμός as engaged habitually in acts of imagination, fantasy, and the like. This explanation may apply as well for the anomalous occurrences of ἦτορ and κῆρ described at the end of the previous section. The general consistency and limitation on the use of these words are unquestionably more remarkable than these exceptions, which are probably unavoidable at times in the range of experience that this vocabulary engages.

This survey of the Homeric 'soul' words comes to an end with κραδίη, a word whose later development is again of importance for ψυχή. κραδίη also offers a test of the validity of the 'life-force' model, since it is manifestly the anatomical heart (Il. 13.442: the spear of Idomeneus fixes itself in the κραδίη of Alcathous) and, with one obviously metaphorical exception (Il. 24.129: Thetis asks how long Achilles will sit 'eating' his κραδίη in grief), all references are consistently to the palpable heart. Thus at Iliad 10.94 the κραδίη 'leaps' from the breast (ἔξω στηθέων ἐκθρῴσκει) while the ἦτορ is 'distraught' and the γυῖα 'tremble'; at Iliad 13.282 the κραδίη of the coward 'beats' (πατάσσει) while the θυμός cannot be kept in control; at Iliad 22.461 Andromache rushes to the wall παλλομένη κραδίην; and at Odyssey 20.13 the κραδίη 'barks' (ὑλάκτει) before Odysseus speaks to it in self-address. This consistency and the lack of shared physical contexts with the 'life-force' words—strength, sustenance, syncope, wasting and waning—serve to differentiate κραδίη as a physical entity from the 'life-force' words, and we therefore expect differences in psychological behavior as well. This is, in fact, what happens. κραδίη is regularly found in doublets with θυμός, where either its use appears to be derived from the identity of θυμός and κραδίη as seats of 'courage' or 'wrath' (Il. 16.266: the Myrmidons pour forth having κραδίην καὶ θυμόν like those of wasps) or it serves to intensify θυμός usages that I have characterized above as neutral 'impulses'. Thus the phrase θυμός κελεύει, regularly used as a formula introducing words spoken with sincerity, becomes at *Odyssey* 8.204 κραδίη θυμός τε κελεύει when Odysseus challenges the Phaeacians to compete with him.

In addition to these phrases almost all instances of κραδίη can be categorized as either 'courage' or 'courage' ambiguous with 'wrath', that is, usages belonging to group II in the 'life-force' model. The number of occurrences listed in the table below as "other" is somewhat deceptive.

κραδίη[71]

		Iliad	*Odyssey*
'Life'			
Periphrasis			
Anatomical part		1^a	
I	(1)		
	(2)		
	(3)		
	(4)		
II[2]	(5)	1	1
	(5a)	7	7^d
	(6)	3	
	(6a)	9^b	6
III	(7)	1^c	
	(8)		
	(9)		
	(9a)	2	
Emotion per se			
Other		5	10

[a] 13.442; but cf. *Il.* 10.94, 13.282, 22.461, and *Od.* 20.13 discussed above.
[b] Group II uses contain 15 doublets with θυμός, making analysis questionable.
[c] 24.129: σὴν ἔδεαι κραδίην.
[d] Includes several passages where the word is used in an extended sense: 5.389 (the κραδίη of Odysseus offshore forebodes destruction), 20.327 (the κραδίη of Penelope and Telemachus is the seat of false confidence in Odysseus' return), and 20.18 (Odysseus restrains his κραδίη from acting in the only Homeric instance of self-address to the κραδίη).

71. (5) *Il.* 13.784; *Od.* 18.61. (5a) *Il.* 1.225, 10.94, 220, 12.347, 13.282 (anat.), 21.547; *Od.* 1.353 (extended), 4.293, 5.389, 8.204, 20.18, 327, 21.198 (6) *Il.* 10.319, 21.169 (?), 551. (6a) *Il.* 2.171, 8.147, 9.635, 646, 15.208, 16.52, 19.220, 23.591 (extended), 24.584; *Od.* 17.489, 18.274, 348 (= 20.286), 20.13, 17. (9a) *Il.* 10.10, 23.47.

Five[72] of those from the *Odyssey* are doublets with θυμός that seem to absorb κραδίη into θυμός as an 'impulse', rather than intensify θυμός. This is strictly true only for 15.395 (Eumaeus tells those whose κραδίη and θυμός bid them go to sleep to do so). The others involve sending a man forth on his travels when his κραδίη and θυμός bid, and it is not impossible that some sense of boldness or daring is involved. Three[73] passages in the *Odyssey* are repetitions of the formula πολλὰ δέ μοι κραδίη πόρφυρε κιόντι, a phrase that may refer, like *Iliad* 21.551, where the same formula is used, to some palpable intensification of emotion associated with the heart in the breast at a moment of crisis (Agenor seeing Achilles bearing down on him, Odysseus after Hermes leaves him on the walk to the house of Circe). Of the rest, *Iliad* 22.461 (Andromache on the wall) may be predominantly physical, two (*Od.* 4.260: Helen's κραδίη wanted to return home from Troy; *Od.* 23.103: the κραδίη of Penelope is harder than stone, if she treats Odysseus as she now does) characterize κραδίη as a powerful seat of feeling like the κῆρ or ἦτορ (*Od.* 4.259 uses κῆρ as well), and four passages, all from the *Iliad*, are distinct anomalies: *Iliad* 1.395 (Achilles sends Thetis to Olympus "if ever she benefited the κραδίην Διός"), 3.60 (Paris tells Hector, after being chided by him, that Hector's κραδίη is like an ax), 16.435 (Zeus' κραδίη is divided over saving Sarpedon), and 21.441 (Poseidon chides Apollo as having an ἄνοον κραδίην).

The point of this pattern in terms of the 'life-force' seems clear. As something palpable and specific—the 'heart'—not an indeterminate force, the κραδίη cannot be 'lost' or 'destroyed', nor can it easily be said to 'waste away' in distress and grief. But the heart can readily be characterized as involved in physical willingness to fight, and feelings of courage and wrath do, in fact, take up most of the uses of κραδίη. κραδίη thus conforms significantly to the 'life-force' model. Its striking lack of group III usages, which would identify it as a more extensive agent of the type of κῆρ, ἦτορ, and θυμός, could not be explained if these words were alternative expressions for 'heart', or for a group of competing organs of any kind, since there would be no basis for singling out κραδίη from among the other words for such exceptional restriction of context. The comparable absence of μένος from these more psychological usages clearly results from its ability to work as a nonhuman force. But the limitation of κραδίη must be seen, I suggest, as a function of its inherent inability to assume the appropriate physical 'life-force' connotations of wasting and waning necess-

---

72. *Od.* 14.517, 15.339, 395, 16.81, 21.342.
73. *Od.* 4.427, 572, 10.309.

ary for it to act as a seat of grief (or joy) not related to 'wrath'. The exception to the general 'life-force' pattern of psychological uses furnished by κραδίη thus seems, on examination, to be understandable in terms of that pattern. And this conclusion is equally obligatory in dealing with the physical uses of κραδίη as against the other words. If κῆρ and ἦτορ were perceived, like κραδίη, as the anatomical 'heart' in Homer, it seems improbable that they would share with μένος and θυμός a substantial number of contexts—sustenance by food and drink, use with φίλος, periphrasis—that κραδίη lacks. If Homeric Greek in fact had several words for 'heart' and extended to the 'heart' certain semantic characteristics based on its role as an organ of physical and psychological importance in the body, logically κῆρ and ἦτορ would have the same pattern as κραδίη, or κραδίη would regularly have all the uses of θυμός and μένος found for κῆρ and ἦτορ. Such parallels, as I have shown, are not found.

Several other points may be added to support the validity of taking 'life-force' as the core meaning of Homeric θυμός, μένος, ἦτορ, and κῆρ. (1) The apparent contradiction of 'leave' and 'destroy' contexts is eliminated. Since the physical description of the 'life-force' is always subject to change, it may 'leave' the body by ceasing to animate it (e.g., λίπε δ' ὀστέα θυμός) or by being 'slain' or 'destroyed'. In addition, if the basic meaning of ἦτορ is not 'heart' but 'life-force', the notion of 'breathing out' one's ἦτορ need not be explained as a late abstraction of 'heart' to 'life' or as the result of an active analogy by which a word that ordinarily means 'heart' is drawn into a death context completely inappropriate to it. In effect, real contradictions arise only when the idea of the 'shade' is introduced, since whatever it is that can be 'destroyed' is at least ostensibly incompatible with whatever it is that survives the body. In the same fashion, the indiscriminate use of θυμός as 'breath', 'blood', and 'heart' need not be regarded as a Homeric nod but as a result of the tendency to use the word for any of the possible manifestations of 'life-force' to which it refers. (2) If the primary meaning of ἦτορ is 'life-force', it is reasonable for Homer to situate the ἦτορ in the κραδίη. The placement of μένος in the θυμός—one 'life-force' within another—is more difficult to understand but may perhaps be explained by the ability of μένος to be felt as both the human 'life-force' and an impersonal 'force' that animates universally; it is as the second of these, perhaps, that it animates the θυμός. (3) Throughout the poems the words are constantly interchangeable in psychological contexts. Similes are particularly valuable for examples of an apparently random pattern of substitution, and this again implies that the words should be seen in terms of a common underlying idea, not discretely drawn bodily attributes. At *Iliad*

11.555ff. a lion frustrated from killing cattle during the night departs at dawn τετιηότι θυμῷ, a formula Homer varies in the next line without discernible change in meaning as ὣς Αἴας τότ' ἀπὸ Τρώων τετιημένος ἦτορ / ἤϊε πόλλ' ἀέκων. Similarly, at *Iliad* 16.264 wasps are described as ἄλκιμον ἦτορ ἔχοντες and the Myrmidons in comparison τῶν ⟨sc. σφηκῶν⟩ τότε ... κραδίην καὶ θυμὸν ἔχοντες. At *Odyssey* 4.538ff. Menelaus describes his grief on learning of the death of Agamemnon with the paired expressions κατεκλάσθη φίλον ἦτορ ... οὐδέ νύ μοι κῆρ / ἤθελ' ἔτι ζώειν. After Proteus encourages him to think of revenge Menelaus recalls ὣς ἔφατ', αὐτὰρ ἐμοὶ κραδίη καὶ θυμὸς ἀγήνωρ / αὖτις ἐνὶ στήθεσσι καὶ ἀχνυμένῳ περ ἰάνθη. This passage may be compared with the syncope of Laertes (*Od.* 24.345), where the sequence λύτο γούνατα καὶ φίλον ἦτορ ... τὸν δὲ εἷλεν ἀποψύχοντα ... ἐς φρένα θυμὸς ἀγέρθη shows that his ἦτορ has collapsed, that he is unconscious and perhaps lacking ψυχή, and that he revives with the restoration of θυμός.[74] It seems obvious that, whatever their differences, the words in question are employed with an extraordinary degree of mutual substitution, which must in turn depend upon a unity of meaning not derived from identification as the same bodily organ or process. If traditional etymologies are used, this conclusion is self-evident in the case of θυμός and ἦτορ. The substitution of κῆρ for ἦτορ (e.g., *Od.* 4.538ff.) is less convincing as a case for 'life-force', since it is possible to argue for the identity of κῆρ and ἦτορ as common expressions for 'heart', if the traditional interpretations are accepted. But one may perhaps doubt whether the poet would vary drastically in successive lines the naming of something perceived as a single concrete entity, if κῆρ and ἦτορ do indeed bring to mind for him the precise image of the beating heart. The difficulty can be removed easily enough by taking κῆρ and ἦτορ as 'life-force' expressions that represent in different words essentially similar but not visually concrete ideas and thus allow for the sense of similarity and difference required by a context like that of *Odyssey* 4 quoted above.

My point has been that the vocabulary of 'soul' words in the Homeric language is deeply shaped by idiosyncratic speech patterns and underlying cultural beliefs that can be approached only empirically, not through etymological inferences or suppositions about primitive logic. Whether the ideas I have suggested, contextual 'thought' and 'life-force', are entirely adequate is less important, as I have said, than that the existence of such fundamental patterning be recognized.

74. Cf. *Il.* 5.399 for the exchange of κῆρ and θυμός in a predominantly physical context.

Most affected by this thesis, perhaps, is the use of the 'soul' words as strongly personified psychological agents. Can one say with certainty that Homeric man imagines himself to have a variety of discrete, persistent entities or agents to which he must constantly attribute his emotional and mental life? In the case of νόος and φρήν/φρένες I have already argued that uses implying the presence of psychological agents are as likely to have come into being by a habit of expression centering on contextual 'thought' as by beliefs about entities that have an organic, hence stable and autonomous, identity. The pattern of the 'life-force' words is even more unsettling to the "organic" treatment of Homeric psychology. We have identified, broadly, three kinds of usages for these words: formulaic or idiomatic expressions like κατὰ θυμόν, κατὰ φρένα καὶ κατὰ θυμόν, and so forth; direct 'life-force' uses in which a clear physical role for the words is seen (groups I and II in the κῆρ model); highly personified psychological uses in contexts of extreme 'life'-affecting feeling (group III). It is surely possible to see in this pattern another tendency for so-called agent uses to arise spontaneously. Even though 'life-force' designates, as has been shown, something both physically and psychologically real to Homeric speakers, it is clear that metaphorical exaggeration is also at work in the use of these words. That is, the words serve not just to locate and account for emotion within the self but to intensify emotional expressions by rhetorical allusion to the vulnerability of the 'life-force' to a given event. But statements introduced to intensify emotional expression by reference to the metaphorical or literal involvement of 'life' or 'life-force' must—like the nominative uses of νόος and φρήν/φρένες—fall into ambiguity with statements made, or able to be made, about strong, independently existing agents, as in the wish of Menelaus to die at *Odyssey* 4.539: οὐδέ νύ μοι κῆρ / ἤθελ᾽ ἔτι ζώειν; and these seeming agents can then persist and spread even without an immediate connection to the idea of 'life'. A semantic development of this kind could explain the odd limitation of θυμῷ and κῆρι to the meaning 'exceedingly'. It seems likely that these idioms are created, as it were, as intensifying uses of θυμός and κῆρ—that is, as something like English "heartily." Like the dative φρεσί in the case of the 'thought' words, however, 'life-force' words used in the dative seem to be less readily felt as agents and are thus able eventually to exhibit idiomatic coloring unrelated to the stronger nominative and accusative uses of θυμός and κῆρ as autonomous entities acting and acted upon. The isolation of θυμῷ and κῆρι could not, at any rate, have arisen out of statements whose purpose was to place emotion "in" the θυμός or κῆρ, as would be the case, surely, if these words originally designated physical or psychological organs.

2

The Homeric 'Soul' Words in the Late Fifth Century

The development of the 'soul' words after Homer is complex, worth studying in its own right, and, I believe, largely misconstrued by attempts to attribute to this vocabulary increasing "intensity" and gradual aware-ness of the soul-body dichotomy.[1] Since the goal of this study, however, is to understand the development and use of ψυχή into the fifth century, it would be superfluous and distracting to examine here the gradual progress of the related words from Homer on. Instead, I will treat their outcome only in prose and poetry of the late fifth century, specifically in the texts of Euripides, Thucydides, and Herodotus.

Two facts about the use of the 'soul' words in the historians are noteworthy. First, except for θυμός and ψυχή, all 'life-force' words and καρδία as well are lacking. The words ἦτορ, μένος, κῆρ, and καρδία do not occur in either Thucydides or Herodotus except for the use of καρδία as 'stomach' in the description of the plague at Thucydides 2.49, and of μένος once in Herodotus in the words of an oracle.[2] Second, the words that are retained tend to decline drastically in frequency of use, to lose their status as psychological agents, and to occur in idioms of an impersonal nature. Thus, of the seven instances of φρήν/φρένες in Herodotus, two appear in the phrase ἐν φρενὶ λαβεῖν in the context of the deliberations of a collective

---

1. See particularly the extensive study of V. N. Jarcho, who, after noting that lyric use of the soul words remains relatively Homeric, turns (p. 155) to the repeated use of θυμός in self-address in Archilochus for evidence of new "Intensität in der Wahrnehmung der Eigenwirksamkeit des 'Geistes'. Die ihrem Wesen nach ganz archaische Steigerung des künstlerischen Effectes ergibt auf rein quantita-tivem Wege etwas qualitativ Neues: Dem Geist werden nicht nur mehr Forderungen gestellt, sondern diese Forderungen machen auch sein Verhalten unvergleichlich aktiver und vielgestaltiger als im Epos."

2. Assmann (1926), pp. 118ff.

council (2.151, 9.10); one of the remaining five is oracular (1.47: the smell of the tortoise strikes the φρένες of the oracle) and therefore cannot attest popular usage; one (3.155 ἐξέπλωσας τῶν φρενῶν) uses a tragic metaphor to describe madness and conveys the Homeric sense of 'wits'; and three are used, curiously enough, in conjunction with the idea that physical changes in the body can affect the mind: Cambyses' epilepsy is such that it would be not at all strange if his mind were sick (3.33 οὔ ἀεικὲς ... μηδὲ τὰς φρένας ὑγιαίνειν), Atossa urges Darius to do something spectacular before his φρένες grow old, since they become feeble along with the body (3.134 αὐξομένῳ γὰρ τῷ σώματι συναύξονται καὶ αἱ φρένες, γηράσκοντι δὲ συγγηράσκουσι), and Xerxes apologizes for his change of mind on the grounds that he has not yet reached the full growth of his φρένες (7.13 φρενῶν τε γὰρ ἐς τὰ ἐμεωυτοῦ πρῶτα οὔκω ἀνήκω). In Thucydides φρήν/φρένες does not occur.[3]

A similar pattern is found for θυμός, which occurs only three times in Thucydides, always as 'anger', 'courage', or 'zeal' rather than as a psychological agent; it is opposed to ἐπιστήμη and λογισμός (1.49, 2.11) in a contrast between rage and reflection (e.g., 1.49, θυμῷ καὶ ῥώμῃ τὸ πλέον ἐναυμάχουν ἢ ἐπιστήμῃ), and it is used to characterize the vigor of the newly formed alliance of the Lacedaemonians and Argives in the year 418 (5.80).[4] In Herodotus the use of θυμός is less consistent, but the pattern is clear enough. Twice it means simply the neutral 'desire' or 'impulse' to act, already discussed for Homer: the women who come to the ship in 1.1 are described as wanting to buy goods pleasing to them (ὠνέεσθαι τῶν φορτίων τῶν σφι ἦν θυμὸς μάλιστα), and at 8.116 the sons of a Thracian king have θυμός to see the war. It is used three times (1.120, 3.85, 7.52) in the phrase θυμὸν ἔχειν ἀγαθόν ('to be cheerful') and four times (1.137, 1.155, 2.129, 3.36) to indicate something that can be taken as either 'anger' or 'the seat of anger'.[5] θυμός may denote 'desire' per se at 5.49 (τὰ θυμῷ βουλόμενοι: Cleomenes is told by Aristagoras that the Spartans can have whatever they want if they conquer the Persians), where the superfluity of θυμῷ argues against interpreting θυμός as a fully personified agent, if it does not again mean 'very much' as in Homer. Similarly, it can be seen as an emotion, not agent, at

---

3. Nor does φρήν/φρένες occur in Xenophon, except for the prayer of *Symposium* 4.55.

4. I omit 3.104, which quotes Homer.

5. 1.137: Herodotus relates that the Persians do not kill a slave until he is demonstrably more trouble than he is worth, and only then οὕτω τῷ θυμῷ χρᾶται; 1.155: Croesus appeals to Cyrus not to indulge his θυμός and destroy Sardis (μὴ πάντα θυμῷ χρέο); 2.129: Mycerinus, the Egyptian king, "appeases the anger" of those against whom he has rendered judgments by compensating them from his own pocket; 3.36: Croesus advises Cambyses not to yield to his youthful age and θυμός by arbitrarily killing his Persian subjects.

8.130, where the Persians recognize that they are inferior in θυμός, or 'courage', to the Greeks at sea (κατὰ μέν νυν τὴν θάλασσαν ἐσσωμένοι ἦσαν τῷ θυμῷ). If we omit the oracular response of 7.140,[6] there remain only four instances of θυμός in Herodotus that unambiguously point to the continued use of the word as a psychological agent. Three of these are the repeated and perhaps colloquial formulation ἐς θυμὸν βάλλειν, in which little personification seems implied; decision is required in a context of immediate action (1.84, 7.51, 8.68). The fourth is a curious statement of Xerxes to Pythius the Lydian (7.39), who has requested that one of his five sons be left behind with him; Xerxes replies that he should know that the θυμός of a man lives in his ears (ἐν τοῖσι ὠσὶ τῶν ἀνθρώπων οἰκέει ὁ θυμός): when it hears something good it fills the body with delight, but hearing the opposite it swells up. This suggests the archaic θυμός, treated now in a highly metaphorical fashion.

νόος, in turn, is used forty-six times in Herodotus, twenty-five of which clearly imply meanings like 'intention' (1.216, 4.131, 7.162, 9.98) or 'wish'.[7] In the twenty-one remaining occurrences νόος always indicates the seat of some kind of mental activity, but of these, thirteen are simply repetitions of ἐν νόῳ ἔχειν.[8] A slightly more ambiguous use is found in νόῳ λαμβάνειν, which occurs five times and varies in meaning from 'perceive' (3.41, 3.51) to 'reflect on' (3.51) to 'recognize' [an idea] (5.91) and 'imagine' [a possibility] (8.19). Last, the phrase ἐκπλώσαντες ἐκ τοῦ νόου (3.155), like ἐξέπλωσας τῶν φρενῶν at 6.12, describes madness. In Thucydides, νοῦς is found ten times: in four places (4.8, 4.22, 4.85, 5.45) we read a form of ἐν νῷ ἔχειν, always with the meaning 'intend'; four times (3.22, 6.93, 7.19, 8.8) there occurs a form of τὸν νοῦν [προσ]έχειν, in which νοῦς is clearly 'attention' (visual, mental, and physical) directed toward an object or endeavor; at 4.120 the phrase κατὰ νοῦν occurs with a meaning similar to that found in Herodotus.[9]

An obvious and important pattern emerges from the use of these words in the historians. Assmann approaches the truth when she points out

---

6. The Athenians are advised to "spread θυμός over their evils" (κακοῖς δ' ἐπικίδνατε θυμόν). This is probably of a type with the injunction elsewhere θυμόν ἔχειν ἀγαθόν, but since the language is oracular the passage cannot be taken to show the prose usage of Herodotus.

7. E.g., κατὰ νόον ('according to [one's] wish'): 1.117; 4.88, 97; 5.106; 6.130; 7.104, 105; 9.45. Cf. σὺν νόῳ ('carefully') 8.86, and ἄνευ νόου ('carelessly') 3.81. Further uses are given by Assmann (1926), p. 122 ("semper fere animus, consilium, voluntas"), and need not be repeated here.

8. Assmann lists only twelve in this category but mistakenly includes 3.143 with the examples for νόῳ λαμβάνειν.

9. I omit 6.59, which is reported as an inscription and shows wider connotations for νοῦς than other usages in Thucydides.

that in Herodotus φρήν is used only in a self-conscious effort to imitate Homeric style.[10] This conclusion is correct but needs to be enlarged. Upon examination of both historians it is clear that, except for functional uses denoting the results of the activities of νόος, φρήν, and θυμός, and except for what seem somewhat colloquial expressions like βάλλειν ἐς θυμόν, ἐν νόῳ ἔχειν, φρενὶ λαμβάνειν, and νόῳ λαμβάνειν, the traditional psychological language virtually disappears. Either the traditional words are no longer used at all or, if used, they have lost their former status as psychological agents of the kind familiar in Homer and in the poets. It is difficult to accept Assmann's view that such differences in usage are simply a matter of style. Since νόος, a word decidedly less restricted to poetry, has undergone a change of the same kind as θυμός and φρήν, what occurs in the early prose authors is apparently the elimination or weakening not of isolated poetic words but of the entire class of traditional words.

To some extent, parallels for these changes can be found in Euripides.[11] As in the historians—and we must conclude, I think, in the spoken language—ἦτορ, κῆρ, and μένος have all but disappeared. There are no occurrences at all of ἦτορ,[12] and κῆρ (κέαρ) appears only twice, both times in the *Medea*, where it is a traditional 'life-force' agent (398 τοὐμὸν ἀλγυνεῖ κέαρ: Medea says that no one will get away with injuring her κέαρ; 911 ἀλλ' ἐς τὸ λῷον σὸν μεθέστηκεν κέαρ: Jason is glad Medea's spirit has turned to something better). On the basis of parallel passages in Sophocles and Aeschylus,[13] however, these uses may perhaps be identified as periphrastic for the person. The decline in the use of κέαρ in Euripides is remarkable and decisive, since the word appears as a traditional psychological agent seventeen times in Aeschylus and five times in Sophocles.[14] Similarly, μένος occurs only twice in Euripides, once as the 'strength' of a storm (*Hr.* 428) and once (*Hipp.* 983) as the emotion 'wrath'. An absolute decline can again be traced, with fifteen occurrences of μένος in Aeschylus in all categories and four in Sophocles.[15]

10. Assmann (1926), pp. 121 and 127.

11. The following analysis is based on the extant plays for all words except φρήν/φρένες, where the sample is drawn from ten plays (*Med., Hipp., Ba., HF, IT, Andr., Rh., Hec., Or., Hel.*). Fragments are not included. The language in question has been examined in detail for tragedy by Assmann (1917), who generally draws only limited conclusions, and, of course, by Meissner. Where I have relied on Assmann I mark [A] below.

12. Only one in tragedy (*Pers.* 991) [A].

13. *Pr.* 390, *Aj.* 686, *OC* 655, *Ch.* 26 [A].

14. Assmann (1917), pp. 246–49. I treat her category of heart proper (*Ag.* 997, *Ch.* 410, *Supp.* 784) as metaphorical.

15. Ibid., pp. 218–21.

The surviving terms, however, are more complicated in both quality and distribution of uses. It is unnecessary to examine again citations that merely repeat Homeric meanings, and I shall instead provide a numerical summary of the pattern of each word in Euripides supplemented, where necessary, by examples. Thus, according to the categories suggested for the 'life-force' words, θυμός has a profile in Euripides summarized in the table below. This pattern is significant, in comparison to Homer, for the sharp decline in absolute numbers of uses, the absence of 'life' uses ('life' occurs only once in tragedy),[17] the decline in anomalous or idiomatic occurrences (i.e., mere impulse to act, personified exchange, and the like), and the rise in uses that can be clearly defined, as in the historians, as emotion per se.

$$θυμός^{16}$$

I	(1) (2) (3) (4)	2
II	(5) (5a) (6) (6a)	2 8
III	(7) (8) (9) (9a)	3
Emotion per se		5
Other		6

καρδία, in contrast, expands considerably in both scope and quality, as can be seen in the table below. The unambiguous use of καρδία as 'life' (Hec. 1026 ἐκπεσῇ φίλας καρδίας / ἀμέρσας βίοτον) is the most surprising development and may be directly correlated, perhaps, with the substantial increase

16. (2) Ba. 620, Rh. 786 (5a) Med. 865, Supp. 480 (metaphorical) (6a) Med. 1056, IA 125, 919, Hr. 924 (all clearly personified); Med. 1079, Hipp. 1328, Pho. 454, HF 1211 (ambiguously agents) (9a) Hipp. 1114 (?), El. 176, 578; Emotion per se: Or. 702, Med. 168, 879, 1152, Hec. 1055 (all anger); Other: Med. 639 (sexual passion), Med. 310, Hipp. 1087 ('impulse'), Andr. 1072 (mantic θυμός: αἰαῖ πρόμαντις θυμὸς ὥς τι προσδοκᾷ), Alc. 829 (βίᾳ δὲ θυμοῦ: idiomatic for 'against my will'; cf. Sept. 612, A. Supp. 798).

17. Ag. 1388 [A]. The use of θυμόν with forms of πνέω twice in Euripides (usages under (2), n. 16 above) to mean 'pant' suggests the complete eclipse of θυμός as 'life' lost at death.

in the representation of καρδία as the seat of deep and vital feeling (9a), an area in which κραδίη is not found in Homer. Further, whereas Homeric instances of κραδίη listed under "other" were either largely formulaic (as in doublets with θυμός) or else compatible with the 'life-force' pattern, such uses in Euripides point toward very general contexts. Thus, καρδία is now linked with altruistic joy and compassion (El. 402: the chorus is 'warmed' at heart at the hope of Orestes' return; IT 344: Iphigenia recalls in self-address to her καρδία the feelings of pity she used to have toward strangers). It is what a man eases by leaving the house when bored (Med. 245 ἔπαυσε καρδίαν ἄσης) and the seat of Clytemnestra's feelings as she lives on at Argos without Agamemnon and Iphigenia (IA 1173 τίν' ἐν δόμοις με καρδίαν ἕξειν δοκεῖς;). It is for Euripides the source of sincerity in speaking (IA 475 ἐρεῖν ... ἀπὸ καρδίας), and it is used in describing moderate feelings of displeasure (Hec. 235: a master is distressed in his καρδία by a slave who speaks out of turn), agitation (Ba. 1321: Pentheus would ask Cadmus in the ordinary course of things whether anyone was troubling his καρδία), and the mere impulse to be up and about (Rh. 770: the charioteer gets up to feed his horses μελούσῃ καρδίᾳ).

$$καρδία^{18}$$

'Life'		2
I	(1) (2) (3) (4)	
II	(5) (5a) (6) (6a)	5 5
III	(7) (8) (9) (9a)	8
Other		13

18. 'Life': Hr. 583, Hec. 1026. (5a) Alc. 837, Med. 858, 1042, 1242, HF 833. (6a) Med. 99, 590, Hec. 1129, Cyc. 349, Rh. 596. (9a) Hipp. 912, Hel. 960 ('seat of compassion'), Alc. 1067, 1100, Med. 1360 (ambiguous with 'life'), Or. 466 (self-address), Hec. 433, Ba. 1288. Other: Med. 432, Hipp. 27, 1274 (sexual passion, but Med. 432 is ambiguous with 'seat of wrath or daring'), Med. 245, 708, Hec. 235, 242, El. 402, IT 344, IA 173, 475, Rh. 770, Ba. 1321.

Such expansion and change of contexts can be observed for
φρήν/φρένες and νοῦς as well. Most important, the singular φρήν as an agent
accounts for nearly half the appearances of φρήν/φρένες in Euripides, as
against one in fifteen for Homer,[19] and there is also substantial extension in
its range and depth. For Euripides, φρήν is regularly the seat of a broad
spectrum of experiences, and in twenty-eight of the forty-two instances
examined there is either no trace of the Homeric ambiguity with 'plan',
'intent', or other contextually limited 'thought' or, if there is, the breadth
of context allows identification of the word as an autonomous agent (e.g.,
Hipp. 1454 οἴμοι φρενὸς σῆς εὐσεβοῦς τε κἀγαθῆς: Theseus to Hippolytus). Of
these twenty-eight occurrences, thirteen[20] treat the φρήν as a seat of deep
emotion (e.g., Med. 143 οὐδὲν / παραθαλπομένα φρένα μύθοις: no word can
warm Medea's 'heart'; IA 1434: Clytemnestra at the sacrifice of Iphigenia
has cause ὥστ' ἀλγεῖν φρένα), three[21] as the source of anger or violence (e.g.,
Med. 38 βαρεῖα γὰρ φρήν, οὐδ' ἀνέξεται κακῶς / πάσχουσ[α]: the nurse's view
of Medea), one[22] as the seat of sexual passion, and nine[23] as a general
psychological agent to which moral blame or praise in some cases can be
extended[24] (e.g., Hipp. 1454 just quoted). The last two occurrences of φρήν
as an agent, both from the Hippolytus, suggest the dichotomy of mind and
body: at 317 Phaedra claims that her φρήν is polluted, not her hands (χεῖρες
μὲν ἁγναί, φρὴν δ' ἔχει μίασμά τι), and at 612 Hippolytus claims that his
tongue swore, not his φρήν (ἡ γλῶσσ' ὀμώμοχ', ἡ δὲ φρὴν ἀνώμοτος).[25] Nine
of the fourteen remaining instances of the singular φρήν[26] imply, as in
Homer, an immediate plan, purpose, general 'intention', or the seat of such
'intention' (e.g., Hipp. 685 οὐ σῆς προυνοησάμην φρενός; Phaedra to the
nurse); three,[27] again all from the Hippolytus, although possibly limited to
contextual 'thought', are perhaps not easily distinguished from the φρήν of
men in general as described by Theseus at 934ff., or from the moral φρήν of

19. See p. 19 above. There are 42 occurrences of φρήν, 62 of φρένες.
20. Med. 143, 599, El. 334, Or. 545, IA 1134, 1580, Or. 1176, HF 745, IT 655, Hec. 85, 300, 590,
Rh. 976.
21. Med. 38, 104, Or. 608.
22. Hipp. 969.
23. Hipp. 1120, Andr. 365, Ba. 427, Rh. 79, and following note.
24. Hipp. 934, 1419, 1454, Med. 1373 (ἀπόπτυστον φρένα), Andr. 181. Cf. esp. Hipp. 534.
25. That this phrase points to an Orphic context for Hippolytus may be suggested. See below,
p. 84.
26. Med. 677, Hipp. 685, IA 67, 327, Andr. 361, El. 1059 ('plan' or 'purpose'), Med. 266, 1052,
Hipp. 1262 ('intention').
27. Hipp. 1268, 1298, 1337.

Hippolytus himself at 1454; in the remaining two passages φρήν is 'intelligence' or the 'seat of intelligence'.[28]

The development of the plural φρένες is not as dramatic as is that of φρήν, but substantial differences from the Homeric pattern can again be found. Again, the Homeric tendency to employ the word φρένες in usages inseparable from contextually defined 'thoughts' evolves toward usages in which it denotes a seat of feeling without the usual Homeric connotations of immediate action, purposeful thinking, or lost ability to think ordinary thoughts (e.g., *Il.* 3.442 ἔρως φρένας ἀμφεκάλυψεν). Thus, when love affects the φρένες at *Hippolytus* 256 the personification is such that it now seems possible to regard the φρένες as the proper agent to respond, not simply as that which is hindered or distorted (εὔλυτα δ' εἶναι στέργηθρα φρενῶν / ἀπό τ' ὤσασθαι καὶ ξυντεῖναι: the nurse to Phaedra);[29] at *Medea* 55 the troubles of the master 'touch' the φρένες of the servant (ξυμφορά . . . φρενῶν ἀνθάπτεται), now something like 'feelings'. Although the distinction is necessarily hard to press, the purposeful φρένες of Homer, ordinarily ambiguous with 'thoughts' in some limited sense, seem to recur in Euripides only in the area described for Homer as 'thoughts' that allow one to act in an ordinary, rational manner. Hence they account sixteen times for madness in Euripides by their absence or distortion,[30] and in perhaps six[31] instances they refer to contextual or externalized 'thoughts' in a manner fully recalling Homeric usage (e.g., *Hipp.* 935: Theseus' λόγοι . . . ἔξεδροι φρενῶν strike terror in Hippolytus; *Hipp.* 390: Phaedra has taken care not to fall τοὔμπαλιν φρενῶν; *HF* 212: Zeus lacks δικαίας φρένας toward Amphitryon). Of the remaining uses, three[32] extend the contrast of mind and body designated by φρήν to the plural as well, three[33] treat φρένες, like φρήν, as intelligence or the seat of intelligence, eleven[34] suggest without further characterization reflective 'feelings' and 'thoughts' (as described for *Medea* 55), not ones focused on action, and no fewer than fourteen[35] additional

28. *Andr.* 482, *Rh.* 266.

29. But cf. continuation of the Homeric reference to φρένες and love at *Hipp.* 765, 775.

30. *Hipp.* 238, 283, 511, 574, 1012, 1230, *HF* 775, 836, 1091, 1122, *Hel.* 1192, *Or.* 1021, *Ba.* 33, 359, 850, 947. Cf. *Hipp.* 689.

31. *Med.* 177, *Hipp.* 390, 473, *HF* 212, *IA* 1359, *Or.* 216.

32. *Hipp.* 188, *El.* 387, *Or.* 1604.

33. *Hipp.* 701, *Ba.* 203, 269.

34. *Med.* 55, 1265, *Hipp.* 256, 1102 (questionable, but σύστασις seems to look to the state of the φρένες, not their goal), *HF* 482, *IT* 815, 1181, *Or.* 297, *Hel.* 732, *Rh.* 863. Cf. *Med.* 316.

35. *Med.* 661, *Hipp.* 926, 1014, 1390, *Hec.* 359, 746, *Or.* 1204, *Hel.* 160, 501, *IA* 359, 394, *El.* 1061, *Ba.* 670, 944.

occurrences of such generalized 'thoughts' and 'feelings' convey, remarkably enough, a sense of persistent moral or behavioral character. For example, Teucer (*Hel.* 160) regards the Egyptian Helen as not having ὁμοίας φρένας to the Greek Helen, Artemis (*Hipp.* 1390) tells Hippolytus that τὸ εὐγενὲς τῶν φρενῶν has destroyed him, and Theseus (*Hipp.* 926) complains that there needs to be a διάγνωσιν φρενῶν to tell true men from false. An examination of comparable passages in Homer for φρένες (above, p. 17, n. 23) shows at once a great increase in the generality of contexts and, hence, in the ability of φρένες to act as a psychological agent in the Euripidean texts.

For νοῦς as well, finally, important changes from Homeric usage can be observed. The typical Homeric seat or function of 'attention' and 'intention' accounts by itself for only six[36] of twenty-nine occurrences. Instead, νοῦς is ordinarily used in esoteric intellectual contexts (*Tr.* 886 Ζεύς, εἴτ' ἀνάγκη φύσεος εἴτε νοῦς βροτῶν ...; *Hel.* 1014 ὁ νοῦς / τῶν κατθανόντων ζῇ μὲν οὔ, γνώμην δ' ἔχει / ἀθάνατον εἰς ἀθάνατον αἰθέρ' ἐμπεσών), when a dichotomy between appearance and reality is intended[37] (*Hel.* 731 τοὔνομ' οὐκ ἔχων ἐλεύθερον, / τὸν νοῦν δέ: the slave to Menelaus explaining his character), and—except for one instance (*Ion* 1370) when it describes the seat of memory—whenever the function or seat of intelligence or reason is at issue. Exactly half the occurrences of νοῦς (fourteen) in Euripides have this last connotation. Thus *IA* 1139, ὁ νοῦς ὅδ' αὐτὸς νοῦν ἔχων οὐ τυγχάνει, which can be translated only "Your νοῦς has no intelligence," is by itself definitive for Euripides. But eight of these fourteen occurrences are, as in Herodotus, forms of ἔχειν νοῦν,[38] three[39] of ὅσοις (etc.) ἔνεστι νοῦς, and one is σὺν νῷ.[40] As in Herodotus, all seem colloquial in tone and no longer equivalent to the Homeric νόος as a highly personified psychological agent.[41]

As against Homeric practice, in sum, only νοῦς, φρήν/φρένες, and καρδία have acquired significant new usages in Euripides. θυμός has declined in scope and frequency. μένος, κῆρ, and ἦτορ have disappeared. This pattern of change is not random, in my opinion, but keyed to the development of ψυχή. For that reason discussion of these results is deferred to the end of part II.

---

36. *Hec.* 603, *Andr.* 237, *IA* 334, *Tr.* 1052 (entity), *Or.* 1181, *Pho.* 1418 ('attention').

37. *Hel.* 122, 731, *Ion* 251, 742, *Pho.* 360.

38. *Hipp.* 105, *Andr.* 944, 252, *IA* 374, 1139, *Tr.* 652, *Ba.* 252, 271 (all ἔχειν νοῦν).

39. *Hipp.* 920, *Andr.* 231, 667.

40. *Or.* 909.

41. The remaining two are *Med.* 529, *Tr.* 988.

P A R T II:

ψυχή and Its Evolution in Popular Usage

Although many of the implicit usages of the Homeric 'soul' language are beyond recovery, close examination of the words in the way I have proposed must call into question the theory that Homeric people possess a childlike or mechanical view of themselves as subjects of unending, random intrusion by a number of discrete mental and emotional agents and organs. Rather, it can be argued that to the extent that Homeric speakers fall short of a vocabulary able to describe the psychological self as a single comprehensive entity, they do so because of the habit of expressing the psychological life as the activity of a 'life-force' or of 'thoughts' occupying an ambiguous position between the mind that knows or thinks and the objects or ideas that are known. The principle feature of this language and the system behind it, I have tried to suggest, is not simply the lack of predictable interaction between reason and emotion, or an excess of sources for psychological activity,[1] but the tendency to make all psychological activity seem constantly dependent upon metaphorical, and sometimes nonmetaphorical, involvement of the 'life' of the person affected. This habit of expression, in particular, is apt to seem to the modern reader to lack subtlety and discrimination. Doubtless much depended for an archaic Greek speaker on gesture and implicit cultural attitudes, now lost to us, which could refine the apparent reliance on dramatic overstatement. Even so, it is not hard to see why this system of psychological description began to fall into disuse, at least in its traditional form, when more sophisticated ways to describe human psychology were sought, as in Thucydides.[2]

ψυχή and its development must be considered against this pattern of 'life-force' words. I shall try to show in this section that the early psychological use of ψυχή results from its natural tendency to be identified as a 'life-force' and that the increasing use of ψυχή in later tragedy depends upon its

1. Dodds, chap. 1.
2. See Huart, pp. 37ff., on the importance of γνώμη in Thucydides.

ability to preempt that meaning from the other 'life' words. The importance of ψυχή in popular usage after Homer is, therefore, not that it reflects the spread of new ideas about the nature of the psychological self but that on the whole it preserves for Greek speech, particularly poetry, the archaic pattern of expression that attributes each human life to the activity of a powerful 'life-force' whose manifestations are both physical and psychological. If this can be demonstrated, the questions surrounding the nature of the Homeric ψυχή itself are considerably simplified; that is, we can try to understand the early uses of ψυχή by assessing their relationship to later meanings of the word that can be examined systematically instead of to supposed pre-Homeric meanings that cannot. To do so, the simplest plan will be to examine first the continuation of specifically Homeric usages of ψυχή after Homer, and then to return to the vexed problem of the origin of the psychological uses of ψυχή after Homer.

I

The Homeric Use of ψυχή and Its Continuation

Despite a lengthy debate in the scholarly literature,[3] the only meanings of ψυχή clearly attested in Homer are the 'shade' and the 'life' destroyed at death. The physical characteristics of the latter are ambiguously 'breath'-like (*Il.* 22.467 ἀπὸ δὲ ψυχὴν ἐκάπυσσε and the statement of Achilles at *Il.* 9.408–09 that the ψυχή of a man cannot be recaptured once it has crossed the ἕρκος ὀδόντων) and 'blood'-like (*Il.* 14.518 ψυχὴ δὲ κατ᾽ οὐταμένην ὠτειλὴν ἔσσυτ᾽ ἐπειγομένη and *Il.* 16.505 τοῖο δ᾽ ἅμα ψυχήν τε καὶ ἔγχεος ἐξέρυσ᾽ αἰχμήν). That these phrases indicate the ψυχή is felt as something objective and is not a sheer abstraction treated metaphorically, as has been suggested,[4] is a reasonable conclusion strengthened by the linkage of ψυχή to μένος in phrases implying physical destruction (λύθη ψυχὴ τε μένος τε), perhaps also by Achilles' phrase ἐν δὲ ἴα ψυχή,[5] by the use of ψυχή uniquely among the 'soul' words as a referent of oaths[6] and with ἴφθιμος in the proem of the *Iliad*,[7] and by the conspicuous absence of ψυχή from the

---

3. See below, p. 92, n.1.

4. Otto, p. 27; Warden, p. 100.

5. A point made by Böhme, p. 112.

6. *Il.* 22.338: Hector asks to have his body returned for burial ὑπὲρ ψυχῆς καὶ γούνων σῶν τε τοκήων. Other Homeric passages of oath taking or supplication employ only concrete referents, as one would expect: children (*Il.* 15.660), mother, father, and child (*Il.* 24.465), knees, (*Il.* 9.451), the great scepter (*Il.* 1.234). For parents, see also Theognis 1330 ἀλλὰ γονέων λίσσομαι ἡμετέρων. In the *Hymn to Hermes* (274) Hermes swears by his father's head (along with the knees also a sacred part of the body according to Onians, p. 97 and pp. 174ff.) and by the προθύραια of the gods (384), while Apollo (460) swears by his own staff. These are all less than serious in tone, but they nevertheless illustrate the importance of concreteness. Also worth noting is *Od.* 15.261–62 (Theoclymenus to Telemachus) λίσσομ᾽ ὑπὲρ θυέων καὶ δαίμονος, αὐτὰρ ἔπειτα / σῆς τ᾽ αὐτοῦ κεφαλῆς καὶ ἑταίρων.

7. *Il.* 1.3 πολλὰς δ᾽ ἰφθίμους ψυχὰς Ἄϊδι προΐαψεν. This phrase might use ψυχάς as a substitution for κεφαλάς (cf. *Il.* 11.55 πολλὰς ἰφθίμους κεφαλὰς Ἄϊδι προϊάψειν) on the grounds that the connotations of

(continued overleaf)

description of animals.[8] None of these points is by itself decisive, but collectively they rule out the possibility of treating *ψυχή* as 'life' in an abstract sense.

In the later period it is clear that *ψυχή* retains this Homeric quality of objective existence. It is still used as the referent for oath taking, not with any frequency but as late as *Oedipus Coloneus*, where Polynices swears to Oedipus by his children and *ψυχή* (ἀντὶ παίδων τῶνδε καὶ ψυχῆς.)[9] A possible addition to such passages, important because of its nonliterary context, is the use of *ψυχή* on two curse tablets, *SIG* 1175 (fourth or third century B.C. from the Piraeus) and *SIG* 1261, which read, respectively,

---

(continued from previous page)

κεφαλάς would conflict with the division of visible and invisible parts the poet intends in the following αὐτούς. But the possibility of a traditional and appropriate connection between ἴφθιμος and ψυχή must be considered, even though this is the only instance in which the words are joined. (1) The connotation of physical 'strength' is hardly possible, since the ψυχή is being sent off to Hades, and ψυχή is never later clearly associated with strength. (2) ψυχάς might be used periphrastically for the men as in later Greek, but no similar usage appears in Homer, and in any case when ψυχή is used in such constructions it designates the living man, not the ghost. (3) In addition to men of great strength (e.g., *Il.* 12.410), ἴφθιμος is applied to things that, if we believe Onians, are 'sacred'—heads, shoulders (*Il.* 18.204), heads of cattle (*Il.* 23.260)—and to gods (*Od.* 10.534), rivers (*Il.* 17.749), and particular women of the highest stature, like the wedded wives of Sthenelus (*Il.* 19.116) and Diomedes (*Il.* 5.415), Penelope herself (*Od.* 16.332), Ictimene, the daughter of Anticlea (*Od.* 15.364), Iphthime, the sister of Penelope (*Od.* 4.797), and the daughter of the king of the Laestrygonians (*Od.* 10.106). The idea of a sacredness or power not simply physical in nature may attach to all these diverse people and things: the head and shoulders according to archaic beliefs about the body, the gods by definition, the rivers as gods (cf. Scamander in *Il.* 20), and the women as members of royal houses. If so, an ἴφθιμος κεφαλή is more likely 'powerful' and 'sacred' than 'strong', and that connotation might reasonably be extended to ἰφθίμους ψυχάς in *Il* 1.3. The broad similarity in usage between ψυχή and κεφαλή tends to support this view: both can be said at some point in Greek speech in periphrasis for the person, both can be that which goes to Hades or the object by which an oath is sworn, and both can mean 'life' in some sense and can be staked in a trial of arms. Examples of these usages are for the most part conveniently collected in Onians, pp. 95–100, who asserts that the ψυχή may once have been thought to dwell in the head.

8. The evidence is not completely consistent. At *Od.* 14.426 a boar is slain in the hut of Eumaeus and the death is told with the familiar τὸν δ᾽ ἔλιπε ψυχή; otherwise, θυμός is used, e.g., *Il.* 23.880, *Od.* 3.455, 10.163, 19.454. Rahn, p. 449, sees the use of ψυχή in *Od.* 14.426 as evidence that the evolution of the term into a presumed later meaning 'life' had already begun to occur between the time of the composition of the *Iliad* and that of the *Odyssey*. A more plausible interpretation is that Homer invented (Snell, [1953], p. 11) the curious image of the θυμός flying from the body in order to avoid giving animals ψυχή. Homer anthropomorphizes animals when he has reason to (*Od.* 10.156ff., 19.454, *Il.* 16.469, 23.880 [examples taken from Rahn, pp. 288ff. and p. 448]), and this treatment extends to psychological vocabulary. Animals may be μεγάθυμοι (*Il.* 4.467, 16.488), and they may occasionally, though not regularly, have φρένες (Harrison, p. 74). That they lack νόος (but cf. νοεῖν at *Od.* 17.301) can be explained as a matter of emphasis, particularly since they have φρένες. The omission of ψυχή is therefore striking.

9. *OC* 1326. Cf. *Or.* 1517 (but a play on 'life') and S. fr. 431, where the ψυχή is set as guardian of oaths (ὅρκου δὲ προστεθέντος ἐπιμελεστέρα / ψυχή κατέστη· δισσὰ γὰρ φυλάσσεται / φίλων τε μέμψιν κεἰς θεοὺς ἁμαρτάνειν).

κατέδησα τὰς χεῖρας καὶ τοὺς πόδας καὶ τὴν γλῶσσαν καὶ τὴν ψυχήν and κατάδῶ δὲ [καὶ Σ] εὔθου γλῶτταν καὶ ψυχὴν καὶ λόγον ὅμ μέλεται καὶ πόδας καὶ χεῖρας, ὀφ[θ]αλμοὺς [καὶ στόμ]α. Although here ψυχή need not have any sense of the sacred or inviolable associated with oaths, its inclusion in a traditional and perhaps formulaic catalogue of vital parts (neglecting λόγος in the second inscription) points to a meaning other than abstract 'life'.[10] ψυχή continues, as in Homer, to be avoided in descriptions of animals. Exceptions are a remark of Herodotus (3.108) attributing multiple births for timid animals of prey (ὅσα μὲν ψυχήν τε δειλὰ καὶ ἐδώδιμα) to divine providence, where ψυχή serves as the 'seat of courage', and three instances in archaic poetry where snakes are said to die by giving up their ψυχαί.[11] This curious attribution of ψυχή to snakes is plausibly a vestige of early Greek belief in 'soul' animals, that is, in creatures whose habitat—like that of snakes—places them in a special relationship to the dead, and which are therefore believed to be possessed by the souls of the dead.[12]

Just as in Homer, it is impossible to find definitive death contexts by which to determine the physical embodiment of this 'life' lost at death. 'Breath' is indicated at *Nemean* 1.47, just mentioned, where the snakes die by breathing out their ψυχαί (ψυχὰς ἀπέπνευσεν), and at Simonides 553, where a child dies (γλυκεῖαν ἐδάκρυσαν / ψυχὰν ἀποπνέοντα). But other passages, some obviously colored by the presence of ψυχή as a psychological agent, do not suggest 'breath'. Predictably, the diction of tragedy and lyric poetry creates phrases that are more exotic than those of epic, and this has generated added suggestions for specifying the primitive substrate of ψυχή. Further evidence for ambiguity with 'blood' is found in Clytemnestra's complaint that Electra has offended her by drinking the blood of her ψυχή (S. *El.* 786 τοὐμὸν ἐκπίνουσ' ἀεὶ / ψυχῆς ἄκρατον αἷμα).[13] That the ψυχή exists in the 'marrow' has been imputed somewhat illogically to the nurse's statement at *Hippolytus* 255 that she is touched to the 'marrow' of her ψυχή (πρὸς ἄκρον μυελὸν ψυχῆς).[14] Pindar's curious and elsewhere unparalleled phrase ἄν περὶ ψυχὰν ἐπεὶ γάθησεν has been thought to demonstrate a crucial transition of ψυχή to the role of a psychological organ modeled after καρδία.[15] Literally interpreted, phrases like ψυχὴν διακναῖσαι (*Hr.* 296) and

10. Possibly semen, as suggested explicitly for *Regimen* I by Joly, pp. 30ff.

11. Pi. O. 8.39, N. 1.47; Hes. fr. 204.139.

12. ψυχή appears in Aristotle as 'butterfly', a meaning that Nilsson (1955), vol. I, p. 198, n. 53, ascribes to the presumed archaic belief that souls depart with the first creature to light on the corpse.

13. LSJ s.v. ψυχή, VII. But the phrase is the subject of a pun at *Clouds* 712, which suggests that it is striking and perhaps anomalous to the fifth-century ear.

14. Onians, p. 118, who takes τὴν ψυχήν ἐκπίνουσιν as possible evidence for 'marrow' as well.

15. Meissner (above, p. 4).

ψύχειν ψυχάν (Pr. 692) might also suggest a material substance that can be injured, but one not as specific as in the previous examples. With its deliberate alliteration, however, ψύχειν ψυχάν is a particularly good example of the way in which physical attributes can be acquired through language that is transparently metaphorical, and it should warn against literal interpretation of any such phrases.

In contrast to these examples, most of the other metaphorical uses of ψυχή after Homer are merely extensions of those found in Homer, and they do not change our perception of the word. In Homer the ψυχή can be 'risked', 'stolen', 'taken away', or 'gained'; schemes can be woven περὶ ψυχῆς, and material wealth can be described as not ἀντάξιον ψυχῆς.[16] In the later period the ψυχή can be 'spared' as well as 'risked',[17] it can be 'saved',[18] a contest can be fought over it or it can be set as the prize,[19] it can be 'stolen',[20] friends may not be more important than it, but children are the very ψυχή to a man.[21] Later contexts allow it to be spoken of as an object to be 'sold' or 'spent', as something that can be 'partially expended', given in payment, 'bargained away', 'thrown away', 'given up', 'given to' or 'for' someone, or as something one can 'bemoan', others can 'prevail over', or by which one can be 'betrayed'.[22] The apparent metaphorical boldness of ψυχῆς ἄκρατον αἷμα and μυελὸν ψυχῆς is, obviously, not repeated in the rest of these examples, and whatever evidence those phrases offer for extension of the metaphorical availability and, perhaps, increasing abstraction of ψυχή receives no further support.

The contradictions implied by the Homeric use of ψυχή continue in these passages. Nothing in the later death contexts excludes continuation of the nonabstract ψυχή as it is found in Homer. Nevertheless, the concrete examples of ψυχή are contradictory if taken literally. This conflict is summed up by the nurse's use of μυελὸν ψυχῆς in the Hippolytus: we have no particular reason to believe that the ψυχή has the kind of spatial, or at least

---

16. 'Risk': Il. 9.322, Od. 3.74; 'fighting': Il. 22.161, Od. 22.245; 'taking away': Il. 22.257, 24.754, Od. 22.444; 'stealing': Il. 11.334, Od. 21.154 (both times with θυμός); others: Il. 9.401, Od. 1.5, 9.423.

17. Archil. 213; Tyrt. 6.14; Sol. 1.46; cf. S. El. 980, Aj. 1270; Thuc. 3.39.8.

18. Alc. 929.

19. S. El. 1492, Ph. 1330, fr. 67.7; Thuc. 8.50.5. Cf. Hel. 946, Or. 847.

20. Ph. 55 (may be periphrasis).

21. Andr. 419; Nauck adesp. fr. 36.2.

22. 'Sell': Ant. 322; 'spend': E. Supp. 777; 'partial expenditure': Andr. 541; 'pay with': Ch. 276; 'bargaining': Ph. 1228; 'throw away': Ion 1499; 'give up': Tr. 1135; 'give to': Or. 662 (Orestes to his father); 'give for': Hr. 550; 'bemoan': IA 1441; 'prevail over': Hipp. 1040, OC 1207; 'betray': E. Supp. 1024.

material, character suitable to possession of a 'marrow', the only logical interpretation of the phrase as it stands; yet, unlike Clytemnestra, it cannot be appropriate for the nurse, who constantly speaks in a gnomic fashion, to introduce into the play a highly poetic metaphor radically at odds with usages familiar to popular speech.

Departures from Homeric 'life' usages are indicated in only two areas. First, by the end of the fifth century the Homeric idea of the 'life that is destroyed' (e.g., λύθη ψυχή τε μένος τε and ψυχῆς ὄλεθρος) eventually leads to a class of expressions that might have been unacceptable to Homer. Whereas Homer could speak of the 'destruction' of the ψυχή and have the μῆνις of *Iliad* 1.1, as a personal agent, send ψυχαί to Hades, in the *Agamemnon* and *Andromache* Helen herself is a personal agent who 'destroys' the ψυχαί of the men who fought at Troy, and in the *Trojan Women* she is said to have 'slain' (ἔκτεινε) the ψυχή of Astyanax.[23] From these usages may be derived the more emphatic idea that the ψυχή itself can die; once in Euripides it is said to have 'perished' (ἀπόλλυται), and once each in Euripides and Sophocles to have 'died' (forms of θνήσκω).[24] These uses may well reflect a more naturalistic sense of the physical 'life' ψυχή than appears in Homer, and a more positive sense of 'life' than 'that which is lost at death' may perhaps be seen in nondeath passages as well. Instances of this second departure from Homeric usage are infrequent and, in one case at least, there is an archaic quality not to be expected for statements that ought to derive from later and more rationalistic thinking about the nature of 'life'. An example is, perhaps, the repetition of Achilles' phrase ἐν δὲ ἴα ψυχή (in an altered form) when Pheres refuses to die for Admetus at *Alcestis* 712 because, he alleges, men live "with only one life" (ψυχῇ μιᾷ ζῆν, οὐ δυοῖν, ὀφείλομεν). The use of the dative in this phrase must indicate something 'with' or 'for' which we live, unless ψυχή has here and here only a temporal meaning equivalent to βίον ζῆν.[25] Less unusual diction is found in a fragment of Sophocles attributing the presence of Aphrodite to all who have ψυχή (ἐντήκεται γὰρ πλευμόνων ὅσοις ἔνι / ψυχή). Whether or not the ψυχή in this passage is also felt as a psychological agent, it is clearly

23. *Ag.* 1455–57; *Andr.* 611; *Tr.* 1214. Cf. also at *Hr.* 296.

24. *Hec.* 21–22; *Hel.* 52; *Ant.* 559. Cf. *Med.* 226 (ἐμοὶ δ' ἄελπτον πρᾶγμα προσπεσὸν τόδε / ψυχὴν διέφθαρκ'), which may be ambiguous with the psychological agent; and *Hipp.* 440, in which Phaedra destroys her own ψυχή for love.

25. E.g., Coleridge (1898), "To live one life, not twain, is our due." Lattimore (Univ. of Chicago, 1955), "We have only one life and not two to live." The Budé editor (Méridier) takes ψυχή as 'person' in some sense, almost exactly translating the scholiast: "C'est pour un être et non deux que nous devons vivre." Cf. S. *El.* 650 ζῶσαν ἀβλαβεῖ βίῳ; *Tra.* 168 ζῆν ἀλυπήτῳ βίῳ. That the phrase is in fact periphrastic, 'for one person', is an attractive suggestion and would eliminate the difficulties of the line.

ambiguous as well with 'life' in a more positive sense than 'that which is lost at death.'[26] A positive sense of the 'life with which or by which we live' is also required in a fragment of the comic poet Melanippides that hails Zeus as ἀειζώου μεδέων ψυχᾶς,[27] a phrase for which the meaning 'immortal life' is necessary to provide the line with a comic point. An important occurrence of ψυχή in Sophocles depends on this new sense of 'life' and unquestionably exhibits a departure from the Homeric restriction of ψυχή as 'life' to death contexts. Ajax tells the infant Eurysaces (*Aj.* 559) that he envies him his inability to perceive evil and all else and that he is to nourish his ψυχή like a young plant, sheltered from the wind, until the necessity to feel joy and pain come upon him (τέως δὲ κούφοις πνεύμασιν βόσκου, νέαν / ψυχὴν ἀτάλλων, μητρὶ τῇδε χαρμόνην). Here too we cannot eliminate ambiguity with ψυχή in its role as a psychological agent, particularly since other passages in which the ψυχή is concerned with forms of sustenance clearly give it that value.[28] But the themes of infancy and growth in this passage are suggestive of physical 'life' in an affirmative way that differs importantly from the Homeric death contexts. Additional confirmation of this new usage is offered by a fragment of Middle Comedy[29] that urges the abandonment of philosophy for drink and pleasure while it is still possible to nourish the ψυχή (Πινώμεν, ἐμπίνωμεν, ὦ Σίκων, Σίκων / χαίρωμεν, ἕως ἔνεστι τὴν ψυχὴν τρέφειν), a text in which the comic thrust obviously depends on the ability to hear τὴν ψυχὴν τρέφειν in a nonphilosophical sense, that is, "while we still have life to provide for." Almost certainly, therefore, "nurturing one's ψυχή" must suggest physical life in some non-abstract sense to fifth and fourth-century speakers. Last, Bacchylides 5.151, in which the ψυχή of Meleager is gradually diminished while the log on which his life depends is burned, may be seen, perhaps, as an extension of this kind.

Continuity of Homeric usage is illustrated, of course, by the presence of ψυχή in the meaning 'shade' in the later texts. The Homeric tension between death descriptions in which the ψυχή is 'destroyed' and those in which it 'leaves' the body but is not necessarily the 'shade' persists, although

---

26. S. fr. 855.8. This proposed development in meaning is placed by Webster, p. 149, as early as Hes. *Op.* 686 (χρήματα γὰρ ψυχὴ πέλεται). That a traditional use of Homeric ψυχή cannot be applied here is not demonstrable. For a death context with a positive sense of 'life', one approaching personification, see *Or.* 1033–34, in which Electra contemplates suicide with the words θανούμεθ᾽ οὐχ οἷόν τε μὴ στένειν κακά / πᾶσιν γὰρ οἰκτρὸν ἡ φίλη ψυχὴ βροτοῖς.

27. Fr. 762 *P.* Edmonds translates (doubtfully for the probable date of 440 B.C.) "ruler of everliving mind."

28. E.g., Hipponax 39.

29. Alexis (Meinecke 3.394).

contexts of 'leaving' are relatively rare and, if similar uses of the other 'soul' words are relevant, need not imply direct thoughts of afterlife survival.[30] But in the case of the 'shade', too, a subtle change in usage—comparable to and perhaps related to the apparent transition from 'life destroyed' to 'life lived' just traced—can be suggested. By this I mean the apparent lack of casual references to the 'shade' of a sort showing that such allusions remained a commonplace. In contrast to the ubiquity of the meaning 'life destroyed', the post-Homeric texts indicate, if anything, that 'shade' had begun to acquire esoteric connotations. Apart from the frequent parody of the 'shade' in Aristophanes and a number of important cultic allusions to it in Pindar, only about twenty references to ψυχή as 'shade' occur after Homer, and all are in highly poetic contexts.[31] Four are found in one poem, Bacchylides 5, which has an underworld setting, two in the context of summoning up the shade of Darius in Persae, three in Alcestis as required by the inherited eschatology of the myth, and one in Pindar, when the underworld journey of Cassandra and the shade of Agamemnon is described.[32] Aside from an additional Pindaric instance of ψυχή which warns that a misanthropic man will pay his ψυχή to Hades without δόξα (I. 1. 68) and a reference to Agamemnon's revenant in the Orestes, every other occurrence of ψυχή as 'shade' is either difficult to interpret or an intentional wordplay. Examples are Antigone's accusation (Ant. 1065) that Creon is making a ψυχή dwell in the tomb while keeping the corpse from the gods below,[33] and the question posed by the chorus to Clytemnestra in Agamemnon 1545–46 whether she intends to sacrifice to the ψυχή of Agamemnon (ψυχῇ τ' ἄχαριν χάριν ἀντ' ἔργων / μεγάλων ἀδίκως ἐπικρᾶναι), a passage in which ψυχή is seemingly Agamemnon's 'shade' but may in some sense be the 'life' that Clytemnestra has just slain. Problematical expressions that allude to the 'shade' are the assertion of Oedipus at Oedipus Coloneus 999 that the ψυχὴν ... ζῶσαν of Laius would not contradict his arguments in defense of

---

30. At Pho. 1553 death results when ψυχαί "leave the light" (πῶς ἔλιπον φάος;), and in four Euripidean passages the dead "let go" the ψυχή (forms of ἀφίημι and μεθίημι). Similarly, the idea of 'departure' rather than 'destruction' is implicit both in an epitaph of Simonides (180.1) on the young Timarchus in which disease begrudges the ψυχή to remain (ἐρατῇ πὰρ νεότητι μένειν) and when Pindar says of the dead father of a laudandus (N. 8.44) that it is impossible to bring back his ψυχή—ψυχὰν κομίξαι—a phrase which, whatever else it may mean, is more compatible with a ψυχή that has 'departed' than one which has been 'destroyed'. Cf. Ag. 96.

31. I omit here Heracl. B 98.

32. Bacch. 5.64, 77, 83, 171; Pers. 630, 687 (ψυχαγωγοῖς); Alc. 301, 461–63, 900; Pi. P. 11.21; also E. fr. 912.9.

33. Ant. 1065; cf. Pi. P. 3.61–62, where Pindar tells his ψυχή not to desire life immortal, and Sept. 1034.

himself and the command of Aeson to Jason at *Pythian* 4.159 to bring back the ψυχή of the dead Phrixus from Colchis (ἐὰν ψυχὰν κομίξαι). In the first, it is difficult to know whether Oedipus imagines the 'shade' or Laius himself (cf. *Orestes* 676); the second, unless we follow the scholiast who suggested an ἀνάκλησις like that of *Odyssey* 9.65,[34] presents the oddly superstitious idea that the ψυχή of Phrixus will follow the ship that brings back his corpse.

It would be rash to conclude from this pattern that the notion of ψυχή as 'shade' was regarded by the fifth century as only a poetic fantasy. But it is fair to say that the meaning 'shade' has less currency than in Homer, and has not in any way enlarged its scope in the semantics of ψυχή after Homer. No importance attached to the 'shade' after Homer has inhibited the late use of 'life-force' expressions. Euripides' statement that Helen killed (ἔκτεινε) the ψυχή of Astyanax is decisive for the late or, perhaps, growing vigor of ψυχή as a physical 'life-force' unaffected by logical inferences from the notion of the surviving 'shade'. As a physical 'life-force', moreover, ψυχή is compatible with the other 'life-force' words both in its Homeric and later uses, although it is not indistinguishable from them. Like them, it is in Homer 'lost' or 'destroyed' at death, ambiguously 'breath'-like and 'blood'-like, and not an abstraction. In Homer it lacks entirely physical usages of the type I have described as group I in the model for κῆρ, but with one exception these appear in later texts along with periphrastic expressions comparable to those found for κῆρ and μένος. The exception is the absence of ψυχή in ordinary 'strength' contexts, although Bacchylides 5.151 perhaps fills this gap. Otherwise, the lack of 'strength' usages in nonpsychological 'life-force' contexts in the later texts distinguishes ψυχή from the pattern traced for the other words.[35]

34. Cf. Farnell, p. 159, n. 89.

35. It is conceivable, although barely, that we should think of ψυχή at *Aj.* 559 as having some of the qualities of the Roman *genius*, and this would be a further point of differentiation. But the ψυχή obviously never achieves the specificity of the *genius*, which is associated with a man's birth (*RE* 7, 1156; Rose, p. 59), transmitted to the successor son with the last breath (Rose, p. 60; Bayet, p. 517), and receives sacrifices (*RE* 7, 1161). Despite these parallels and Onians's strong assertion of the connection, the evidence seems insufficient.

2

ψυχή as a Psychological Agent after Homer

LYRIC POETRY AND TRAGEDY

The analysis of *ψυχή* as a psychological agent must begin with its use in periphrasis, since, as in the cases of *περὶ κῆρι* and *θυμῷ* above, it can be argued that failure to take this idiom into account greatly distorts our view of the evidence. Webster notes that "in Sophocles and Euripides *ψυχή* may also simply mean a person without any further emphasis on the soul as distinct from the body than the implied recognition that the soul controls the body." [1] This judgment understates, I think, the importance of periphrasis for *ψυχή* and, in its conclusion about the relationship of body and soul, misstates entirely the nature of the periphrasis encountered.

The most convincing example of periphrasis with *ψυχή* is found at *Hecuba* 87–88. Hecuba enters and asks where she can find the divine *ψυχή* of Helenus or Cassandra to interpret her dream (*ποῦ ποτε θείαν Ἑλένου ψυχὰν | καὶ Κασάνδραν ἐσίδω;*). Unless we are to believe that Euripides has here arbitrarily introduced an arcane reference to religious or philosophical notions of *ψυχή*, it seems certain that the noun-adjective combination *θείαν ψυχάν* is not meant to signify a thoughtful connection of soul and divinity. But one must still ask whether *θείαν* modifies the periphrastic word or whether it is felt to apply solely to the subject of the periphrasis, that is, Helenus. Although it is not possible to reach a decisive answer to this question, comparable expressions are of some help. These fall into two groups, namely, expressions using 'force' or 'life-force' words (*Il.* 2.851 *Παφλαγόνων δ' ἡγεῖτο Πυλαιμένεος λάσιον κῆρ*; *Il.* 14.139 *Ἀχιλλῆος ὀλοὸν κῆρ*; *Od.* 2.409 *ἱερὴ ἲς Τελεμάχοιο*; *Od.* 7.167 *ἱερὸν μένος Ἀλκινόοιο*; *Il.* 23.720

1. Webster, p. 151.

κρατερὴ ἲς Ὀδυσῆος; *Ch.* 893 φίλτατ᾽ Αἰγίσθου βία) and expressions using κάρα (*Ag.* 905 φίλον κάρα in address; *Ant.* 1 ὦ κοινὸν αὐτάδελφον Ἰσμήνης κάρα; *OT* 40 ὦ κράτιστον πᾶσιν θἰδίπου κάρα; S. *El.* 1164 ὦ κασίγνητον κάρα; *OC* 1657 τὸ Θησέως κάρα; *OT* 1207 ἰὼ κλεινὸν Οἰδίπου κάρα; *Hipp.* 651 ὦ κακὸν κάρα; E. *Supp.* 163 ὦ καθ᾽ Ἑλλάδ᾽ ἀλκιμώτατον κάρα; *Hec.* 676 τὸ βακχεῖον κάρα . . . Κασάνδρας; *HF* 1046 τὸ καλλίνικον κάρα = Heracles; *Or.* 481 ἀνόσιον κάρα = Orestes). The examples demonstrate that adjectives in 'force' expressions may remain open to a literal connection with the word in question—for example, ἱερὴ ἲς, κρατερὴ ἲς—although it is possible for an adjective to incline toward the subject and not the periphrastic word, as in Ἀχιλλῆος ὀλοὸν κῆρ. Periphrasis in tragedy with κάρα, on the other hand, seems to drop all literal connection with the periphrastic word, since κράτιστον κάρα, αὐτάδελφον κάρα, κλεινὸν κάρα, βακχεῖον κάρα, ἀνόσιον κάρα, and the like make sense only by reference to the subject undergoing periphrasis. A logical conclusion, therefore, is that periphrastic expressions using κάρα are sufficiently colloquial to repress the literal meaning of κάρα. From the equivalence of τέθνηκε θεῖον Ἰοκάστης κάρα at *Oedipus Tyrannus* 1235 and θείαν Ἑλένου ψυχάν at *Hecuba* 87–88, it follows that ψυχή can also be used in periphrasis of the κάρα type. By analogy to κάρα, therefore, such expressions must imply suppression of the ordinary meanings of ψυχή where they occur, not that the "soul controls the body."

A more difficult problem, then, is to know the limits of such periphrasis and the differences, if any, between κάρα and ψυχή when used in this way. On the evidence of κάρα, all uses of ψυχή in address to others can be counted as potentially periphrastic, whether phrases with single modifiers like *Philoctetes* 712 and *Iphigenia Taurica* 881 (ὦ μελέα ψυχά both times), comparable to κάρα at *Hippolytus* 651 (ὦ κακὸν κάρα), or phrases with extended modifiers like *Iphigenia Taurica* 837 (ὦ κρεῖσσον ἢ λόγοισιν εὐτυχοῦσά μου ψυχά) and perhaps Sophocles' *Electra* 1127 (ὦ φιλτάτου μνημεῖον ἀνθρώπων ἐμοὶ / ψυχῆς Ὀρέστου λοιπόν), to which Euripides' *Supplices* 163 (ὦ καθ᾽ Ἑλλάδ᾽ ἀλκιμώτατον κάρα) and *Oedipus Tyrannus* 950 (ὦ φίλτατον γυναικὸς Ἰοκάστης κάρα) may be compared. Unlike these instances of address to the ψυχή of another, however, when a speaker addresses his own ψυχή the pattern followed is that of epic address to a personified agent, not periphrasis. Orestes' appeal to himself at *Orestes* 466 (ὦ τάλαινα καρδία ψυχή τ᾽ ἐμή) confirms this by doubleting ψυχή with the nonperiphrastic καρδία. Furthermore, all such instances of self-address occur at moments of great distress, for example, Creusa at the moment she learns of Ion's adoption (*Ion* 859 ὦ ψυχά, πῶς σιγάσω), and three may have connotations of the 'life' ψυχή as a function of their proximity to death—

Pindar's appeal to his ψυχή not to desire immortality (*P.* 3.61–62 μή, φίλα ψυχά, βίον ἀθάνατον / σπεῦδε), Antigone's injunction to her ψυχή to share the troubles of the dead Polynices (*Sept.* 1034 τοιγὰρ θέλουσ' ἄκοντι κοινώνει κακῶν, / ψυχή, θανόντι ζῶσα συγγόνῳ φρενί), and Heracles' plea to his ψυχή to endure as he is placed on the funeral pyre (*Tra.* 1260–63 ὦ ψυχὴ σκληρά, χάλυβος / λιθοκόλλητον στόμιον παρέχουσ' / ἀνέπαυε βοήν ...). In none of these cases can we infer periphrasis.

Comparison with κάρα suggests two additional periphrastic idioms. First, the use of κάρα with the possessive pronoun at Euripides' *Electra* 1196 (τίς ... ἐμὸν κάρα προσόψεται / ματέρα κτανόντος) and *Heraclidae* 539 (ὦ τέκνον, οὐκ ἔστ' ἄλλοθεν τὸ σὸν κάρα / ἀλλ' ἐξ ἐκείνου ...) may imply a periphrasis with ψυχή at *Oedipus Tyrannus* 64 (ἡ δ' ἐμὴ / ψυχὴ πόλιν ... στένει) and when Philoctetes accuses Odysseus of corrupting Neoptolemus (*Ph.* 1013 ἡ κακὴ σὴ διὰ μυχῶν βλέπουσ' ἀεὶ / ψυχή νιν ... προὐδίδαξεν). Both uses of the word, however, also conform to otherwise ordinary meanings. Second, periphrasis of the person with a kinship term as at *Phoenissae* 612 (ἀθέμιτόν σοι μητρὸς ὀνομάζειν κάρα) might explain the expression of Oedipus in the *Oedipus Coloneus* (999) that his father, if alive, would not refute his claim of innocence (ὥστ' ἐγὼ οὐδὲ τὴν πατρὸς / ψυχὴν ἂν οἶμαι ζῶσαν ἀντειπεῖν ἐμοί). A further use of periphrasis, one not paralleled in the surviving texts by κάρα, may perhaps be seen in the statement of Oedipus in the same play that one person may accomplish a sacrifice for many if he is well disposed (498–99 ἀρκεῖν γὰρ οἶμαι κἀντὶ μυρίων μίαν / ψυχὴν τάδ' ἐκτίνουσαν, ἢν εὔνους παρῇ). Taken literally, the idea that the ψυχή can make a sacrifice is bizarre, and it is worth noting that in at least one other occurrence of ψυχὴν μίαν periphrasis seems an equally, if not more, likely explanation of ψυχή than does psychological characterization. At *Medea* 247 Medea complains that, although a man is able to turn to a friend when troubled (πρὸς φίλον τινα), it is necessary for women to look to only one ψυχή (πρὸς μίαν ψυχὴν βλέπειν). If the theme of isolation is taken into account the phrase seems intended to show not that she has her ψυχή to talk to but that she has no one to talk to except herself, expressed by a periphrastic use of ψυχή. Possible support for this interpretation is offered by one of the remaining instances of ψυχὴν μίαν, *Hippolytus* 259 (τὸ δ' ὑπὲρ δισσῶν μίαν ὠδίνειν / ψυχὴν χαλεπὸν βάρος: the nurse complains that it is harsh for one ψυχή to bear the sufferings of two), where both periphrastic and psychological usage seem allowable.[2]

2. In *Or.* 1046 ψυχὴν μίαν is used to describe, perhaps metaphorically, the idea of a shared 'life' and name for Orestes and Electra.

These periphrastic expressions constructed with ψυχή raise an important question. Meissner's belief that the psychological use of ψυχή originated in the attachment of qualitative adjectives to ψυχή in periphrastic constructions doubtless stems from the fact that, with few exceptions,[3] uses of ψυχή with an unusual or highly characterizing adjective can be interpreted as periphrastic. Thus, fragment 97 of Sophocles, which says that a ψυχὴ εὔνους καὶ φρονοῦσα τοὔνδικον is a better discoverer than any sophist, corresponds to the use of εὔνους with the periphrastic μίαν ψυχήν in the line of *Oedipus Coloneus* just quoted. Similarly, the description of Phaedra at *Hippolytus* 159–60 as bound to her bed in grief (λύπᾳ δ᾽ ὑπὲρ παθέων / εὐναία δέδεται ψυχά) is acceptable as a periphrasis but awkward if εὐναία is taken as directly modifying the ψυχή itself. Additional expressions of this type are found at *Medea* 110 (μεγαλόσπλαγχνος δυσκατάπαυστος / ψυχή = Medea), *Ajax* 154 (μεγάλων ψυχῶν = 'great men'), and *Phoenissae* 1296–97 (φόνιαι ψυχαὶ δορὶ παλλόμεναι = Eteocles and Polynices) and can, like *Hippolytus* 259, be taken either periphrastically or as poetic enhancements of traditional usages. The list of such instances of ψυχή is completed by fragment 388 of Euripides—a discussion of which I shall defer for the moment—and two very unusual occurrences of ψυχή with genitive plural nouns which may or may not be extensions of periphrastic usages. In the Euripidean *Supplices* (1102–03) Iphis laments the death of Evadne by saying that nothing is sweeter to an old man than a daughter, for although the ψυχαί of males are 'greater', they are 'less sweet in endearments' (ἀρσένων δὲ μείζονες / ψυχαί, γλυκεῖαι δ᾽ ἧσσον ἐς θωπεύματα). Similarly, Hermione at *Andromache* 159–61 accuses Andromache of having made her unattractive to her husband and of injuring her womb, skills in which the Asiatic ψυχή of women is practiced (δεινὴ γὰρ ἠπειρῶτις εἰς τὰ τοιάδε / ψυχὴ γυναικῶν). The plural genitives are difficult to explain, since similar constructions that appear to be periphrastic always use the singular. In these instances, to look ahead, it is possible that the use of ψυχή reflects late fifth-century belief that types of ψυχαί can be generically grouped. One might compare, for example, the speculations of the writer of *Airs, Waters, Places* on the feeble nature on the ψυχαί of those who live in hot climates. ψυχή treated in this way is clearly biological in nature, and therefore the case for a tie to the Euripidean passages is anything but decisive. Yet there is a ring of similarity that seems worth noting.

3. *Hipp.* 1006 παρθένον ψυχήν, see below, p. 84; Bacch. 11.47–48 παρθενίᾳ ψυχῇ; Hipponax 39 τὴν πολύστονον ψυχήν; *Peace* 1068 δόλιαι ψυχαί. I regard S. *El.* 218 δυσθύμῳ ψυχᾷ and the ἀγαθή/κακή phrases as having an obvious traditional attachment to ψυχή.

If such ambiguity is in fact present in these two passages, the case for psychological overtones in singular constructions that are periphrastic in appearance may perhaps be strengthened. On balance, however, the isolation of unusual or potentially generalizing usages of *ψυχή* by a single idiomatic category—here periphrasis—must be suspect. As in the use of *θυμῷ* and *περὶ κῆρι*, periphrasis for *ψυχή* seems to be an idiom that depends upon the suppression of significant meaning for *ψυχή*. That *ψυχή* and *κάρα* are used identically with *θεῖος* and that *κάρα* is then used elsewhere with complete freedom from literal denotation imply that partial or complete suppression of rational connection between *ψυχή* and its modifier is possible whenever *ψυχή* designates the 'person'. That *ψυχή* appears with *θεία* as late as *Hecuba* argues that the ability of such periphrases to accept inapposite modifiers was never diminished, much less eliminated, as would be expected if a development of the type proposed by Meissner had occurred. But our ability to penetrate the nuances of these constructions is admittedly limited, and in the following discussion I have avoided dogmatism on this point.

With this in mind it is possible at last to examine in detail the psychological use of *ψυχή* after Homer and to assess the reasons for the development of *ψυχή* as a psychological agent. It will be clear, I believe, that almost all psychological uses of *ψυχή* not identifiable as periphrases adhere in general to the 'life-force' pattern. For the lyric poets and tragedy this can be shown by direct application of the *κῆρ* model.

Group I Uses. The most obvious citations in this category are those that speak of the *ψυχή* as benefited by food and drink. Occurrences of this kind that may be ambiguous with the notion of a more general psychological agent as well are Hipponax 39, where wine is a *φάρμακον πονηρίης* for the *ψυχή*, and *Cyclops* 340, where the Cyclops speaks of the meal he is about to make of Odysseus as one that will 'do good' to his *ψυχή* (*τὴν ⟨δ'⟩ἐμὴν ψυχὴν ἐγὼ / οὐ παύσομαι δρῶν εὖ—κατεσθίων τε σέ*). A more casual context, and one which therefore tends to isolate appetite by itself as a function of *ψυχή* is that of *Ion* 1170, where the chorus is told that those who attended the feast satisfied the *ψυχή* with rich food (*εὐόχθου βορᾶς / ψυχὴν ἐπλήρουν*).[4] The more general idea of giving material gratification of any kind to one's *ψυχή* is found first in Semonides 29 and on an Eretrian inscription, passages we shall examine below when the very earliest psychological uses of *ψυχή* are discussed together. A later use of this idea is found at *Persae* 841, where it

---

4. Worth adding in this context is the *Deipnon* of Philoxenus Leucadius 836 (b) 5, thought to date from the end of the fifth century, which speaks of dishes of food as *ψυχᾶς δηλεασμάτοισι*.

is perhaps ambiguous with the 'shade', since the ghost of Darius advises the chorus to furnish daily pleasure to the ψυχή (ψυχῇ διδόντες ἡδονὴν καθ' ἡμέραν), given the uselessness of wealth to the dead.[5]

A direct extension of this interest in the material well-being of the ψυχή is its importance as the center or source of sexual desire. Apart from passages in Anacreon and Sappho, also to be discussed with the earliest usages, the first text that seems to impose an erotic context on ψυχή is fragment 123 of Pindar. Addressing his θυμός, Pindar declares that one must "pluck loves in season." Whoever does not swell with desire looking into the eyes of Theoxenus either has a black heart forged in a cold fire of adamantine steel, or, dishonored by Aphrodite, toils angrily for possessions, or γυναικείῳ θράσει | ψυχὰν φορεῖται πᾶσαν ὁδὸν θεραπεύων. Although ψυχάν is written only by emendation it is nevertheless almost certain. A sensible translation is possible only if the word is treated as an erotic psychological agent that demands gratification: "With woman's lust the jaded man is borne down every path serving his ψυχή."[6] This interpretation is further supported by the possible appearance of the phrase "serving the ψυχή" in Euripides.[7] ψυχή is not found in an erotic context in Aeschylus, which should not be surprising in view of the inappropriate subject matter of the surviving plays, and it occurs only once in Sophocles, in fragment 855.8, a use discussed earlier as an extension of the Homeric 'life'. Kypris is said to be "melted into the lungs of all who have ψυχή" (ἐντήκεται γὰρ πλευμόνων ὅσοις ἔνι | ψυχή), a typical way of saying simply "those who are alive," but in view of the erotic involvement of ψυχή elsewhere the meaning here may be ambiguous. In the plays of Euripides,

5. Nontragic passages from the fifth century also show this use of ψυχή. Cf. Epicharmus B 45 and Diocles K 14, who recommends that one die young "having experienced something good for the ψυχή (ἀγαθόν τι τῇ ψυχῇ παθών) rather than live to a toothless old age." Also relevant, perhaps, is ψυχή in the story of Polycrates at Hdt. 3.40ff., and remotely, Aj. 559.

6. Just prior to writing ψυχράν, the copyist had read ψυχρᾷ φλογί and therefore corrupted ψυχάν. Attempts to preserve ψυχράν are absurd. See Farnell's discussion, pp. 441–43, who quotes Sandys: "with woman's courage is borne along a path that is utterly cold," a translation that leaves out θεραπεύων in any case. The thought of these lines, following Farnell, must be that the man who feels no desire is either frigid, consumed with monetary greed, or sexually indiscriminate and jaded. Farnell seems rightly to take γυναικείῳ θράσει as 'with lust' rather than 'modestly', and to reject attempts to render θεραπεύων without an object. But it is impossible to accept the bizarre resolution of the line in which he destroys the natural coherence of φορεῖται πᾶσαν ὁδόν in order to avoid what undoubtedly seem to him the ethical difficulties of the phrase θεραπεύων ψυχάν: thus the lustful man is "driven hither and thither" in his soul, "courting love along every highway and by-way," a rendering that is scarcely convincing. These difficulties are resolved if we give ψυχή the meaning suggested by its use elsewhere and its parallelism to the other 'life' words, namely, the 'life-force' that craves and demands various kinds of physical gratification, including sexual. θεραπευών necessitates, however, emendation to ψυχᾷ.

7. E. fr. 220, below, nn. 12 and 13.

however, where appropriate situations are common, *ψυχή* is readily found in such contexts. Most directly sexual is the occurrence of *ψυχή* in a fragment of the lost *Danae*, in which Danae speaks to her father of a lover who would leap into her arms and with a "crowd of kisses possess my *ψυχή*" (fr. 323 τάχ' ἂν πρὸς ἀγκάλαισι καὶ στέρνοις ἐμοῖς / πηδῶν ἀθύροι καὶ φιλημάτων ὄχλῳ / ψυχὴν ἐμὴν κτήσαιτο) and concludes that intercourse is the greatest love potion among men. Another fragment, attributed to the *Phaedra* of Sophocles by Stobaeus but to Euripides by Clement of Alexandria, asserts that the *ψυχαί* of the gods as well as men are subject to ἔρως (fr. 431 Ἔρως ... θεῶν ἄνω / ψυχὰς χαράσσει).[8] In the *Hippolytus* the *ψυχή* is repeatedly mentioned in contexts suggestive of erotic feeling. It is perhaps possible to include here—if it is also felt as a psychological agent and not simply periphrastic—Phaedra's εὐναία *ψυχή*, bound to the bed in grief (159–60) as the result of hearing a report from Crete about Theseus. Phaedra herself replies to the nurse's suggestion that she do something to carry out her desires toward Hippolytus by saying that clever and persuasive words will lead her to destruction thanks to the power of ἔρως over, or in, her *ψυχή* (504–05 ὡς ὑπείργασμαι μὲν εὖ / ψυχὴν ἔρωτι). The chorus comments on this scene with an ode to the power of ἔρως over *ψυχή* (525–27 Ἔρως, Ἔρως, ὅ κατ' ὀμμάτων / στάζεις πόθον, εἰσάγων γλυκεῖαν / ψυχᾷ χάριν ἐπιστρατεύσῃ), and finally, Hippolytus proclaims his innocence to Theseus by asserting that his virgin *ψυχή* defends him against interest in sexual matters (1006 παρθένον ψυχὴν ἔχων). This last phrase in particular has led to the conclusion that *ψυχή* is now able to encompass the general 'character' of a man,[9] but a connection to the earlier erotic uses of *ψυχή* in the play is certainly possible. For reasons to be taken up below, however, this is an important and perhaps unique appearance of the word.

Group II Uses. From Pindar on, *ψυχή* is often translated 'courage'. Although courage is frequently implied, and perhaps properly characterizes *ψυχή* as an emotion per se, most occurrences of *ψυχή* in this sense look simply to a force that generates violence, and hence are plainly 'life-force' uses like those of *μένος* and *θυμός*. This essential ambiguity can be illustrated from *Pythian* 1.47–48, where the military prowess of Hiero is invoked with the thought that the sentiments uttered will remind him how he stood in conflict with an enduring *ψυχή* (οἵαις ἐν πολέμοισι μάχαις / τλάμονι ψυχᾷ παρέμεινε). That this 'enduring' *ψυχή* was common for the description of military excellence is made certain by Aeschylus'

8. The fragment is assigned by Nauck to the first *Hippolytus*.
9. E.g., Webster, p. 150.

description in *Persae* of the Persian host on its departure to Greece as terrible in the reputation for endurance and courage (A. *Pers.* 27–28 φοβεροὶ μὲν ἰδεῖν, δεινοὶ δὲ μάχην | ψυχῆς εὐτλήμονι δόξῃ), and such usage is thought to derive from phrases like that of Tyrtaeus 12.18 (ψυχὴν καὶ θυμὸν τλήμονα παρθέμενος), where an analogy of ψυχή and θυμός may have functioned.[10] It is natural to think of the enduring ψυχή in battle as the emotion 'courage' itself or its sources in the man, but the statement of Apollo at *Pythian* 3.40–42 that he will not 'endure' in his ψυχή to allow Asclepius to die on account of the envy of Artemis (οὐκέτι | τλάσομαι ψυχᾷ γένος ἀμὸν ὀλέσσαι | οἰκτροτάτῳ θανάτῳ) shows a less specific meaning appropriate to the 'life-force'. What the ψυχή furnishes Apollo is clearly not only 'courage' but also anger and the disposition to act violently. Other passages in drama in which ψυχή describes ambiguously an emotion itself and the seat or source of such emotion illustrate the inappropriateness of 'courage' alone, at least in drama, as a discrete value for ψυχή. Thus, the chorus at *Heraclidae* 922ff. celebrates the success of the suppliant children and the restraint placed upon the ὕβρις of the man whose θυμός demanded δίκη— here, surely retribution—and closes with the hope that its own φρόνημα and ψυχά may not be insatiable (μήποτ᾿ ἐμοὶ φρόνημα ψυχά τ᾿ ἀκόρεστος εἴη). 'Courage', or the 'seat of courage', would here have to be a connotation directly opposed to the sense of criticism in the lines, and what must be intended is therefore only 'anger' or 'violent passion'. Similarly, at *Hippolytus* 1039–40 Theseus' question whether Hippolytus thinks that he is a 'juggler' or 'magician' able to overpower his ψυχή (ὃς τὴν ἐμὴν πέποιθεν εὐοργησίᾳ | ψυχὴν κρατήσειν) suggests again 'anger' or 'passion' or its source in the man, in addition to an ambiguity with ψυχή as 'life'.[11] In most of these passages 'courage' is far too ethically weighted and sententious as a translation of ψυχή, and 'passion' or 'boldness' must be understood instead.

A number of psychological uses of ψυχή in addition to those just discussed can be grouped around these ideas or their source in the person. The ψυχή in this sense may account for naive daring, as in Bacchylides 11.47–48, where the daughters of Proteus are led by their παρθενίᾳ ψυχᾷ (a phrase that might be compared to ἀρσένων ... ψυχαί in Euripides) to enter the precinct of Hera and there boast of the wealth of Proteus. Or it can account for more self-conscious pride, as in fragment 924 of Euripides, where the speaker accuses his ψυχή in direct address of boasting too much,

10. Cf. Webster, p. 150. I take εὐτλήμονι as a transferred epithet.
11. Cf. OC 1207, where μηδεὶς κρατείτω τῆς ἐμῆς ψυχῆς can mean only, "Let no one have control over my life."

asking it why it puts on such airs (ψυχή, / τί περισσὰ φρονεῖς;). Further, a fragment of Euripides' *Antiope*, which with the words γνώμῃ φρονοῦντες οὐ θέλουσ᾽ ὑπηρετεῖν / ψυχῇ has been thought to invite a Platonic interpretation of ψυχή, can be understood in traditional terms by reference to ψυχή as the seat of a disposition to violence.[12] Despite some ambiguity,[13] the passage can be read as contrasting γνώμῃ and ψυχῇ with ψυχή taken as the natural object of ὑπηρετεῖν here as in Pindar fragment 123. The sentiment in that case is familiar from Thucydides. Like Pericles, who in the funeral oration (2.40.3) says that those who know most clearly the "sweet and the terrible" and yet do not as a result turn away from risks are rightly judged κράτιστοι ... τὴν ψυχήν, Euripides seems most likely to mean that rationalization can turn one away from acts of boldness: "Reasoning things through they do not wish to serve the spirit that moves them to boldness, for the most part deferred by [thoughts of] things dear to them." I would also compare here a fragment from the *Erechtheus* of Euripides (E. fr. 360.44–45) in which Praxithea says that no one will destroy the ancestral institutions of the city without the consent of her ψυχή (ἑκούσης τῆς ἐμῆς ψυχῆς ἄτερ), as she prepares to sacrifice her own daughter for the salvation of the city. Two passages that invite the notion of ψυχή as 'character' in a general sense but in which the word is easily associated with 'boldness' may be noted here without discussion. Theognis 529–30 simply contrasts the 'courage' or 'boldness' of the free man with the cowardice of the slave (οὐδέ τινα προύδωκα φίλον καὶ πιστὸν ἑταῖρον / οὐδ᾽ ἐν ἐμῇ ψυχῇ δούλιον οὐδὲν ἔνι); at *Phoenissae* 1296–97 the duel between Polynices and Eteocles moves the chorus to cry φεῦ δᾶ φεῦ δᾶ, δίδυμοι θῆρες, / φόνιαι ψυχαί δορὶ παλλόμεναι, either a reference to the penchant of the ψυχή for violence and battle, or else periphrasis. Three passages in which there is no possible ambiguity with emotion per se, and which offer a more demonic and destructive sense of ψυχή like that of *Heraclidae* 926–27, describe the motivation of vengeful women. At *Medea* 110, again a possible periphrasis, the nurse wonders what Medea's violent ψυχή will drive her to do, describing it as μεγαλόσ-πλαγχνος δυσκατάπαυστος / ψυχὴ δηχθεῖσα κακοῖσιν; in the Sophoclean *Electra* 219 the chorus warns Electra that she has brought an excess of evil on

12. πολλοὶ δὲ θνητῶν τοῦτο πάσχουσιν κακόν· / γνώμῃ φρονοῦντες οὐ θέλουσ᾽ ὑπηρετεῖν / ψυχῇ τὰ πολλὰ πρὸς φίλων νικώμενοι. A rationalistic interpretation of ψυχή in this passage is supplied in the translation of Snell (1964), p. 65: "Many mortals suffer this evil—filled with reasonable insight they do not wish to subject themselves to the soul, because they are for the most part defeated by what is dear to them."

13. Meissner (pp. 66–67) translates," Viele wollen, obwohl sie vernünftig sind, ihrer besseren Einsicht nicht nachkommen, da sie in ihrer Seele meist dem Lustvollen unterliegen," a rendering that makes ψυχή properly emotional.

herself by breeding wars in her ψυχή (σᾷ δυσθύμῳ τίκτουσ' αἰεὶ ψυχᾷ πολέμους);[14] last, at *Antigone* 930 the chorus says of Antigone as she goes to her death that winds of the soul hold her: ἔτι τῶν αὐτῶν ἀνέμων αὗται | ψυχῆς ῥιπαὶ τήνδε γ' ἔχουσιν.

'Courage' without the notion of violence is implied, though not without ambiguity, whenever the ψυχή is described as good or bad. This meaning can be validated outside drama by the passage from Thucydides just mentioned and the phrase ἀγαθὴ ψυχή at Herodotus 7.153, where military success is said to be beyond the province of every man and to come only πρὸς ψυχῆς τε ἀγαθῆς καὶ ῥώμης ἀνδρηίης. In tragedy, Polyxena at *Hecuba* 579–80, who faces her executioners without having to be bound, is described by the onlooking Argives as τῇ περίσσ' εὐκαρδίῳ | ψυχήν τ' ἀρίστῃ, and at *Agamemnon* 1643–46 Aegisthus is abused as being ἀπὸ ψυχῆς κακῆς for leaving the murder of Agamemnon to Clytemnestra instead of doing it himself. The consistency of such expressions is important for *Philoctetes* 1013–14, in which Platonic overtones, perhaps evoked by Odysseus' corrupting of the youthful Neoptolemus, are seen in Philoctetes' accusations that the κακὴ ψυχή of Odysseus (ἡ κακὴ σὴ διὰ μυχῶν βλέπουσ' ἀεὶ | ψυχή) has taught Neoptolemus to be "wise in evils."[15] Even if ψυχή is not periphrastic, it is unnecessary to go beyond the traditional functions of the ψυχή—greatly elaborated by διὰ μυχῶν βλέπουσα—as the seat of 'courage', here ambiguous with 'endurance', to explain what Philoctetes means.

Group III Uses. The limitations on ψυχή in this category are striking in that, even more than κῆρ, ἦτορ, and θυμός, the word is found only in instances of crucial feeling. It is used, in effect, only by protagonists to describe moments of extreme crisis for themselves or by supporting figures to express their sympathetic feelings for endangered friends and loved ones. For Ajax, in a fragmentary speech from a play of unknown authorship, nothing so 'bites' the ψυχή of a man as dishonor, and this sentiment is placed at what must be the moment of his return to sanity.[16] The ψυχή of Oedipus, again possibly a periphrasis, is moved by grief for himself, his

14. For δυσθυμία, ὀργή, and ψυχή cf. also E. fr. 822, where it is said that a woman is sweetest for her husband in troubles and sickness if she takes care of the house, soothes his passion, and "lifts his ψυχή out of anger" (ὀργήν τε πραΰνουσα καὶ δυσθυμίας ψυχὴν μεθιστᾶσ').

15. Cf. Jebb: "But thy base soul, ever peering from some ambush, had well trained him—all unapt and unwilling as he was—to be cunning in evil."

16. Adesp. fr. 110. Nauck reads for the first lines οὐκ ἦν ἄρ' οὐδὲν πῆμ' ἐλευθέραν δάκνον | ψυχὴν ὁμοίως ἀνδρὸς ὡς ἀτιμία. The variant ἐλευθέρου is unquestionably better, given the ordinary absence of strongly characterizing modifiers with nonperiphrastic uses of ψυχή. According to one of the sources, Ajax is about to commit suicide.

country, and his people on account of the plague (*OT* 64 ἡ δ᾽ ἐμὴ ψυχὴ πόλιν
τε κἀμὲ καὶ σ᾽ ὁμοῦ στένει). In *Ion* Creusa cries out to her ψυχή at the moment
she learns of Ion's adoption and then says that her ψυχή grieves at having
become the object of plots by men and gods (*Ion* 876–77 στάζουσι κόραι
δακρύοισιν ἐμαί | ψυχὴ δ᾽ ἀλγεῖ κακοβουλευθεῖσ᾽ | ἔκ τ᾽ ἀνθρώπων ἔκ τ᾽
ἀθανάτων). The ψυχή of Admetus (*Alc.* 354) suffers grief over the death of
Alcestis. Hecuba feels horror in her ψυχή over the plight of the Trojan
women (*Tr.* 182 ὀρθρεύουσαν ψυχὰν ἐκπληθεῖσα). Finally, at *Heraclidae*
644–45 Iolaus speaks to Alcmena of the return of endangered loved ones
for whom she has wasted away in her ψυχή (πάλαι γὰρ ὠδίνουσα τῶν
ἀφιγμένων | ψυχὴν ἐτήκου νόστος εἰ γενήσεται), and in the Euripidean *Electra*,
Electra (208) describes herself as 'wasting away' in her ψυχή while exiled
from the palace (αὐτὰ δ᾽ ἐν χερνῆσι δόμοις | ναίω ψυχὰν τακομένα).
Sympathetic statements involving the ψυχή include *Prometheus* 690–92,
where the chorus considers the horrors it has heard from Io to be the worst
it has ever encountered, ones that chill its ψυχή (οὐδ᾽ ὧδε δυσθέατα καὶ
δύσοιστα | †πήματα, λύματα, δείματ᾽ ἀμφήκει κέντρῳ ψύχειν ψυχὰν ἐμάν†); the
chorus of *Oedipus Tyrannus*, which, like Oedipus himself, feels its ψυχή
consumed by sorrow for the distress of the country (*OT* 665–66 ἀλλά μοι
δυσμόρῳ γᾶ φθίνουσα τρύχει ψυχάν …);[17] and the chorus of *Alcestis* 601ff.,
which says that its ψυχή has θάρσος that the man who honors the gods will
prosper. This statement is clearly an expression of hope that the life of
Alcestis can be saved through her husband's piety. A comparable passage is
found at *Heraclidae* 173, in which the herald tells Demophon not to let his
ψυχή be raised (εἰ τοῦτό σε | ψυχὴν ἐπαίρει) by the hope that the sons of
Heracles will be able to save Athens from Argos when they grow up. Other
statements having the same quality of deep sympathy are found at
Choephori 743–50, where the nurse calls Orestes, whose death she has just
reported, the supreme source of grief in her life now and the burden of her
ψυχή since his childhood (τῆς ἐμῆς ψυχῆς τριβήν), and at *Hippolytus* 255,
where Phaedra's nurse, as mentioned above, declares that one should feel
φιλία for others only in moderation, not πρὸς ἄκρον μυελὸν ψυχῆς—an idea
that may be developed at 259 if the expression ὑπὲρ δισσῶν μίαν
ὠδίνειν | ψυχήν is not felt as periphrastic. Again in *Hippolytus* the chorus says
that its ψυχή longs to know what is the matter (*Hipp.* 173 τί ποτ᾽ ἔστι μαθεῖν
ἔραται ψυχή), and in the Euripidean *Electra*, that its ψυχή shares Orestes'
desire to know the plight of Electra (E. *El.* 297 κἀγὼ τὸν αὐτὸν τῷδ᾽ ἔρον

---

17. Pearson's reading of λῆμα for mss. ψυχάν is gratuitous but shows the difficulties editors have
with ψυχή.

ψυχῆς ἔχω). ψυχή in this sense, but ambiguous with death connotations, is, as mentioned, also found in Antigone's words to her ψυχή at *Septem* 1034.

This listing exhausts the easily categorized uses of ψυχή in lyric poetry and tragedy, and it can be seen that in general they fall into close agreement with the basic 'life-force' pattern proposed for the psychological uses of κῆρ and the other 'life-force' words. Sixteen remaining occurrences must be classified initially as falling outside these categories. Of these, five appear at first to extend the traditional meaning of ψυχή, but on closer examination it is clear that they do not in fact do so, although the contexts are often too vague to allow a precise interpretation of the word. The most unusual of these is the phrase ἂν περὶ ψυχάν at *Pythian* 4.122, where Aeson rejoices on seeing his son—a passage that caused Meissner to regard ψυχή as an organ of consciousness like the καρδία. As we have seen earlier, θυμός has acquired 'heart' connotations at *Iliad* 7.216 (θυμὸς ἐνὶ στήθεσσι πάτασσεν), and it must be evident by now from the general argument I have made that without consistent repetition such anatomical expressions are of little value. This single instance of ψυχή as a spatial, and hence "organic," entity may simply demonstrate again the anatomical flexibility of these expressions, not the specific analogy of καρδία and ψυχή. Other uses, suggestive of innovation, are found in Sophocles, where ψυχή is used in contexts that seem to comment directly on the character of a central figure in the play, giving rise to translations and commentary that accept ψυχή as a kind of philosophical 'soul' or 'self'.[18] At *Oedipus Tyrannus* 726–27 Oedipus cries out, after learning of the exposure of the infant child, that wandering of his ψυχή and agitation of his φρένες have taken hold of him (ψυχῆς πλάνημα κἀνακίνησις φρενῶν). The close parallelism of ψυχή with a use of φρένες implying madness[19] may be taken to suggest the direct attribution of mental functions to ψυχή as well. But *Troades* 640 (ψυχὴν ἀλᾶται τῆς πάροιθ᾿ εὐπραξίας: one who has fallen from good fortune to bad wanders in his ψυχή from his former prosperity), another passage that can be included here, points up the vagueness of the expression and the range of ambiguities to which it may be subject. Although ψυχή is not associated with syncope in tragedy—no suitable contexts come to mind—ψυχῆς πλάνημα could easily describe the loss or weakening of physical and emotional strength to endure, not an immediate decline in rationality as a function of ψυχή. Less difficult to interpret is *Ajax* 1361. When Odysseus seeks permission to bury

18. I omit *Ph.* 55, already discussed, but taken by Webster and others as a new use of ψυχή.
19. Cf., e.g., *HF* 749 φρενῶν οὐκ ἔνδον ὤν.

Ajax he is asked by Agamemnon whether he would recommend having as friends those who are friends now but may become enemies later, and he answers that he does not praise an unyielding ψυχή (σκληρὰν ἐπαινεῖν οὐ φιλῶ ψυχὴν ἐγώ). This usage may be periphrastic or may be explained, like the use of ψυχὴ σκληρά at the end of *Trachiniae*, as a reference to the penchant of the ψυχή for violent, bold, or overbold acts—here, of course, in an unfavorable sense as at *Heraclidae* 927.

The remaining uses of ψυχή in tragedy need detailed explication and can be grouped as follows:

(1) ψυχή occurs twice in *Antigone* in difficult but possibly traditional uses. In his opening address to the citizens, Creon declares that it is impossible to know the 'plan', 'thought', or ψυχή of a man before he is manifest in his rule (175–77 ἀμήχανον δὲ παντὸς ἀνδρὸς ἐκμαθεῖν | ψυχήν τε καὶ φρόνημα καὶ γνώμην, πρὶν ἂν | ἀρχαῖς τε καὶ νόμοισιν ἐντριβὴς φανῇ), and later, Haemon tells his father that a man who thinks himself alone wise and possessed of ψυχή and a tongue unlike that of others will be exposed (707–09 ὅστις γὰρ αὐτὸς ἢ φρονεῖν μόνος δοκεῖ, | ἢ γλῶσσαν, ἣν οὐκ ἄλλος, ἢ ψυχὴν ἔχειν, | οὗτοι διαπτυχθέντες ὤφθησαν κενοί). Typical translations of ψυχή and γνώμη in the first text are 'soul' and 'mind'.[20] Webster translates the three nouns more conservatively as 'courage and wisdom and eloquence',[21] although he provides no support for his interpretation and offers in 'eloquence' a somewhat odd rendering of γνώμη. For the fifth century, φρόνημα is apt to be a specific intent[22] and not a desired quality of character, and it is perhaps relevant to cite here again μήποτ' ἐμοὶ φρόνημα ψυχά τ' ἀκόρεστος εἴη at *Heraclidae* 926–27, where the linkage of ψυχή and φρόνημα defines φρόνημα in an unfavorable sense. It is useful to compare also fragment 220 of Euripides, in which, as discussed, an opposition between γνώμη and ψυχή that defines ψυχή in its traditional role as a seat of passion and boldness is implied. Since this is Creon speaking in praise of himself, the intended meaning may be 'courage', although there may also be a more threatening tone. In either case a traditional value, supported directly by the Euripidean fragment and *Heraclidae*, accounts for Creon's diction

---

20. "You cannot learn of any man the soul, the mind, and the intent" (Wyckoff). Cf. Jebb: "No man can be fully known, in soul and spirit and mind." Müller comments (p. 65), "Als allgemeinstes Wort für das Bewusstsein (wie etwa 227, 559, *El.* 903, *Tr.* 1260) wird ψυχήν hier durch τε καὶ mit φρόνημα und γνώμην als den speziellen Funktionen oder als den Teilen des Bewusstseins verbunden."

21. Webster, p. 151.

22. *LSJ* s.v. φρόνημα.

without recourse to ψυχή as a comprehensive psychological self. The second passage from *Antigone* has caused even greater difficulty.[23] But it is apparent in the preceding line (ὡς φὴς σύ, κοὐδὲν ἄλλο, τοῦτ' ὀρθῶς ἔχειν) that Haemon is appealing in a warning manner to his father to avoid the excesses of the tyrant, and it is consistent with this statement and the earlier warning (692–93) about popular dissatisfaction with Creon to conclude that lines 707–09 list, with some irony, the qualities of the successful politician—planning, eloquence, and 'boldness'. It is superfluous, therefore, to give this use of ψυχή an intellectual cast, and extensions in meaning along the lines of 'self' or 'character', despite the metaphorical suggestiveness of διαπτυχθέντες ὤφθησαν, would be meaningless. The sense of the passage is thus traceable to a traditional use of ψυχή, and specifically to the same political context as that of Creon's own use of ψυχή earlier.[24]

(2) A few instances of ψυχή in tragedy have shamanistic or ecstatic connotations. These occurrences are paralleled for tragedy not only by θυμός[25] but by φρήν/φρένες. A line of Sophocles that speaks of the "gate of the ψυχή" (fr. 360 ψυχῆς ἀνοῖξαι τὴν κεκλημένην πύλην) and might therefore be thought to have a philosophical ring to it comes from the lost *Manteis*, and it is not an unreasonable guess, insofar as anything can be said on the basis of the five words left to us, that the elaborate metaphor has prophetic connotations. A similar figure (κλῇδα φρενῶν) is found at *Medea* 661. Twice in the *Bacchae* ψυχή occurs as the personal agent of Dionysian ecstasy. At the beginning of the play the chorus finds a man to be 'blessed' who knows the mysteries of the gods, lives piously, and revels in his ψυχή (*Ba.* 72–76 θιασεύεται ψυχὰν / ἐν ὄρεσσι βακχεύων), and toward the end of the play Cadmus asks Agave whether her ψυχή is still agitated (1268 τὸ δὲ πτοηθὲν τόδ' ἔτι σῇ ψυχῇ πάρα;)—language that is parodied by Strepsiades during his quasi-religious initiation into the φροντιστήριον (*Clouds* 319 ταῦτ' ἄρ' ἀκούσασ' αὐτῶν τὸ φθέγμ' ἡ ψυχή μου πεπότηται). Parallels with φρήν/φρένες can be found in βακχεύει φρένα (E. *Alex.* fr. 7) and ἐπτοημένοι φρένας (*Pr.* 856). But the infrequency of such usages in tragedy suggests that the idea of

---

23. Jebb tries to avoid the issue by using "soul" in the English sense of "person": "Wear not, then, one mood only in thyself; think not that thy word, and thine alone, must be right. For if any man thinks that he alone is wise—that in speech, or in mind, he hath no peer—such a soul, when laid open, is ever found empty." Cf Mazon (1955): "Les gens qui s'imaginent être seuls raisonnable et posséder des idées ou des mots inconnus à tout autre, ces gens-là, ouvre-les: tu ne trouveras en eux que le vide."

24. *Ant.* 175–77.

25. *Andr.* 1072 πρόμαντις θυμός. Cf. *Pers.* 11, A. fr. 243 N.

an ecstatic ψυχή was not an everyday connotation of ψυχή, and this conclusion may be strengthened by the ability of Aristophanes to use such ideas for comic effect.[26]

(3) Three instances of what may be nonrational knowledge attributed to the ψυχή are found in tragedy. Orestes replies to Electra's sudden assertion that she has a plan to save them by saying that he knows there is τὸ συνετόν in her ψυχή (*Or.* 1179–80 θεοῦ λέγεις πρόνοιαν. ἀλλὰ ποῦ τόδε; / ἐπεὶ τὸ συνετόν γ᾽ οἶδα σῇ ψυχῇ παρόν). Over the lifeless body of Astyanax, Hecuba says that had he grown to manhood and died he would have been blessed by the prosperity of his father's house, but now he will know it only in his ψυχή (*Tr.* 1171 νῦν δ᾽ αὖτ᾽ ἰδὼν μὲν γνούς τε σῇ ψυχῇ, τέκνον, / οὐκ οἶσθ᾽, ἐχρήσω δ᾽ οὐδὲν ἐν δόμοις ἔχων). In the Sophoclean *Electra* the sight of Orestes' lock of hair is said to have burst upon the ψυχή of Electra (903 κευθὺς τάλαιν᾽ ὡς εἶδον, ἐμπαίει τί μοι / ψυχῇ σύνηθες ὄμμα). These passages, particularly the first, are taken to support the belief that ψυχή begins to have a special connection with knowledge in late fifth-century drama.[27] But the last passage seems simply to refer to the emotional ψυχή, which responds vigorously to the return of Orestes as it recognizes in its feelings what is seen with the eyes. Neither the context nor ἐμπαίειν suggests intellectual activity. The use of τὸ συνετόν in the first quotation reflects the tendency in the late fifth century to employ articular adjectival constructions[28] which inevitably force upon ψυχή a sense that it is internally divided. But the context as a whole looks more to inspired knowledge than to reflective or calculative intelligence. The use of ψυχή in the case of Astyanax is unprecedented but also set in a curious context if it is a consequence of developments in the use of ψυχή. It is perhaps more plausible to see in these lines a poetic extension of the ψυχή that enjoys material blessings and joys, a connotation I have already suggested in the address of Ajax to the infant Eurysaces.[29] Hecuba may mean in addition that the blessings of his birth, which Astyanax has seen and known in his ψυχή, are all that he will know, because his ψυχή is all that is left to him. Such an oblique use of ψυχή as 'shade', however, is unusual.

(4) Another curious and unique passage that seems nevertheless to look backward rather than forward in the semantic history of ψυχή is the guard's report of a conversation with his ψυχή at *Antigone* 225ff. The guard

26. See below, p. 87.
27. Meissner, p. 67; Webster, p. 151.
28. Kühner-Gerth II i, pp. 267–68.
29. Cf. *Aj.* 559.

doubts his judgment in allowing himself to be the one who brings bad news to Creon (ψυχὴ γὰρ ηὔδα πολλά μοι μυθουμένη· | τάλας, τί χωρεῖς οἶ μολὼν δώσεις δίκην;). Although it is true, as Webster points out, that this ψυχή apprehends plans and places alternatives before the guard, it is difficult to believe that it would be to the guard, and not to other Sophoclean figures, that so uncommonly intellectual a usage of ψυχή would be given. The closest parallels for this passage are in fact the instances of personified exchange in epic involving θυμός, and a reasonable guess is that, for dramatic reasons, ψυχή here exhibits a function of the θυμός in Homer. The Homeric setting of the passage, in any case, is unmistakable and must act to limit the interpretation of ψυχή.

(5) There remain, finally, two very intriguing occurrences of ψυχή in tragedy. The first is in fragment 388 of Euripides, which asserts that there is another sort of love among men—that of a ψυχή which is just, moderate, and good—in accordance with which wise men should abandon sex and love only the pious: ἀλλ᾽ ἔστι δή τις ἄλλος ἐν βροτοῖς ἔρως | ψυχῆς δικαίας σώφρονος τε κἀγαθῆς. | καὶ χρῆν δὲ τοῖς βροτοῖσι τόνδ᾽ εἶναι νόμον | τῶν εὐσεβούντων οἵτινές τε σώφρονες | ἐρᾶν, Κύπριν δὲ τὴν Διὸς χαίρειν ἐᾶν. This fragment is used by Meissner, Webster, and most recently Adkins[30] to show the general attribution of moral and intellectual qualities to ψυχή in fifth-century popular usage. It must be pointed out, however, that the words δικαίας σώφρονος τε κἀγαθῆς alone have a formulaic quality to them, since a similar phrase is found at Septem 610. It is not, therefore, out of the question that ψυχή is being used in periphrasis, and, together with the unusual connotation of chastity for ἀγαθός,[31] this possibility must caution us against reading the passage, as Adkins does, as clear evidence for wide-spread changes in the use of ψυχή. These reservations do not apply, however, to what is undoubtedly the most striking occurrence of ψυχή in tragedy—already singled out by Burnet—namely, Hippolytus' claim to Theseus, in defense of his sexual purity, that he has a παρθένον ψυχήν. Here, of course, there can be no possibility of periphrasis, since the ψυχή is something one 'has', and, indeed, the phrase may well depend directly upon the Orphic attachments of Hippolytus alleged only a few lines earlier by Theseus[32]—a juncture of context and usage that otherwise seems

---

30. Adkins (1960), p. 192, n. 13, who does not see the passage as radically new in content, translates, "a mind which is *dikaios*."

31. Adkins (1960), pp. 172ff.

32. Barrett, pp. 342–43, correctly discredits the interpretation of Hippolytus as a practicing Orphic. That his portrayal is meant to suggest Orphic (or non-Orphic) asceticism remains unaffected. Without it Theseus would not be able to make his point at 952–55.

improbably coincidental. But this is, it must be pointed out, the one context that comes to mind in which a highly characterizing adjective that apparently implies an internalized moral code can be applied to *ψυχή* in a nonperiphrastic way and yet remain ambiguous. For if Hippolytus is in fact an Orphic figure, his sexual abstinence is to some extent a matter of ritual morality. This phrase may therefore demonstrate not that in late fifth-century tragedy a whole spectrum of human character traits can properly be attached to the *ψυχή*, but only that Orphics spoke of the *ψυχή*, as the object of hope for the afterlife, in terms of sexual chastity. It is not absolutely certain, therefore, that the phrase shows the moral qualities of the whole man attributed to the *ψυχή* and thus the creation of the comprehensive use of *ψυχή*. But, on balance, it seems likely that Euripides supplies in this instance an unmistakably new use of *ψυχή* and attempts to gain a deliberate and striking effect by placing the word in an Orphic context. This is a fact of considerable importance for the history of the word. The appearance of an "Orphic" use of *ψυχή* where a characterizing adjective is first used without periphrasis, it should be noted, helps to confirm the case for caution in interpreting constructions that do involve periphrasis.

OLD COMEDY

There are thirteen occurrences of *ψυχή* in fifth-century comedy[33] that are perhaps not simply unambiguous instances of traditional usage.[34] These will bear particularly close examination, since in comedy *ψυχή* seems a word deliberately sought out for its ambiguities. Possible Socratic references for *ψυχή* in Aristophanes will be examined in the last section of the book in conjunction with Xenophon and Plato.

33. *ψυχή* in Aristophanes is treated by Handley (1956).

34. The meaning 'life' is found in five places, all in Aristophanes: Dicaeopolis (*Ach.* 357) speaks nostalgically of his *ψυχή* as he is about to lay his head on the block (*καίτοι φιλῶ γε τὴν ἐμὴν ψυχὴν ἐγώ*) in a passage that may carry overtones of a *φίλη ψυχή* like that of *Or.* 1034 and similar passages; at *Wasps* 376 the chorus tells Philocleon not to be afraid, since it will make Bdelycleon run the race for his life if he speaks out (*τὸν περὶ ψυχῆς δρόμον δραμεῖν*); at *Peace* 1301 one of the boys throws away his shield and thus "saves his *ψυχή*," a usage that may involve a play on *ψυχή* as 'courage'. Penia (*Pl.* 524) asks rhetorically whether if a man were rich he would run the risk of his *ψυχή* by becoming a kidnapper (*κινδυνεύων περὶ τῆς ψυχῆς*); *Thesmophoriazusae* 864 repeats the rather strange diction of *Hel.* 52–53: *ψυχαὶ δὲ πολλαὶ δι'ἔμ' ἐπὶ Σκαμανδρίαις/ῥοαῖσιν ἔθανον.* Unambiguous references to *ψυχή* as the 'seat of courage' are found when Dicaeopolis (*Ach.* 393) says, as he sets out to find Euripides, that his *ψυχή* must be strong (*ὥρα 'στὶν ἤδη καρτερὰν ψυχὴν λαβεῖν*); in a fragment of Hermippus, where in a personal attack Pericles is asked why he chooses words over warlike deeds, "having promised the bravery of a Teles" (K 46 *ψυχὴν δὲ Τέλητος*

(continued overleaf)

The uses in question can be organized as follows:

(1) At *Acharnians* 375 Dicaeopolis, who is about to put his head on the block, says that he fears the τρόποι of rustic people who want to hear the city and themselves praised without regard to truth, and that he fears too the ψυχαί of old men who think only of the vote (τῶν τ' αὖ γερόντων οἶδα τὰς ψυχὰς ὅτι / οὐδὲν βλέπουσιν ἄλλο πλὴν ψηφηδακεῖν). If *Clouds* 94 is relevant, Dicaeopolis intends an insult to the old men of the chorus when he suggests that they physically resemble the ψυχή as 'ghost' or 'shade';[35] at the same time, of course, he fears the ψυχαί of the old men in a tragic sense as irrational and violent seekers after vengeance, just as the ψυχή of Eurystheus is feared at *Heraclidae* 927. Two passages in *Wasps* also come under this rubric. Shortly after Bdelycleon is threatened with a race for his ψυχή, the chorus encourages Philocleon to let himself down from the window by rope, "having filled his ψυχή with Diopeithes" (*Wasps* 380 τὴν ψυχὴν ἐμπλησάμενος Διοπείθους). Since Diopeithes was a soothsayer,[36] the joke may turn on the combination of ψυχή as the seat of courage and as an alleged source of occult knowledge. An equally complicated passage is found later in the same play (756) when Philocleon calls to his ψυχή in mock tragic tones to come to his aid, wishing that he were back in court casting the last ballot: σπεῦδ' ὦ ψυχή. ποῦ μοι ψυχή; / πάρες ὦ σκιερά. This appeal to the ψυχή must be referred to the parallel instances of self-address in tragedy noted above—for example, *Trachiniae* 1260, where Heracles speaks ambiguously to his 'courage' and his 'life' at the moment of death, and *Ion* 859, where Creusa addresses her ψυχή as a sympathetic listener to her troubles. If Philocleon's words invite these associations, the tone thus established might in itself account for comic effect. By addressing the ψυχή

(*continued from previous page*)

ὑπέστης); and in a fragment of Eubulus (K 101 εἰ μὴ σὺ χηνὸς ἧπαρ ἢ ψυχὴν ἔχεις). The quotation is made by Athenaeus (IX 384c) in the context of a discussion of goose liver as a Roman delicacy. Since we find anger situated in the ἧπαρ (e.g., Archil. 234 χολὴν γὰρ οὐκ ἔχεις ἐφ' ἥπατι), sense can be made of the quotation only if it alludes to the passion of the individual in question. (Edmonds *ad loc.* translates ψυχή as 'mind'.) The meaning 'shade' is unambiguous in a quotation from Plato Comicus (from the scholiast on *Birds* 471) in which a ghost is made to swear that his body is truly dead even though his shade "like that of Aesop has come back up" (K 68 ψυχὴν δ' ἀνήκειν ὥσπερ Αἰσώπου). Diocles K 14, discussed above, adduces the familiar idea of "doing good" to one's ψυχή before old age sets in. Additional uses of ψυχή that will not be discussed are *Knights* 482, where the chorus asks the sausage seller to reveal his plans: ἄγε δὴ σὺ τίνα νοῦν ἢ τίνα ψυχὴν ἔχεις; (the reading is uncertain since R has γνώμην but in any case ψυχή would mean only 'courage'), and Cratinus K 384, which gives us ἀνεπτερῶσθαι τὴν ψυχήν, "to have the ψυχή excited," a phrase that is without context and can only be compared to *Ba.* 1268 and *Clouds* 319.

35. Cf. Dover (1968) at line 91.
36. Nilsson (1940), pp. 133–34.

as σκιερά, however, Aristophanes succeeds in adducing the 'shade' as well, and this deliberate transformation may be taken to show that 'shade' is not ordinarily felt in such instances in tragedy.

(2) An extremely elaborate use of ψυχή implying ecstasis is found at *Peace* 827ff., where the servant of Trygaeus asks his master what he has seen while traveling in from the heavens, and he is told, "two or three ψυχαί of dithyrambic poets flying about collecting songs" (ξυνελέγοντ᾽ ἀναβολὰς ποτώμεναι). To the servant this suggests that the belief that men become stars when they die is false, but Trygaeus reassures him that in fact they do, citing the example of Ion of Chios, recently deceased and now known by a rather unwieldy joke as 'Daystar'. On the simplest level the afterlife activity of the 'shade' seems to be what is meant, and that is how the servant obviously takes Trygaeus' words. At *Acharnians* 395ff., however, the servant of Euripides tells Dicaeopolis that his master is both at home and not at home, since his νοῦς is abroad collecting songs while the master himself is within, writing tragedy (ὁ νοῦς μὲν ἔξω ξυλλέγων ἐπύλλια / οὐκ ἔνδον, αὐτὸς δ᾽ ἔνδον ἀναβάδην ποιεῖ / τραγῳδίαν). The parallel use of συλλέγειν in the two passages suggests that the ψυχαί of the dithyrambic poets are undergoing poetic ecstasies and not death. It is appropriate that for Euripides the νοῦς and not the ψυχή should undergo poetic transport of this kind, but if these scenes allude to anything more substantial than the poet's imagination it was surely ψυχή, not νοῦς, that was capable of poetic ecstasis. But of course neither text can be taken as a reliable witness to a serious theory of poetic creation, traditional or otherwise, involving ecstasis and the ψυχή. The interpretation of the passage from *Peace* is further complicated by the fact that one of the fragments of Ion of Chios refers to Pythagorean belief in metempsychosis.[37]

(3) At *Birds* 465–66 Pisthetairos, having completed elaborate ritual preparations for his oration to the chorus, tells Euelpides that he wishes to speak a great speech that will shatter the ψυχή of the birds (μέγα καὶ λαρινὸν ἔπος τι / ὅ τι τὴν τούτων θραύσει ψυχήν). Since his purpose is to stir a sense of injustice in them that will make them act against the gods, ψυχή must be felt as the seat of 'courage' and 'boldness' and, with θραύω, the seat of feeling regularly spoken of metaphorically in tragedy as the object of quasi-physical duress. There may be a more obscure ambiguity, however, given that Pisthetairos is attempting to exhibit the form, if not the substance, of rational discourse in dealing with the ψυχή of the birds. It is perhaps possible, in view of the late date of the play (414 B.C.), that we are meant to

37. B 4: see below, p. 116.

hear a parody of the Gorgianic claim that the speaker can move the ψυχή
with the power of λόγος.

(4) If we compare with the passage from *Birds* the claims of Gorgias
that λόγος is able to 'charm' and 'persuade' the ψυχή (B 11.14) and that
tragedy is an ἀπάτη (B 23), there is a remote possibility that such Gorgianic
aesthetic theories are also parodied at *Lysistrata* 959–65, where the chorus of
old men commiserates with the sexually aroused and frustrated Cinesias,
just after he is deserted by Myrrine, for being 'worn out' and 'deceived' in
his ψυχή (ἐν δεινῷ γ' ὦ δύστηνε κακῷ / τείρει ψυχὴν ἐξαπατηθείς). But there
are, of course, far more obvious ideas appropriate to ψυχή in the passage:
the seat of grief, of sexual desire, and the 'life' of the man. As in other
instances,[38] a first mention of ψυχή directly sparks a second, a fact
demonstrating, perhaps, the possibilities for punning offered by the word
in the fifth century. Here the chorus goes on in mock tragic style to a series
of rhetorical queries that effectively reduce the ψυχή to the level of a
material 'life-force' able to be compared to kidneys, testicles, and the like
(κἄγωγ' οἰκτίρω σ' αἰαῖ / ποῖος γὰρ ἂν ἢ νέφρος ἀντίσχοι, / ποία ψυχή, ποῖοι δ'
ὄρχεις / ποία δ' ὀσφῦς, ποῖος δ' ὄρρος / κατατεινόμενος).

(5) An ambiguous passage that plays on entirely traditional meanings but exhibits the persistent comic value of ψυχή for Aristophanes is
found at *Frogs* 1331ff. Aeschylus parodies Euripidean style by describing a
dream sent from Hades—itself, of course, nearly a ψυχή—as having a
ψυχὰν ἄψυχον.

(6) The phrase ψυχὴν ἄριστος, which always refers in tragedy to
physical courage, occurs as such in the exchange between the two λόγοι at
Clouds 1044ff. The unjust λόγος asks which of the sons of Zeus was ἄριστον
ψυχήν, thus initiating a joke about the effect of the warm baths of Heracles
on the stamina of the young. The rhetorical question of line 1052 (καίτοι
τίς ἀνδρειότερος ἦν;) confirms that 'courage' is intended, although any
reference to ψυχή in a play about Socrates should perhaps be regarded with
curiosity. A possible pun on ψυχή as body and 'soul'—an important early
reference, if so—is found in an exchange between the chorus and the
sausage-seller at *Knights* 451ff., in which the latter is urged to beat
Paphlagon with his wares (παῖ' αὐτὸν ἀνδρειότατα, καὶ / γάστριζε καὶ τοῖς
ἐντέροις / καὶ τοῖς κόλοις) and is then addressed with tragic solemnity, after
the beating has taken place, as 'noblest flesh' and 'best in ψυχή' (ὦ γεν-
νικώτατον κρέας ψυχήν τ' ἄριστε πάντων, / καὶ τῇ πόλει σωτὴρ φανεὶς ἡμῖν τε
τοῖς πολίταις). κρέας is humorous in itself, as it is at line 421 of the same play,

38. *Clouds* 712 and 719.

since a word that denotes only edible meat is utilized to mock the tragic use of κάρα and κεφαλή, but the juxtaposition of κρέας and ψυχή is possibly a parody as well of σῶμα and ψυχή, found by this date with an entirely naturalistic meaning in the medical texts. Unfortunately, the passage does not permit us to do more than speculate. A third instance of ψυχὴν ἄριστος is found at *Peace* 675, where Hermes asks Trygaeus who is the greatest lover of peace in the city. Again, a pun may be intended. Trygaeus replies that it is Cleonymus, who is ψυχὴν ἄριστος in military affairs, except that whenever he enters battle he throws away his shield. It is unnecessary, of course, to go beyond the traditional meaning 'courage' for the joke, but it is tempting to hear a play on ψυχή as 'soul' or 'character' to the effect that Cleonymus is a man whose 'character' is indeed 'best' in Trygaeus' eyes because he is totally lacking in military valor. Taken together, these three passages may show, at least around the period of *Knights*, *Clouds*, and *Peace* (424–421 B.C.), the usefulness for comedy of the phrase ψυχὴν ἄριστος.

(7) ψυχή as an "inner self" has been alleged for *Frogs* 1468, where Dionysus declares that he will choose whichever poet his ψυχή wishes (ὅνπερ ἡ ψυχὴ θέλει).[39] When reminded in the next line of his oath to take Euripides with him he replies that only his tongue swore: ἡ γλῶττ' ὀμώμοκ', Αἰσχύλον δ' αἱρήσομαι. This statement parodies *Hippolytus* 612 (ἡ γλῶσσ' ὀμώμοχ', ἡ δὲ φρὴν ἀνώμοτος), as lines 101–02 of the same play do earlier. In itself the line is unexceptional; we can probably place this use of ψυχή with various occasions in Euripides in which it is the seat of deep sympathy and feeling for others. The apparent equation of φρήν and ψυχή is an innovation, however, that would give ψυχή a rationalistic and reflective quality like that of φρήν. But it is unclear whether we are meant to take ψυχή as the equivalent of φρήν or as a carefully wrought alternative to it, or whether the phrases are juxtaposed accidentally. A simpler comic point may lie in the fact that what elsewhere guards oaths is here what breaks them. At best, the passage is, like those involving ψυχὴν ἄριστος, suggestive of innovation but not certain. An apparent connection of φρένες and ψυχαί is also seen at *Peace* 1068, where foxes are said to have tricky ψυχαί and φρένες (ὧν δόλιαι ψυχαί, δόλιαι φρένες). The strongly characterizing modifier with a non-periphrastic use of ψυχή is striking and untraditional. The speaker is the soothsayer Hierocles, a man whose interest in ψυχαί may be somewhat technical and hence subject to punning, but unless there is a meaning in this passage we are unable to ascertain, the connection of φρένες with ψυχή and the use of δόλιαι must be seen as evidence of semantic development.

39. Handley, p. 215.

HERODOTUS AND THUCYDIDES

In Herodotus ψυχή is used twenty-one times. In 2.123 Herodotus describes the Egyptian origins of belief in the immortality of the soul. In four instances ψυχή means 'courage', 'boldness', or the source of such emotions,[40] and in twelve, the word is used to denote 'life' either metaphorically or in death contexts.[41] Details of these passages will be omitted since they add nothing to the present discussion. The remaining occurrences are of some interest. At 7.16 Artabanus takes the role of a sophistic adviser to Xerxes and reproaches those who have encouraged the ψυχή of the Persians, or perhaps of Xerxes, to become acquisitive, concluding that evil counsel has prevented Xerxes from following his own nature. When alternatives were presented to him—the one likely to increase ὕβρις, the other likely to diminish it by showing that it is harmful to 'teach' the ψυχή always to seek more than it has (ὡς κακὸν εἴη διδάσκειν τὴν ψυχὴν πλέον τι δίζησθαι αἰεὶ ἔχειν τοῦ παρεόντος)—Xerxes chose wrongly. Another apparently psychological usage of ψυχή is repeated three times in the story of Polycrates of Samos (3.40–3.43). After concluding an alliance with Polycrates, Amasis advises him to temper good fortune with bad by deliberately throwing away the treasure he would most regret losing (ἐπ' ᾧ σὺ ἀπολομένῳ μάλιστα τὴν ψυχὴν ἀλγήσεις), instructions that Polycrates follows when he has decided which treasure it would most pain him in his ψυχή to lose (μάλιστα τὴν ψυχὴν ἀσηθείη). When the ring is providentially returned, Amasis foresees trouble and withdraws from the alliance in order not to suffer in his ψυχή for Polycrates, as he would for a guest-friend, when disaster eventually strikes him (ἵνα μὴ ... αὐτὸς ἀλγήσειε τὴν ψυχὴν ὡς περὶ ξείνου ἀνδρός). We must ask, first, why these passages and no others use ψυχή as an important psychological agent, and second, why the use of ψυχή in Herodotus has declined so sharply from that in tragedy.

There is no clear answer to the first question. In the first three passages ψυχή appears loosely related to the ψυχή that seeks physical and material gratification. In the fourth, the ψυχή involved in the description of Amasis' feeling for Polycrates is comparable to the ψυχή in tragedy that feels grief and sympathy for a friend at moments of crisis. But the repetition of ψυχή

40. 3.14, 7.153, 3.108, 5.124. In 3.14 Cambyses decides to try the ψυχή of Psammenitus (διαπειρᾶσθαι τῆς ψυχῆς) by enslaving his daughter and killing his son in a public spectacle. This is more than the mere 'battle courage' implied in the other passages and suggests a blending of ψυχή as 'seat of courage' and the place in which grief of life-and-death proportions is experienced, an ambiguity familiar from tragedy.

41. 1.24, 1.112, 2 31, 3 119, 3.130, 4.190, 5.92ε, 7.39, 7.209, 8.118, 9.37, 9.79

in the story of Polycrates is obviously stylistic, particularly since we find repetition of the entire phrase in ἀλγήσεις/ἀλγήσειε, and it must be concluded therefore that Artabanus' warning and the story of Polycrates are the only events in the whole course of the history that Herodotus imagines in terms of the ψυχή as an expression of any complexity. Since traditional meanings of ψυχή seem to apply in both instances, it is obvious that whatever the intention of Herodotus in using ψυχή, neither the traditional ψυχή nor any new use of the word has an important place in his language. These isolated instances of ψυχή must also be seen alongside the almost total absence of ψυχή in Thucydides, who uses the word in all meanings only four times—once in the funeral oration of Pericles (2.40 quoted above), where it is said that men who discriminate about danger yet do not retreat from it are rightly thought best in courage (κράτιστοι ... τὴν ψυχὴν); once in Cleon's speech on Mytilene (3.39), where he warns that if Mytilene is not punished the Athenians will have to risk their money and ψυχαί against state after state; and twice in the general narrative, where the simple phrases περὶ τῆς ψυχῆς κινδυνεύειν (8.50) and σωτηρίας τῆς ψυχῆς ἀποστερῆσαι (1.136) are used.[42] It is an inescapable conclusion that for Herodotus ψυχή has all but lost its traditional role as an independent psychological entity and that for Thucydides any such usage is entirely obsolete. This conclusion, in turn, reaches beyond the context of Herodotus and Thucydides in showing that exactly when ψυχή, as the term with the most important future, ought to be extending its meaning to embrace new aspects of the psychological life and character of the individual, it is in fact being eliminated from common prose usage. Assmann's observation on the poetic quality of φρήν in Herodotus can be extended not only to the other Homeric 'soul' words but to ψυχή as well.

42. 8.50 and 1.136 may not show narrative use, since ψυχή occurs in passages of reported speech.

3

The Homeric Use of ψυχή and the Development of ψυχή as a Psychological Agent

Although a number of difficulties remain to be considered, it will be evident by now that the Homeric use of ψυχή and the early use of ψυχή as a psychological agent must be interpreted in terms of the 'life-force' pattern that characterizes the other Homeric 'soul' words meaning 'life' and the post-Homeric uses of ψυχή as well. It would be superfluous, therefore, to review in detail all the theories that have been put forward to account for Homeric ψυχή.[1] In my judgment, only two proposed interpretations of Homeric ψυχή are sufficiently specific and serious to warrant independent consideration before I attempt to explain Homeric ψυχή and its later development as a 'life-force' expression. These are, first, Warden's quite

---

1. Rohde's early theory that all Homeric occurrences of ψυχή were manifestations of the Doppelgänger was destroyed by Otto, who pointed out Rohde's failure to cite direct Homeric instances of ψυχή used in this manner and his unwarranted substitution of αἰών from Pi. fr. 131b. Otto treated Homeric ψυχή as both 'abstract life' and the underworld 'shade', with no direct semantic connection between the two usages (pp. 10–31). For Bickel (pp. 211–15, p. 297ff.) the Homeric 'life' ψυχή represented the process of respiration (as θυμός meant circulation: pp. 261–62) and underwent metamorphosis into the 'shade' at cremation. For Böhme (pp. 111–13) it was the 'last breath', whose departure signaled death but whose relationship to the underworld shade could not be rationally accounted for. Wilamowitz (1927), pp. 192–94, and (1931), pp. 370–76, proposed an etymology from ψύχειν ('make cool') and accordingly made ψυχή the 'cold breath of the dead' which continued a disembodied existence in Hades. Regenbogen (pp. 384–87), more recently, has attempted to see in Homeric ψυχή at least some sense of the Doppelgänger; he emphasizes the vivid representation of the afterlife ψυχή and, like Böhme, gives particular importance to the phrase ἐν δὲ ἴα ψυχή as suggesting continuity of the ψυχή in life with the ψυχή in death. The ψυχή is thus the sine qua non of all bodily, intellectual, and emotional activity, an entity whose presence is felt through such physical events as the return of consciousness after sleep. From this being the later uses of ψυχή could rationally develop. Onians (pp. 94–122 and pp. 129ff.) attempts to equate Homeric ψυχή with the Roman *genius* and thus associates it with sneezing, the fluid contents of the head, the cerebrospinal fluid and the semen, and finally the *anima*, or vital spirit.

logical argument that ψυχή developed by analogy with θυμός in shared death contexts from an original meaning 'shade' ('Totengeist' in his terminology) to the meaning 'life', and then finally to shared psychological uses with θυμός.[2] Second, we must reconsider the view, carefully argued by Nehring, that ψυχή retains in Homer an active connection with the supposed etymological meaning 'breath'.[3]

The objections to the proposal of a direct analogical relationship between θυμός and ψυχή can be seen, I think, if we isolate for a moment the earliest appearances of ψυχή as a psychological agent—that is, those found down to the beginning of the fifth century.[4] There are, in fact, only six, in addition to a single occurrence of ἄψυχος in Archilochus: (1) Semonides (29.13)[5] tells the listener to do good to the ψυχή while alive, recognizing the shortness of life. I have already traced the recurrence of this idea in a variety of later texts, and there is some reason to believe, therefore, that it is a traditional folk idea, not an invention of the lyric poets. (2) A similar phrase, and perhaps the most important evidence on this point, is provided

2. Warden, pp. 95–103.

3. Nehring, pp. 106ff. See now Schnauffer, pp. 191ff., whose analysis closely follows that of Nehring. An Indo-European etymology in *bhes- ('souffler') through Greek ψύχω is accepted now by Boisacq (conditionally: "éléments de derivation peu clairs"), Benveniste (1932), pp. 165–68, and Frisk. Frisk follows Benveniste in reducing ψύχω to ψύ-χω on the model of *ter- τρύω > τρύχω > τρῦχος: [*bhes- ψύω > ψύχω > ψῡχή]. This is of little help in resolving the Greek evidence. All instances of ψύχω in Homer except ψύξασα at Il. 20.440 have to do with 'coldness', not 'breathing' or 'blowing'. Benveniste explained this development as the product of two verbs, ψύχω ('cool') from a stem ψῡχ-, and ψύχω ('breathe') from ψῡ- (as above). But since the outcome is the same (ψύχω = ψύχω), no proof can be given. The traditional notion of a semantic development ψύχω 'blow' > ψύχω 'cool by blowing' remains plausible, and Frisk's suggestion of sailing as the context for this progression is sensible. (The transition is essentially demonstrated by Il. 11.621 for ἀποψύχω). Nevertheless, Homeric πνείω has all but eliminated ψύχω as 'breathe' or 'blow', a fact that leaves ψυχή without active etymological cognates for 'breath' in Homer. On the analogy of the other 'soul' words it is not impossible that the suppression of ψύχω ('breathe') was connected with the specialization of ψυχή into soul functions since the disappearance of ψύχω in this meaning ended the association of ψυχή with a concrete physical function. If so, the fact that there is only a single surviving instance of ψύχω ('breathe') in ψύξασα shows not that ψυχή means 'breath' (cf. Frisk: "Hauch, Atem, Lebenskraft, Seele des Verstorbenen, Abbild des Toten") but that it no longer means 'breath'.

4. ψυχή is found in Theognis at 530, 568, 710, and 910. In 730 and 568 it is clearly the Homeric 'life'. Line 710 speaks of the 'souls' of the dead refusing (ἀναινομένας) to be imprisoned in Hades. Line 910 refers to a man as "bitten in his ψυχή" over deciding the course of his life and has been assigned to the fourth century by Diehl, although it is taken as earlier by others (references in Regenbogen, pp. 391–92). Line 530, where the poet protests that he has never betrayed a friend since οὐδ' ἐν ἐμῇ ψυχῇ δούλιον οὐδὲν ἔνι, could well be genuine and attest ψυχή as the 'seat of courage'. The dating of all these passages is not sufficiently trustworthy to include them here.

5. The poem is quoted by Stobaeus (4,34), who attributed it to Simonides of Ceos, as does now West. Bergk, Wilamowitz, and many others have given it to Semonides. Cf. Lesky (1966), p. 114.

by a sixth-century Eretrian funerary inscription (SIG XII 9.287):[6] ἔνθα⟨δε⟩ Φίλον κεῖται· τόν δὲ κατὰ γαῖ' ἐκάλυσφεν ναυτίλον· ἢ ϕσυχεῖ παῦρα δέδοκ' ἀγαθά. "Here lies Philo. Although a sailor, the earth covers him. He gave few goods to his ψυχή." Unquestionably this use of ψυχή is exactly like that of Semonides. The sailor's hard life prevented him from experiencing the pleasures of ease and comfort. Now that the ψυχή has gone, Philo can have no other pleasures. (3) Sappho (62.7–8) uses the word in what is, to judge from the rest of the fragment, an erotic context,[7] but the construction to which it belongs cannot be determined. (4) Alcaeus F3(b)34 is uninter-pretable. The poem is an invective, and the surrounding words, κάκων ἔσχατ'[. . . ψύχαν . . . αἴει δακ[ρυσι]ν, may suggest that the ψυχή is troubled or consumed by tears. (5) In Anacreon 360 the ψυχή is, ambiguously with 'life', the source of sexual desire: ὦ παῖ παρθένιον βλέπων | δίζημαί σε, σὺ δ' κλύεις, | οὐκ εἰδὼς ὅτι τῆς ἐμῆς | ψυχῆς ἡνιοχεύεις. (6) In poem 39 of Hipponax, the ψυχή, surprisingly personified by the adjective πολύστονος, can be appeased with wine: κακοῖσι δώσω τὴν πολύστονον ψυχήν, | ἢν μὴ ἀποπέμψῃς ὡς τάχιστά μοι κριθέων | μέδιμνον, ὡς ἂν ἀλφίτων ποιήσωμαι | κυκεῶνα πίνειν φάρμακον πονηρίης. (7) To these last instances of ψυχή must be added the unique use in lyric poetry of the adjective ἄψυχος in a brief erotic fragment (193) of Archilochus: δύστηνος ἔγκειμαι πόθῳ | ἄψυχος, χαλεπῇσι θεῶν ὀδύνῃσιν ἕκητι | πεπαρμένος δι' ὀστέων.

These earliest psychological uses of ψυχή raise several serious objec-tions to the theory that ψυχή developed uses other than 'shade' by analogy to θυμός. First, on chronological grounds alone, the operation of this analogy after Homer can hardly account for the appearance of ἄψυχος as early as Archilochus. That we should have, moreover, isolated before us in the text of Homer, predictive conditions for the linguistic analogy thought to be responsible for the psychological development of ψυχή but not the development itself, is hard to believe. Clearly, something other than a period of chronological evolution is called for to explain the difference between the Homeric and lyric use of ψυχή. Second, it is apparent that the earliest psychological instances of ψυχή are too restricted in meaning to be accounted for by θυμός. Whereas θυμός is in Homer a varied psychological agent, these earliest uses of ψυχή have only material and erotic connota-tions. If ψυχή did indeed develop by analogy to θυμός, this difference must mean that although ψυχή was fully analogized to θυμός in its death usages, it

---

6. Schwyzer, n. 801. I take hó according to Schwyzer's second alternative, that is as ὅς = [Philo].

7. Reconstructed in Lobel-Page as μύγις δέ ποτ' εἰσάιον ἐκλ[| ψύχα δ' ἀγαπάτασυ.[

was only selectively analogized as a psychological agent. Moreover, although comparable to certain uses of θυμός, the idea of "doing good to one's ψυχή," which seems important in the early period, is an expression not explicitly known for θυμός and thus not demonstrably one that arose by analogy to θυμός. Finally, when ψυχή does become a commonly used psychological agent in the fifth-century poets, its tendency to appear only in crucial situations makes it closer in some respects to Homeric κῆρ and ἦτορ, as I have described them, than to θυμός; but there are for these words no shared Homeric death contexts with ψυχή of the kind found for θυμός and μένος. The conclusion to be drawn from these points must be that analogy with θυμός cannot by itself explain the development of ψυχή, and we are, I think, directed again to the more generally pervasive 'life-force' pattern.

The theory that ψυχή is still actively connected to an etymological meaning 'breath' in Homer is contradicted by the use of the word to imply 'blood'. Nevertheless, Nehring has argued in his comprehensive study of all Homeric scenes describing syncope that, in two occurrences of ψυχή and one of ἀποψύχω, ψυχή "has its original function as the human breath." [8] The scenes in question are Iliad 5.696ff. (Sarpedon, as the spear is withdrawn from his body: τὸν δὲ λίπε ψυχή, κατὰ δ᾽ ὀφθαλμῶν κέχυτ᾽ ἀχλύς. / αὖτις δ᾽ ἐμπνύνθη, ⟨mss. ἀμπ-⟩ περὶ δὲ πνοιὴ Βορέαο / ζώγρει ἐπιπνείουσα κακῶς κεκαφηότα θυμόν); Iliad 22.466ff. (Andromache on the wall: τὴν δὲ κατ᾽ ὀφθαλμῶν ἐρεβεννὴ νὺξ ἐκάλυψεν, / ἤριπε δ᾽ ἐξοπίσω, ἀπὸ δὲ ψυχὴν ἐκάπυσσε. / ... ἡ δ᾽ ἐπεὶ οὖν ἔμπνυτο καὶ ἐς φρένα θυμὸς ἀγέρθη); and Odyssey 24.345ff. (Laertes on recognizing Odysseus: τοῦ δ᾽ αὐτοῦ λύτο γούνατα καὶ φίλον ἦτορ, / ... ἀμφὶ δὲ παιδὶ φίλῳ βάλε πήχεε· τὸν δὲ ποτὶ οἷ / εἷλεν ἀποψύχοντα πολύτλας δῖος Ὀδυσσεύς. / αὐτὰρ ἐπεί ῥ᾽ ἔμπνυτο καὶ ἐς φρένα θυμὸς ἀγέρθη).

Closer examination suggests that only the two instances of ψυχή itself are significant. ἀποψύχω is here used uniquely in connection with syncope, and since all other occurrences of it have been remodeled, like those of ἀναψύχω, to meanings centering on coldness,[9] it is impossible to establish its meaning objectively in Odyssey 24.[10] In the passages with ψυχή itself, the

8. Nehring, p. 108.

9. E.g., Il. 13.84 ἀνέψυχον φίλον ἦτορ.

10. In Sophocles (Aj. 1031) we find ἀπέψυξεν βίον, but on the model of μή μ᾽ ἀπογυιώσῃς μένεος, already found at Il. 6.265, it is rash to see ἀπέψυξεν βίον as retaining an active physiological value as late as Sophocles. ἀποψύχειν in fragment 104 of Aeschylus is taken to mean 'die', but without direct evidence. It does appear as 'die' in Thucydides (1.134.3) and later prose writers, which shows the final loss of its

(continued overleaf)

important point is that ψυχή seems to replace words and phrases used in other scenes of syncope to describe physical breathlessness—ἄπνευστος, used of Odysseus as he crawls ashore at *Odyssey* 5.455ff., and ἀργαλέῳ ἔχετ' ἄσθματι, used of Hector in *Iliad* 15.9ff. after he has been struck by a stone. There is no reason, however, to see this substitution as one in which ψυχή means 'breath' as a function of its etymological history. An equally valid argument is that it replaces breath in instances of syncope where breathlessness is *not* the significant point of attention. This interpretation is borne out by the observation that in eight passages not using ψυχή, syncope is initiated by manifest physical exhaustion of the kind experienced by Odysseus after swimming to Phaeacia. In the passages with ψυχή, however, no equally violent physical cause for breathlessness exists. A spear is gently removed from the body of Sarpedon. Andromache sees the dead Hector. Laertes is overcome with the joy of Odysseus' return. Of these, the first is obviously a physical event, but it takes place only after Sarpedon has been carried to safety and thus lacks the simple connection to breathlessness of, for example, the blow that strikes Hector. If anatomical precision is sought, what is more likely in this context is, rather, general bodily weakness caused by loss of blood.

Although a statistical sample of eleven instances is scarcely adequate to resolve the issue, these collected passages on syncope tend to show not that the ψυχή is physical breath but that it is a substitute for it in contexts where loss of breathing and cessation of other life signs are observed but not directly accounted for. The argument that the physical similarities of fainting and death would impress the Homeric mind is perfectly plausible and can be applied to suggest that the ψυχή is used in unaccountable swoons because it fills the need for something invisible and self-moved, able to cause a deathlike state by simply ceasing to act. The loss of ψυχή may entail the loss of breath, but the loss of breath does not necessarily or satisfactorily explain the selective use of ψυχή in these passages, and there is no binding argument, therefore, on this evidence, that Homeric ψυχή can mean 'breath'.

(*continued from previous page*)

original meaning and points, probably, to a change of meaning under the influence of the noun ψυχή as 'life'. The suppression of ψύχω as 'breathe' in Homer and the single appearance here of ἀποψύχω in a context strikingly and memorably used for ψυχή elsewhere suggest that the original meaning of ἀποψύχω may already be contaminated semantically with ψυχή as 'life' in some sense not directly physical. It follows that on the level of Homeric meaning, as opposed to probable etymology, ἀποψύχω itself cannot be taken as decisive evidence for a Homeric verb ἀποψύχω ('breathe'), much less for active retention of etymological 'breath' for ψυχή in Homer.

A better explanation of the Homeric and early psychological use of ψυχή can be based on the reasoning that, whatever its origins, it has already been largely absorbed by Homeric times into the 'life-force' category of words and that it therefore shares with the other words a natural ability to act as a psychological agent of the 'life-force' type. The argument can be stated simply: (1) It seems an inherent ability of Homeric 'life-force' words other than ψυχή to function as psychological agents—that is, to be used in expressions in which emotion is treated as a function of an individuals 'life'. (2) ψυχή already has such a role in the earliest remains of lyric poetry—if we extrapolate from Archilochus' use of ἄψυχος—but in the early lyric poets ψυχή is largely restricted to self-gratification and erotic contexts. (3) In the poetry of the fifth century these 'life-force' usages are developed in that ψυχή becomes most directly comparable to κῆρ and ἦτορ; that is, most of the possible 'life-force' categories of use can be applied to it except those involving physical 'strength' and what we have seen as the more idiomatic uses of θυμός. (4) Apart from its use as 'shade', ψυχή is clearly recognizable as a physical 'life-force' in Homeric death contexts: it can be 'destroyed' or 'lost'; it has no decisive physical identification but is ambiguously 'breath'-like and 'blood'-like; it is 'lost' in certain types of syncope; it appears to be linked indiscriminately with θυμός, μένος, and αἰών in death descriptions. It is not, apparently, bound by a definite value like 'breath'. (6) After Homer, in addition to its psychological role, it is modified by φίλος, a usage perhaps comparable to its Homeric appearance in oaths, and finally, it exhibits periphrasis of the type common to μένος and κῆρ in Homer.

From these comparisons there can be no doubt that ψυχή has a relatively consistent 'life-force' identity from Homer on in popular usage and that this identity cannot readily be explained by post-Homeric analogy to any one of the related words. Although ψυχή does not have any significant physical or psychological uses denied to the other words, its pattern of usage in and immediately after Homer is too idiosyncratic and restricted to be the product of analogy to any one word. It is possible, of course, to see the further development of ψυχή in lyric poetry and tragedy as influenced by later analogy to θυμός and the other 'soul' words, but these later analogies, if they occurred, cannot account for the character of ψυχή in the early lyric poets. By far the most economical course is to see the early psychological uses of ψυχή as a pattern struck sui generis as a result of the natural tendency of 'life-force' words to act as emotional agents. Archilochus' use of ἄψυχος seems decisive on this point. At the least, it must indicate that if ψυχή developed by analogy to θυμός or other 'soul' words, it did so not after Homer but in some context outside the Homeric poems.

The appropriate question is, therefore, not why ψυχή becomes a psychological agent after Homer but why it has failed to act as one in Homer. What is it in Homer that has inhibited the presumably normal use of ψυχή as 'life' in some pattern of emotional usage?

The answer to this question can be found in only one area of usage, namely, in the disparity between the nature of the psychological ψυχή when it does appear in lyric poetry and the demands that Homer himself, as opposed to later poets, makes of the word. As I have pointed out, the use of ψυχή as 'shade' is infrequent, if not eclectic, in fifth-century literature, and the potentially contradictory use of ψυχή as the physical 'life-force' in death contexts is strong enough after Homer to permit a phrase like the one in which (*Tr.* 1214) Helen is said to have 'slain' the ψυχή of Astyanax. In contrast, the ψυχή as 'shade' is a subject of great importance for the Homeric poet. Here attention should be drawn not only to the *Nekyia* and to the definitional treatment of ψυχή in that context[11] but, more important, to the confrontation of Achilles with the shade of Patroclus at *Iliad* 23.103–04, lines in which he looks upon the meeting with astonishment since it confirms for him the existence of an underworld populated by ψυχαί (ταφὼν δ᾽ ἀνόρουσεν Ἀχιλλεὺς / . . . ἔπος δ᾽ ὀλοφυδνόν ἔειπεν / "ὢ πόποι, ἦ ῥά τι ἔστι καὶ εἰν Ἀΐδαο δόμοισι / ψυχή καὶ εἴδωλον, ἀτὰρ φρένες οὐκ ἔνι πάμπαν"). What is impressive about these lines is not that they explain the particular nature of the shade but that they show a *need* to explain and define. It is difficult to imagine such statements occurring in an atmosphere in which the shade and its fate did not matter. It is true that the Homeric afterlife offers no compensation for the loss of life, but it is false to equate this feeling on the part of Homeric men with a lack of interest in the ψυχή as 'shade'. In both frequency and intensity, rather, Homeric interest in the underworld ψυχή exceeds that of any subsequent literary source to the end of the fifth century.

Against this attitude toward the 'shade' must be set the fact that whenever ψυχή, or any of the 'life-force' words appear as psychological agents, their range of meanings is largely involved with physical satisfaction and violent passion. Again, the limitation of ψυχή to material and erotic contexts in its earliest uses must be stressed. A natural result of this limitation is that opportunities for suggestive or inadvertent ambiguities between ψυχή as 'shade' and as the emotional 'life-force' are, almost by definition, impossible. That is, the archaic Greek poet cannot assign emotion to the ψυχή except as a function of its bodily attachment and

11. *Od.* 11.218–22.

manifestations, and these emotions are bound to be of the 'life-force' type. This discontinuity is particularly noteworthy in Pindar, for example, where, despite apparent interest in Orphic ideas of ψυχή, which might be expected to color from time to time the way in which the emotional ψυχή is perceived, the surviving psychological uses of the word are the usual 'life-force' ones: the ψυχή is erotic, bold, and so forth.

In terms of the 'life-force' thesis I have proposed, it is precisely this lack of plausible integration between the 'shade' and the inherent qualities of ψυχή as 'life-force' that can best explain the ostensible development of ψυχή after Homer. That ψυχή also expresses the idea of 'shade' apparently cannot at any point affect the *nature* of ψυχή as a 'life-force' of psychological importance by giving it, for example, new categories of psychological usage unavailable to the other 'life-force' words. It seems reasonable, therefore, to argue that a strong connection with the 'shade' will work to inhibit any inherent instinct the poet might have to use the word in psychological contexts appropriate to the 'life-force'. In effect, the dignity accorded the ψυχή as 'shade' in Homer is by nature incompatible with much of what must be said of any 'life-force' when it is personified as an emotional agent. In the lyric texts, where, more as a matter of style and interest than intellectual development, the aura of dignity and numinosity accorded the Homeric 'shade' is lacking or of less consequence, there is simply no inhibition against attributing psychological activity to the ψυχή. I do not wish to claim certainty on this point, obviously, but, in contrast to theories of post-Homeric development—whether analogy to θυμός or changing intellectual attitudes—it seems more likely that what appears to us a development in scope is the ordinary and popular use of ψυχή, while the restricted usage came about in answer to the needs of epic poetry.

Remarkably good evidence for this thesis can be found, I think, in the fifth-century outcome of ψυχή and the other Homeric 'soul' words. Here we may at length draw the point of the evidence assembled at the end of part I. The theory that ψυχή expands its psychological uses in fifth-century poetry as a function of its ability to be felt as the familiar archaic 'life-force' in death contexts, devoid of religious overtones, can account surprisingly well for the relative movement of all the 'soul' words between Homer and Euripides. The changes are summarized in the table below.

	Homer	*Euripides*
νόος	Contextually limited 'thought' or general psychological agent	Acquires 'reason' and 'mind–body' usages
φρήν/φρένες	Contextually limited 'thought' or 'thoughts'	Adds emotional and moral usages that define it as a more extensive and autonomous psychological agent
καρδία	Physical heart; seat of courage or wrath	Becomes the physical 'life'; expands in range as an emotional agent
θυμός	Ubiquitous agent for personified exchange; highly personified 'life-force' with extensive usages	Declines in range of psychological usages; no longer denotes personified exchange; becomes increasingly an emotion per se
μένος	'Wrath' or battle-centered 'life-force'	
κῆρ	Highly personified, extensive 'life-force' agents	All disappear
ἦτορ		

To these may now be added

ψυχή	'Life' in death contexts; 'shade'	Acquires 'life' usages in a more positive sense; becomes a highly personified, extensive 'life-force' agent of the κῆρ/ἦτορ type

This pattern of the development of the 'soul' words in popular usage from Homer to Euripides exhibits one unmistakable criterion for success or failure after Homer: all words that do not have a connection with 'life' or 'life-force' expand in some way, and all words except for ψυχή that do have such a connection—θυμός, μένος, κῆρ, ἦτορ—are eliminated or diminished in importance. If this phenomenon can be explained, we will have made some progress toward understanding the history of ψυχή.

What, then, has caused this shift in meanings, the elimination of competing 'life-force' expressions, and the success of ψυχή? Unduly precise conclusions on matters of this kind are to be doubted on principle, but if the discussion of ψυχή and the 'soul' words above may now be drawn together, a strong conclusion is perhaps warranted. Three points count against the possibility that ψυχή has succeeded against the other words by acquiring— through changing attitudes toward the personality or new afterlife beliefs and the like—a psychological character that the other words lack. (1) With the possible exception of periphrastic constructions, most occurrences of ψυχή in fifth-century popular usage involve wholly traditional meanings.

Some texts may be regarded as ambiguous, like *Antigone* 708, in which Creon's ψυχή is 'unfolded', and some probably real anomalies can be seen—notably phrases like ἠπειρῶτις ψυχή γυναικῶν (*Andr.* 159–61) and παρθένον ψυχήν (*Hipp.* 1006). Yet, for the most part it is very difficult to see ψυχή as developing in any way from traditional 'life-force' usages. I have tried to make this point as fairly and exhaustively as I could in the preceding text and will not reiterate the evidence. The adherence of ψυχή to archaic ideas, moreover, is the only explanation I can find to account for the decline of the word in Herodotus and Thucydides. (2) καρδία, φρήν, ψυχή, and θυμός constitute a system of multiple psychological entities in Euripides not altogether unlike Homer's system; they retain continuity with important Homeric expressions, and many such usages are shared from word to word. There is no clear reason, therefore, why as a psychological agent any Homeric word should be eliminated. (3) There are in the lyric poets and in Aeschylus about eight times as many instances of θυμός in psychological contexts as there are of ψυχή. If a gradual concentration of psychological expression onto a single word had occurred as a result of competition among the words as psychological agents, it is probable that θυμός, not ψυχή, would have prevailed.

If we cannot explain the success of ψυχή in terms of some unique appeal as a psychological agent, it is worthwhile, I think, to look again at the role of ψυχή as the physical 'life' of a man after Homer. As we have seen, ψυχή exhibits a number of changes: it becomes 'life' in a more positive sense as something one lives with (Ajax to Eurysaces to "nourish his young ψυχή"); in phrases like ἠπειρῶτις ψυχή it is, possibly, drawing on the medical notion that there are certain biological types of ψυχή; it can now be 'slain' and thus treated more naturalistically in death contexts than it can in Homer. Behind these poetic expressions may lie the gradual adoption into popular speech of ψυχή as the word of choice to designate the natural animator of the body, a usage available—although I make no assumptions about influence—throughout the fifth century in Presocratic and medical sources. If my argument is correct that θυμός, μένος, ἦτορ, κῆρ, and ψυχή act as psychological agents because of expressions in which there is an implicit connection with the 'life' or 'life-force' of a man, it follows that the success of ψυχή, against other 'life-force' words, as the biological 'life', whatever the cause, would lead to its success against the other words in psychological contexts as well. In this view, therefore, the most important fact that the psychological development of ψυχή is to be coordinated with is simply that in all of Greek tragedy there is only one occurrence of a 'life-force' word other than ψυχή in a death context: θυμός at *Agamemnon* 1388. In contrast, of course, ψυχή appears in such contexts repeatedly to the end of the fifth century. By the time of Euripides, in effect, ψυχή is the only word by which the poets can refer to 'life' in the archaic sense as 'that which is destroyed at death', and it is this fact on which its psychological use in tragedy manifestly depends. The change in θυμός is definitive. Although it continues to have available to it in Euripides all Homeric contexts except 'life', it has simply begun to fade away in frequency of use and to be absorbed into the role of an emotion per se.

This conclusion must demonstrate, in retrospect, that the emphasis placed throughout on 'life-force' in the analysis of these words is correct; and finally, that if the success of ψυχή as the archaic 'life-force' is what accounts for its expansion of usages in the fifth century, it is very likely the same meaning, unaffected by afterlife speculation, that accounts for its development into a psychological agent after Homer.

PART III:

The Development of the Philosophical Use of ψυχή before Plato

I

Problems of Method and Interpretation

So far we have dealt only with texts belonging to the largely homogeneous tradition of Greek literature from Homer to Euripides. For the philosophical and scientific uses of ψυχή, on the other hand, that occurred during the same period and on into the early fourth century, the sources on which we depend for information become far more varied in both the kind and quality of evidence they provide. The several hundred entries for ψυχή in the Diels–Kranz index to the Presocratic fragments and *testimonia* are of mixed value at best. The doxographical materials collected in the A fragments are all but useless for semantic purposes; for the most part they are concerned only with the material composition of soul and with general theories of cognition and animation.[1] These difficulties are already fully

---

1. The A fragments contribute little or nothing to a discussion of semantic nuances, and they are not dealt with in detail here. The paucity of information actually conveyed by the many alleged *testimonia* given in Diels–Kranz is worth noting. Many fragments, including some mislabeled as B, have been produced by dismembering the brief synopsis in *De Anima*: Heraclit. A 15 (soul is the ἀρχή, an exhalation, least corporeal, and in flux); Emp. A 78 (soul is related to the proportion of bodily parts); Hippon A 10 (soul comes from water); Democr. A 101, 104, 104a, 113 (soul and mind are the same, soul moves the body by the motion of the spherical soul atoms); Diog. Apoll. A 20 (soul is identified with air and knows as the ἀρχή); Anaxag. A 100 (soul as mind is the moving principle). Here should be added also Orph. B 11 (soul enters with breathing) and Pythag. B 40 (Pythagorean stories say that any soul can enter any body); of course, neither of these is a quotation. The remaining fragments, not from *De Anima*, generally concern (1) the connection of sensation and knowledge: Protag. A 1, Parm. A 1, 45 (soul and mind are the same); Democr. A 1, 106 (the soul is made up of the same atoms as sun and moon; the air contains atoms Democritus calls soul and mind); Democr. A 105, 135 (perception takes place throughout the whole body; intelligence depends on the composition of body); (2) the composition and nature of soul: Pythag. A 4, B 15, B 4, Eurytus 2, Hippasus 11 (soul is number); Heraclit. A 15 (soul is an exhalation from moisture); Parm. A 45 (Parmenides, Hippasos, and Heraclitus made the soul fiery); Hippon A 3, 10 (soul is brain and water); Parm. A 45 (soul is from earth and fire); Epich. Enni. B 48 (mind is from the fire of the sun); Xenoph. A 1 (soul is breath), A 50 (soul is from earth and water);
(continued overleaf)

apparent in the *De Anima* of Aristotle, the work that serves, of course, as the origin of much of the doxographical information that has come down to us. The ipsissima verba of the B fragments seldom yield to straightforward interpretation and, in some cases, survive only in epigrammatic phrases that cannot be penetrated with any certainty. Philolaus B 14, for example, reports the Orphic idea that for the sake of certain punishments "the soul is yoked to the body and buried in it as though in a tomb," language that recurs explicitly in the *Gorgias* and *Cratylus* of Plato.[2] But before one can discern in the ψυχή of this fragment the attributes of the comprehensive soul found, say, in the closing myth of judgment in the *Gorgias*, it is essential to know whether the punishments and sin alluded to in Philolaus are matters of ritual experience or personal conscience, and for this sort of information the fragment in question is of little or no help. Other significant *testimonia*, like the *Memorabilia* of Xenophon and the early dialogues of Plato, refer to the ψυχή repeatedly but cannot be said to show in any self-evident way how the transition in meaning to the comprehensive soul as self took place.

Despite the difficulty of using these very dissimilar sources, however, some fairly intimate sense of the development of ψυχή can perhaps be based on the semantic evidence of the surviving sources. In order to present this material coherently, the chronological sequence of texts must again be handled somewhat freely and the history of the word approached as much as possible independently of traditional philosophical formulations that assume some certainty about its semantics. Here also I shall be following the general plan of Burnet's study, but again the scale of evidence must be greatly enlarged as against his efforts before empirical conclusions can be suggested.[3] The texts considered will consist mainly of the Presocratic B fragments, the earlier Hippocratic treatises, the fifth-century *testimonia* on Socrates, and the earlier dialogues of Plato as far as *Gorgias*—the work I

(continued from previous page)

Zeno A 1 (soul is a mixture of elements); Heraclit. B 12 (soul is an exhalation αἰσθητική); Pythag. B 41, Echecrates 4, Philol. A 23 (soul is a harmony); Democr. A 108 (soul is mortal); Democr. A 103 (soul is a spirit implanted in the atoms whose ease of movement allows it to go throughout the body). Other alleged *testimonia* include references to the Hippocratic text *Regimen* I (Hippocr. C 11) and titles from Diogenes (Democr. A 33, 34). Of greater interest are the reports in Aristotle (*Resp.* 471b30) on the connection of breathing and soul in Democritus (Democr. A 106) and on Lycophron's belief (*Metaph.* 1045b10) that knowledge is a συνουσία of the soul with knowing (Lycophron A 1).

2. Pl. *Grg.* 493a; *Cra.* 400c.

3. A brief review of ψυχή and of Burnet's thesis appears in Guthrie (1971), pp. 147–53, and it generally supports Burnet. Like his predecessor, however, Guthrie bases his conclusion on a comparison of a random group of fifth-century texts with the uses of ψυχή in *Alcibiades* I, where the importance of ψυχή is not in keeping with other early Platonic texts.

take to be the most natural stopping point for this study. The *Gorgias* is, in any case, as far into Plato as it is possible to go without undertaking a full-scale treatment of the Platonic doctrine of the soul.[4]

Before turning to these texts, however, some mention must be made of the short but influential history of the Presocratic doctrines of soul given in Aristotle's *De Anima*, since Aristotle does in fact purport to give an objective account of the earlier use of ψυχή. Happily, the reputation of *De Anima* does not rest on this brief foray into philosophical history (403b20–405b32), for it must be said that the disservice of *De Anima* to the particular semantic history we are trying to recover here is not small. Aristotle's summary incorporates two fundamental misrepresentations. First, and most simply, any explanation of what are regarded by him as the universally recognized 'soul' functions of motion and cognition are treated in *De Anima* as doctrines of ψυχή more or less formally propagated by his predecessors. Thus, the inherited doctrine of ψυχή most extensively discussed in *De Anima* is the one ascribed to Empedocles, whose cognitive theories best fit the materialist epistemology Aristotle intends to dismiss.[5] Yet the writings of Empedocles survive in fragments on a scale sufficient to guarantee that ψυχή cannot have been used by him with philosophical meaning.[6] Democritus, similarly, is alleged (404a27ff.) to have equated soul (ψυχή) and mind (νοῦς), because he identified sense perception, a function of ψυχή in some sense from Heraclitus on, with truth, which must be regarded as properly a function of νοῦς. Although this statement has value as a philosophical critique, and points out a central problem of atomist thought, it is formulated entirely by deduction and as a result is linguistically without value. Even though the *testimonia* make clear that Democritus believed mind and soul to consist of similar atoms,[7] nothing in the fragments can justify the implication of the sense-truth statement—that the functional identity of ψυχή and νοῦς is philosophically at issue for Democritus, much less that he could have used the words ψυχή and νοῦς as Aristotle himself does. Owing to the breadth of reference that ψυχή has in his own thought,[8] Aristotle is insensitive to the need to recognize the more limited character of the psychical functions his predecessors attributed to

4. See now the study of Robinson (1970).

5. Cherniss (1935), pp. 294–95.

6. An exception, discussed below, is B 138, where ψυχή appears as 'life lost at death'. Mansfeld, p. 23, conjectures ψυχή as the subject of B 105, but there is no evidence for this in the text.

7. A 106 (*Resp.* 471b30); A 1 (D.L. 9.44) Parm. A 45 (Aët. IV 5,5).

8. Randall, p. 62, succinctly describes *De Anima* as an introduction to "the sciences which deal with living things, with especial reference to human living." Aristotle's own sophisticated psychophysical doctrine is, as Hardie points out (pp. 77–79), constantly at odds with the dualistic implications of his inherited language.

the ψυχή. He simply assumes that every Presocratic he mentions addressed his ideas to soul in a comprehensive sense, although emphasis might shift about from cognition to animation. This assumption appears throughout the language of *De Anima*, as in his dismissal of the materialist doctrines of self-motion or like-to-like cognition (411a26ff.):

> From what has been said it is evident that it is not because the soul is compounded of the elements that knowledge belongs to it, nor is it correct or true to say that the soul is moved. Knowledge, however, is an attribute of the soul, and so are perception, opinion, desire, wish and appetency generally; animal locomotion also is produced by the soul; and likewise growth, maturity and decay.[9]

The point at issue is greatly complicated by the inherent tendency of Greek thought to adopt theories of panpsychism[10] and by the fact that from Heraclitus on ψυχή exhibits in the ipsissima verba a contingent relationship to all these functions, and that even in popular usage it is in some sense the sine qua non of human activity.[11] But nothing in the text of *De Anima* addresses the historical difficulty raised by the changing meaning of ψυχή, and nothing suggests that Aristotle himself saw any reason to give thought to this problem.

A second and perhaps even more pervasive distortion descending from *De Anima*—which emphasizes our ignorance of oral speech—is its fundamental assumption that the history of ψυχή can properly be traced only through a sequence of ideas attributable to the Presocratic philosophers. That many of the Presocratics spoke about the ψυχή is true, but that their ideas answer one another or gradually anticipate later theories of soul is another matter altogether. Burnet rightly and effectively disposed of this assumption in its most naive form by pointing to the apparent discontinuity in the meaning of ψυχή as it was used before and after Socrates. But even Burnet's theory of Socratic "invention," in execution at least, tends to give the history of ψυχή an Aristotelian sweep in that it rests more on deduction from logical inferences than on empirically established patterns and cultural idiosyncracies. To recapitulate points made earlier, for the philosophical use of ψυχή three such inferences have held sway: (1) that

---

9. Hicks's translation. Cf. 413a20ff. for the same generalizing view: whatever is ἔμψυχον will have one or more of the characteristics of living things, among which may be νοῦς.

10. Guthrie (1969), p. 69 (on Parmenides); p. 377 (on Diogenes).

11. Regenbogen, p. 387.

whatever survives at death in religious or mystical doctrines must some-how have acquired as a result of such survival the personality of the man as a whole, (2) that the association of ψυχή with knowledge in Presocratic epistemologies in accordance with the account given in *De Anima* would gradually and inevitably have matured into the doctrine of ψυχή as the moral self, and (3) that if Socrates is portrayed in Plato as speaking about the ψυχή as self in a tentative tone not found elsewhere, he must have invented, so to speak, both his ideas and linguistic usage. Any or all of these theories may explain the development of ψυχή, and they remain important touchstones for the following discussion, but it must be said at the outset that all of them result, like much else that has been said about ψυχή and the Greek 'soul' words, from the application of rather casual deductive models to a very incomplete body of texts. By contrast, I shall argue here that it is not possible to know how the soul acquires its comprehensive powers unless we also direct some attention to the contexts, within the philos-ophical record or outside it, in which those powers matter. If ψυχή acquired significant usages in unreported or largely unreported contexts falling somewhere between the traditional motifs of poetry and the notices and quotations that survive in the philosophical fragments, the deductions just described, however plausible, are apt to be misleading. Equally important, they do not allow for the role of conceptual analogy[12] in the development of ψυχή or for oblique connections between the use of the word and the particular social or intellectual environment in which such use might have taken place.

What I shall propose is that there are two demonstrably important groups of philosophical or technical contexts for ψυχή in the fifth century, both of which stem semantically from the archaic 'life-force' and both of which are therefore able to merge more or less invisibly with one another and with popular usage at the end of the century. The first group consists of contexts in which ψυχή is essentially the impersonal animator of the body, whose connection to rationality is largely oblique, although in that ca-pacity it is treated with great speculative interest at least by Heraclitus. The second group, into which I put the fragments of Democritus and Gorgias, the Hippocratic texts *Airs, Waters, Places* and *Regimen* I, and Xenophon's *Memorabilia*, attests to a newly personal and in that sense "Socratic" use of ψυχή based, somewhat unexpectedly, on strongly psychophysical rather than dualistic ideas. For this group of texts, I believe, ψυχή is to be seen as

---

12. These possibilities are well summarized in the brief but thoughtful study of Ingenkamp (1975).

something influenced, if not created, by analogy to scientific or medical notions of body, and in this context the interactions of soul and body occur in a naive or pragmatic way that assumes the two parts of the composite to be highly symmetrical, not ontologically or qualitatively different.[13] In a word, despite certain "Socratic"-sounding claims for soul in these texts,[14] there is in them a constant sense that body and soul are alike in nature and that this underlying likeness is, in obvious contrast to the ascetic beliefs of Socrates, the virtue of soul. For it is through this likeness that theories of soul and body can be addressed to pragmatic ends like health and self-discipline. Because of the variety of sources in which this notion of soul and body is found and, most important, the frequency and specificity with which it is addressed in the early dialogues of Plato, the use of ψυχή in this sense has some claim to be regarded as generally pervasive in the period surrounding the teaching of Socrates. Dependence on the literary record, or on Aristotle's history, has tended to obscure this essential antecedent to the Socratic and Platonic use of ψυχή. On this reading of the evidence, therefore, it is possible to see the identification of soul and self, which rightly or wrongly we identify with the name of Socrates, as something other than semantic whimsy, the progressive assimilation of nonnaturalistic ideas of soul,[15] or the doctrinal fusion, so to speak, of Ionian rationalism and Pythagorean mysticism.[16] The Socratic contribution to ψυχή must be seen, rather, on the basis of the evidence developed here, as the moralization of many traditional contexts of ψυχή, a process focused initially, if not exclusively, on medical or therapeutic interest in the ψυχή as 'life-force'.[17]

13. See the discussion of the general constants of the relationship of mind and body in Hardie, pp. 83–93, especially p. 88, for the notion that since the soul can only cause change in something that preexists whereas the body may in fact create, or seem to create, a psychical response, body and soul have a natural asymmetry that evokes philosophical attempts to describe the relationship of soul and body as a dualism. To adapt the terms used by Hardie, the point here is that this asymmetry cannot be attached to ψυχή and body until ψυχή becomes the soul in a comprehensive sense.

14. Democr. B 187; Gorg. Hel. (1): σοφία is the κόσμος for ψυχή.

15. Gulley, p. 196.

16. Guthrie (1971), p. 150.

17. Vlastos (1945), p. 579 (esp. n. 10), stresses the importance of the Democritean fragments on soul as antecedents to Socrates and sees them in light of medical ideas. Although I take the nature of the connection between ethics and the ψυχή in a more pragmatic and therapeutic sense than does Vlastos (below, p. 146), the significance of scientific medicine for the development of the ψυχή in Democritus is clearly and persuasively argued by him.

2

Eschatological Uses of ψυχή: Pythagoras, Orphism, Empedocles

Since the time of Rohde, Pythagoras and early Orphism have been associated with the most profound changes in the Greek idea of the self, specifically with belief in the existence of an occult self in human beings—a conception arising under the influence of shamanistic cults and practices.[1] In some sense, of course, such influence is undeniable. One need look no further than to the figure of Socrates transfixed for hours by his thoughts at the opening of the *Symposium*,[2] or to the ecstatic journey of Parmenides to Being,[3] for significant reflections in Greek philosophy of the figure of the shaman. Yet the early connection of ψυχή with such phenomena is far from proven, despite the claim that we owe to Pythagoras or his followers the "association of moral behavior and also of the personality of a man with his soul."[4] Direct evidence for linguistic usage by Pythagoras and his follow-

---

1. On Pythagoras and shamanism the authoritative account is that of Burkert (1972), pp. 120–64, whose reexamination of the earlier Pythagorean tradition and its *testimonia* is now indispensable to any discussion of the subject. Burkert's evocation of Pythagoras as a practitioner of primitive religious ideas of the sort reflected in the *acusmata*, who nevertheless gives such ideas a unity hitherto unknown (p. 136), is persuasive. Cf. Kahn (1960), pp. 30–35, for a somewhat comparable view, which, however, assigns Pythagoras more philosophical rigor. For a skeptical treatment of Pythagoras as shaman see Philip, pp. 159–62. Morrison, pp. 349–50, stresses the importance, against Burkert, of the founding of a Pythagorean society.

2. Pl. *Smp.* 175a–b.

3. For this point see Burkert (1972), pp. 284–85.

4. I take this phrase from Gulley, p. 196, who presents the familiar view of the soul as progressing from Homeric 'shade' and 'life' to intellectual value in the Presocratics, and then cites Orphic-Pythagorean attachment of "moral significance . . . to the behavior of the soul," and the broad association, seen from the Gorgianic *Helen*, of ψυχή with "intellectual activity" in the last quarter of the fifth century. Cf. Jaeger, p. 83, who sees the ψυχή of the Pythagoreans as bringing about the "complete coalescence of the life-soul and consciousness as a presupposition of their doctrine of the so-called transmigration of souls," and Burkert (1972), p. 134, n. 78, who believes "it is beyond doubt that metempsychosis, or at any rate, related religious concepts, played a significant role in the development of the notion of ψυχή . . . but they do not presuppose it." Philip, p. 154, takes the unusual view that metempsychosis was "the natural product of the evolution of the notion of personality" and that it antedates Orphism.

ers has not survived, however, and the only fifth-century instances of ψυχή that might be thought to represent actual Pythagorean or Orphic diction are found at *Hippolytus* 1006, already discussed above,[5] and in fragment B 14 of the Pythagorean Philolaus—a text, as noted, that simply recounts without benefit of explanatory context the σῶμα-σῆμα doctrine attributed to the Orphics at *Cratylus* 400c.[6] Whether this fragment is authentic, much less what it means, cannot be decided.[7] It follows that an evaluation of the influence of Orphic or Pythagorean ideas about the ψυχή can be made only through reported evidence, and this evidence must include, of course, the much later texts of Empedocles. For even though ψυχή appears in the fragments of Empedocles just once, and then only in the popular sense of 'life lost at death' (B 138 χαλκῷ ἀπὸ ψυχὴν ἀρύσας), the *Katharmoi* is our only primary source for the nature of ideas of metempsychosis in Greece before Plato.[8] Not surprisingly, given such uneven and inadequate evidence, the problem of terminology has been neglected,[9] even though the influence of metempsychosis and allied beliefs—like those of the *Katharmoi*—in primal sin, ascetic purification, punishment and reward of souls after death, and the existence of an occult personality are taken to be crucial to the semantic history of ψυχή.[10]

At the heart of the issue is the nature of the relationship between the ψυχή as it appears in certain Platonic texts and the soul, or ψυχή, as we imagine it to have been understood in earlier religious or ascetic doctrines. It is from these texts—the myths of the *Gorgias, Phaedo, Republic,* and *Phaedrus*[11]—that we obtain our only intimate knowledge of the

5. See above, p. 84. On the relationship of Orphism and Pythagoreanism, see Burkert (1972), pp. 125ff., who suggests (p. 133) that metempsychosis was introduced to Orphism by the Pythagoreans. It is clear at least that a logical progression like that supposed by Rohde, from simple "Orphic" tenets to Pythagorean doctrine, is undocumentable.

6. B 14: μαρτυρέονται δὲ καὶ οἱ παλαιοὶ θεολόγοι τε καὶ μάντεις ὡς διά τινας τιμωρίας ἁ ψυχὰ τῷ σώματι συνέζευκται καὶ καθάπερ ἐν σήματι τούτῳ τέθαπται.

7. Burkert (1972), p. 248, n. 47.

8. Kahn (1960), p. 30.

9. Burkert (1972), pp. 132–33: "And how important is the word ψυχή? Was there present at its beginning the significant semantic innovation whereby the 'soul', as distinguished from the body and independently of it, is regarded as the 'complete coalescence of life-soul and consciousness' ... or is 'soul' primarily a mysterious, meta-empirical Self, independent of consciousness, as some important witnesses seem to indicate?" Despite this accurate framing of the question, the point is abandoned quickly because it will not yield, obviously, to historical analysis. Guthrie (1962), pp. 317–19, discusses the issue of language with sensitivity but then draws the conclusion that ψυχή could be used for both the 'life-soul' and the transmigrating δαίμων "as it was by Plato." The ψυχή of the Platonic myths thus predominates as a tool for understanding the Pythagorean ψυχή.

10. Cf. Introduction nn. 8 and 10, and above, n. 4.

11. Pl. *Grg.* 523a; *Phd.* 113d; *R.* 614a; *Phdr.* 248c.

Pythagorean or Orphic ψυχή, which, if they are to be believed, survives as a personality, acquires knowledge through recollection, and undergoes judgment and a clearly ethical form of metempsychosis after death. That in some form these ideas and even more specific details[12] have their origins in earlier doctrines of the surviving soul is beyond doubt and confirmed in any case by Plato's own appeal in the *Phaedrus* and elsewhere to ancient authority, including οἱ ἀμφὶ 'Ορφέα.[13] But ostensibly similar ideas may have profoundly different meanings. In the version of metempsychosis reported in Herodotus, for example, the soul does not undergo moral advancement, as in Empedocles, but wanders aimlessly through animal bodies until, at last, it resumes human life; at the least this should remind us that in a period of restricted literacy no doctrine of this kind can escape modification from place to place and from speaker to speaker.[14] That demonstrations of memory began in magical rather than epistemological contexts, a profound division, surely, between early and late ideas, is stressed by Burkert.[15] Above all, for our purposes, it is extremely difficult to know whether there is true common ground between the Platonic treatment of the soul as the mechanism for survival of a psychological personality of some sort and the earlier ideas of survival. The Platonic soul is itself flawed, so to speak, by contradictory tendencies toward personal and impersonal qualities,[16] and these contradictions attach not just to the attainment of rationality but to the soul's experience of transmigration, as the epistemological arguments of the *Meno* and several of the arguments for immortality in the *Phaedo* show.[17] These problems aside, however, the

12. On the close numerological correspondences between *Phdr.* 248e–49b, Pi. *O.* 2 and fr. 133, Emp. B 115 and B 129, and Hdt. 2.123 see von Fritz (1963), cols. 190–91. That these correspondences have a common origin is highly plausible. The ascending destiny of the soul in Emp. B 146 and in *Phdr.* 248c–e almost certainly suggests that Plato has drawn here on Empedocles; so, too, the correspondence of the feasting motif in B 147 with *Phdr.* 247, as Kahn (1960), p. 25, n. 67, observes.

13. Pl. *Phd.* 70c, *Cra.* 400c, *Ep.* VII 335A.

14. Hdt. 2.123; Emp. B 146. Bluck, pp. 411–12, suggests that Plato has eliminated from the underlying myth of Pi. fr. 133 requital for the dismemberment of Dionysus-Zagreus in favor of a doctrine based on general moral virtues. The evidence for weakening of metempsychosis after Plato is given in Burkert (1972), pp. 123–24. But see Solmsen (1968), pp. 631–32, for evidence of Orphic use of the term ἀμοιβή.

15. Burkert (1972), pp. 213–15.

16. The soul that survives as a recognizable self or person must somehow retain feelings that make sense only if they have physical concomitants; for the dissolutionist view, it is only pure intelligence devoid of individuality that survives. The multiplicity of contradictory senses in which Plato uses ψυχή from *Phaedo* on is discussed by Crombie, pp. 293–325.

17. "The memory implied in Plato's theory of *anamnesis* . . . is an impersonal memory, the same for all men" (Cornford [1970], p. 35). *Phd.* 103c–105e offers the second argument from opposites: the soul entails life, the opposite of life is death, the soul cannot admit the opposite of what it entails, hence it is immortal.

"Pythagorean" myths of Plato clearly treat the soul as a comprehensive psychological replica of the man who was once alive, something which was the agent, as well as the object, of the moral life for which the soul is to be judged after death. How exactly this comprehensive afterlife soul in Plato is related (beyond obvious similarities of detail) to historically earlier ideas of the surviving soul is thus the real problem on which any discussion of terminology must turn. There are no obvious or decisive answers to this question, but the earlier evidence for the use of ψυχή in contexts of survival is nevertheless worth examining closely.

Because they invoke, rather than report, a doctrine of metempsychosis and contain what is presumably an explicit reference to Pythagoras,[18] the fragments of Empedocles are most likely to provide whatever insight we can hope to have into the linguistic milieu of early Pythagoreanism and metempsychosis. Of these fragments three are particularly important for the question of diction.[19] In B 117 the speaker, who claims to have been boy, girl, bush, bird, and fish, has no designation except the personal pronoun (ἤδη γάρ ποτ' ἐγὼ γενόμην). In B 115, the fragment that most closely corresponds in detail with the myth in *Phaedrus*, a wandering of 30,000 seasons is imposed on wrongdoers who belong to the long-lived δαίμονες (δαίμονες οἵτε μακραίωνος λελάχασι βίοιο), and of these Empedocles is himself one (τῶν καὶ ἐγὼ νῦν εἰμι, φυγὰς θεόθεν καὶ ἀλήτης). In B 112 he describes himself as a θεὸς ἄμβροτος, οὐκέτι θνητός, wreathed and honored by the citizens of Acragas, followed by thousands who seek the path to gain, dispensation of oracles, or the "word of healing" for their diseases.[20] It can be taken as certain from these passages that for Empedocles the occult self that survives physical death, acquires knowledge through metempsychosis, and eventually seeks to withdraw from the cycle of birth and death is not the ψυχή common to all men but something described by paraphrase or as a θεός or δαίμων.[21] Whether this conclusion should be extended back in time to the earlier Pythagoreans is open to question, since

18. B 129. For a bibliography on the question of attribution see Guthrie (1962), p. 161, n. 1.

19. Other texts on metempsychosis are B 125, 128, 134, 136, 146. The most exceptional paraphrase is B 134, which speaks of the φρὴν ἱερὴ καὶ ἀθέσφατος.

20. The language and style of the shaman-healer are taken up by Gorgias in the *Helen* and by Plato at *Charmides* 156d, where they are directed to the ψυχή (discussed below). It is worth pointing out here that the shaman-healer must have directed his attention to the δαίμων, which causes the disease (cf. *RE Suppl.* 7 (1950), cols. 109–10), and that in the later texts ψυχή takes the place of the δαίμων. It would be interesting to know whether as scientific medicine took hold a direct substitution of ψυχή for δαίμων occurred. Cf. Democr. B 171.

21. Cf. especially B 146 for θεός.

the possibility cannot be ruled out that Empedocles had reasons for rejecting rather than preserving Pythagorean terminology. Because he is the
only early source whose writings actually promulgate a doctrine of
metempsychosis, however, his choice of language cannot easily be dis-
regarded. That he calls the soul a δαίμων, a word extensively documented
in the Pythagorean *testimonia*,[22] but not, to our knowledge, a ψυχή, may
therefore be an indication of Pythagorean usage. It is difficult, moreover, to
reconcile the use of ψυχή in the meaning 'life lost at death' with a tradition
that seeks to honor Pythagoras.

We must thus look elsewhere than to Empedocles for new uses of
ψυχή itself. In fact, only ten citations found before the end of the fifth
century report ψυχή in contexts that can be construed as Orphic or
Pythagorean. The earliest of these texts, Xenophanes B7 (παῦσαι μηδὲ
ῥάπιζ᾽, ἐπεὶ ἦ φίλου ἀνέρος ἐστὶν ψυχή, τὴν ἔγνων φθεγξαμένης αἴων), has been
taken to illustrate directly, as I have said before, the transference of
personality to the ψυχή.[23] The fragment is our oldest Pythagorean text,[24]
and it shows clearly that already in the sixth century Pythagorean belief in
metempsychosis was sufficiently well known to be parodied. But the
fragment is less helpful as a guide to linguistic usage, and it is important to
resist the assumption that we find in it the language as well as the doctrine
of Pythagoras. The linguistic value of the fragment, as I have mentioned
earlier, is largely negated by the fact that ψυχή is the ordinary word by
which any Greek of the archaic or classical period would refer to that which
survives death. This is shown by the Homeric *Nekyia* and the scattered
references to the 'shade' in the post-Homeric texts discussed above, and also
by the inscription from Potidaea[25] (432 B.C.), which says that the ψυχαί of
the dead are given to the αἰθήρ, and their bodies to the ground. Relevant
here too is a recently published tablet from Hipponion in which the ψυχαί
of the dead are vividly portrayed as descending to the vicinity of the Lake
of Memory.[26] Xenophanes' use of ψυχή may be determined, therefore, by
this tradition, by the desire perhaps to satirize the Pythagorean claim to be a

22. A collection of later texts is assembled by Detienne, pp. 171–77, but see Burkert (1964), pp.
563–67.

23. Furley, p. 11; Long, p. 27, who concludes, "Pythagoras' soul was what gave him his
personality as Pythagoras." Burkert (1972), p. 120, n. 1, furnishes a bibliography on the problem of
attribution.

24. Burkert (1972), p. 120.

25. *IG* I, 442, discussed in Guthrie (1950), pp. 262–63, with the important parallels E. *Supp.* and
E. fr. 971 N, in both of which it is πνεῦμα and not ψυχή that ascends to the αἰθήρ. Cf. Epich. B 9.

26. The text is published in Foti, pp. 110–11, who puts its date at the end of the fifth century.

δαίμων or θεός with a comical reference to ψυχή, or possibly by the wish to reflect a genuine new use of ψυχή among the Pythagoreans that called for a systematic connection between the ψυχαί of the living and the surviving ψυχαί of the dead. There are no good grounds for choosing any one of these alternatives. The notion of personality can be attached to the ψυχή described in this fragment only by drawing—as Xenophanes obviously does in a crude way—logical inferences from the doctrine of metempsychosis and by ignoring the very limited nature of the semantic information actually before us. The same argument applies to Ion B 4, in which it is said that if Pythagoras is right, Pherecydes will be rewarded for his decency and courage in life by a τερπνὸν βίοτον for his ψυχή after death—a pseudoepitaph that combines the notion of survival with a pun on the sort of usage found on the epitaph of Philo the sailor.[27] The much-cited passage (2.123) in which Herodotus tells his readers that the Egyptians were the first to believe that the ψυχή is immortal and transmigrates into other living creatures at death—a text in any case lacking both a moral idea of transmigration[28] and any sort of explicit psychological connotation for ψυχή—is again obviously a popular rendering of metempsychosis and therefore not philosophically important.

Passages of similar ambiguity are found in Pindar, for example, fragment 133, where it is said that in the ninth year Persephone returns to the light the ψυχαί of those who have paid the penalty for the ancient πένθος and that from these ψυχαί 'arise' the higher orders of men in this life (ἐκ τᾶν ⟨sc. ψυχαί⟩ βασιλῆες ἀγαυοὶ | καὶ σθένει κραιπνοὶ σοφίᾳ τε μέγιστοι | ἄνδρες αὔξοντ᾽· ἐς δὲ τὸν λοιπὸν χρόνον ἥροες ἁγνοὶ πρὸς ἀνθρώπων καλεῦνται). There can be no doubt that quite specific religious beliefs, his own or those of his patron, have caused Pindar to intensify the moral drama of the soul's passage through Hades, and this journey is obviously comparable in a general way to the one described in the new cult material from Hipponion. But it is not easy to see how either of these apparently innovative underworld portraits of the soul significantly changes the character of the ψυχή itself. The important question is again whether the more moralized vision of the underworld ψυχή is now linked in Pindar's imagination with the

27. Cf. above, p. 93, and Epich. B 45, where the man who gives no goods to his ψυχή is not one whom the poet calls blessed.

28. Cameron, p. 15, sees the lack of moral content as reason to doubt the historical accuracy of Herodotus, but the point is that Herodotus is not reporting Pythagorean doctrine or language per se but the popular rendering of such ideas. The Zalmoxis passage (4.95), rich with the kind of curious detail that suggests authentic antiquarian information, says nothing directly about the ψυχή or, for that matter, transmigration. The dead merely go to the happier abode, which may, as Cameron suggests, imply a doctrine of immortality. But see Burkert (1972), pp. 156ff.

ψυχή of the living man in a way not true for believers in the Homeric 'shade'. In favor of a new connection is, perhaps, the appeal to self in *Pythian* 3.61 (μὴ, φίλα ψυχά, βίον ἀθάνατον σπεῦδε), but such use of self-address is common for ψυχή in drama, and so the most that can be argued is that a familiar use of ψυχή has been placed in a context where ambiguity with the ψυχή that survives is possible. But there is no outright innovation that cannot otherwise be accounted for.[29] A more impressive text is found at *Olympian* 2.68ff., where religious devotion to the ψυχή is undeniable: ὅσοι δ' ἐτόλμασαν ἐστρίς | ἑκατέρωθε μείναντες ἀπὸ πάμπαν ἀδίκων ἔχειν ψυχάν, ἔτειλαν Διὸς ὁδὸν παρὰ Κρό- | νου τύρσιν· ἔνθα μακάρων | νᾶσον ὠκεανίδες | αὖραι περιπνέοισιν.[30] Because the use of ψυχή here includes a reference to justice as well as to survival and reward after death, these words come as close as any to supplying an early instance of ψυχή that seems to anticipate directly the Platonic soul as self. But there are several important arguments against a Platonic reading. First, as in the other texts considered, there is no explicit indication that the ψυχή itself engages in acts of justice or injustice, and that it has thus become for Pindar an agent of consciousness or will. For the passage to be understandable, the ψυχή need be no more than an object of moral concern or of hope for life after death, a being of some sort that is peculiarly one's own and that offers a kind of mechanism for continuity from one life to another. Second, Pindar's regular use of ψυχή in traditional contexts, as described in the previous section, cannot be entirely disregarded in trying to assess the usage in *Olympian* 2, despite the new afterlife ideas. Third, αὐξάνεσθαι in fragment 133 does not suggest the continuous existence of something Platonic in character but, taken literally, the survival of a kind of immaterial seed, so to speak, of interest not for its own sake but as a point of continuity from life to life. Last, this text must be contrasted with the most compelling passage about the soul in Pindar, fragment 131b, the text Rohde used anachronistically to ground his theory of the Homeric ψυχή: καὶ σῶμα μὲν πάντων ἕπεται θανάτῳ περισθενεῖ, | ζωὸν δ' ἔτι λείπεται αἰῶνος εἴδωλον· τὸ γάρ ἐστι μόνον | ἐκ θεῶν· εὕδει δὲ πρασσόντων μελέων, ἀτὰρ εὑδόντεσσιν ἐν πολλοῖς ὀνείροις | δείκνυσι τερπνῶν ἐφέρποισαν χαλεπῶν τε κρίσιν. The phrase αἰῶνος εἴδωλον plainly confirms the diction of Empedocles: that is, where an explicit and thoughtful connection is

---

29. Theognis 710 refers to souls in the underworld 'refusing' (ψυχάς ... ἀναινομένας) when they are held by the gates of the underworld. This lively personification of the ψυχή in the underworld can be contrasted with the apparent lack of personification in the Pindaric texts having the same context. Unfortunately, the passage in Theognis cannot be dated.

30. The dedication to Theron of Acragas, the home of Empedocles, is obviously significant for a Pythagorean connection. See von Fritz (1963), col. 189.

actually made in the mind of the speaker between the surviving soul and something that acts as a mental agent in the living man, a word or phrase other than ψυχή is instinctively sought.

The consistency with which these texts treat ψυχή is encouraging. If we add to them the fragments of Philolaus, taken in accordance with Burkert's recent reassessment, the pattern seems to be confirmed. The σῶμα-σῆμα fragment of Philolaus, B 14, which tells us nothing more than that the ψυχή is the focus for hopes of survival and accordingly is at odds with the body, cannot be authenticated or rejected.[31] B 11, a long fragment which, in the course of a discussion of Number, does treat the ψυχή as a cognitive agent that 'knows' and thus implies the soul in a comprehensive sense, is now convincingly discarded as a later forgery.[32] B 13, which assigns νοῦς to the head, ψυχή and αἴσθησις to the heart, and the animal functions to the navel and genitals, is regarded as genuine. But here, obviously, ψυχή is perceived only in a physiological mode, since the fragment goes on to make "the brain the ruler of man, the *heart* of animal, the navel of plant, the genital of all."[33] Finally, a last epistemological fragment in which ψυχή appears, B 22, already rejected as spurious by Diels, is condemned by Burkert too as a later forgery.[34]

These scattered notices and quotations are, of course, not adequate to support hypotheses of any great subtlety or precision about the Pythagorean use of ψυχή. But together they form a pattern that is more impressive than might be expected, since it draws on a variety of sources. Briefly, in the texts we have considered, ψυχή is never used to designate an occult self in the living man, and no text shows a connection between the surviving ψυχή and the ψυχή as an agent of consciousness in the living man. Either there is no connection (Herodotus 2.123, Ion B 4, Pindar fr. 133) or the texts are too epigrammatic (Xenophanes B 7, Philolaus B 14) or ambivalent (Pindar O. 2.68ff.) to demonstrate that such usage has come into being. Moreover, ordinary 'life-force' uses of ψυχή occur throughout these same authors (Empedocles B 138, Philolaus B 13, Pindar, passim), and where the idea of an occult self is intended a word or phrase other than ψυχή is used (Empedocles B 112, 115, Pindar fr. 131b).

31. Burkert (1972), p. 276.

32. Ibid., p. 273.

33. Ibid., p. 270. Burkert compares Critias A 23 for the point that αἴσθησις means little more than the capacity of the body to respond to stimuli. It is alive, not dead.

34. Ibid., p. 247.

It is one thing to identify this pattern, however, and another to account for it. As in the case of the Homeric ψυχή, a somewhat iconoclastic interpretation of the evidence may be more defensible than seemingly conservative notions of gradual change or natural ambiguity. Certainly any belief in the surviving or transmigrating soul and in the occult δαίμων (or αἰῶνος εἴδωλον and the like) could have influenced the treatment of ψυχή as a psychological entity in the living man, and in Plato at least this potential for change is fully realized. Nevertheless, by itself the earlier material suggests not the gradual falling together of ψυχή with, say, the Empedoclean δαίμων but resistance to such assimilation—like the relationship of Homeric ψυχή and θυμός, a resistance keyed perhaps to some crucial habit of distinction that the new ideas did not change. If such a distinction was made it is unlikely to have arisen from the practice of restricting attribution of the powers of the δαίμων exclusively to the shaman or cult leader and his adepts, although that is the first explanation that comes to mind. Such patterns would imply a more rigorous linguistic environment than we can reasonably suppose, at least for the earlier Pythagoreans.[35] A more satisfactory interpretation, I think, is simply that traditional ideas of the nature of the surviving soul may have persisted even where, thanks to metempsychosis, they ought logically to have faded. I rely here on Kahn's succinct discussion of this issue in connection with Empedocles.[36] Although a precise reconciliation of the two poems of Empedocles is unlikely, Kahn's theory that the apparent contradiction between the poems is owed in part at least to the fact that they are subjected to more rationalized ideas of immortality than fifth-century minds—even that of Empedocles—could imagine, bears directly on the use of ψυχή. The absence of comprehensive uses of ψυχή coupled with the new importance of the ψυχή in passages like Xenophanes B 7, *Olympian* 2, fragment 133 of Pindar, and the σῶμα-σῆμα fragment of Philolaus suggest, perhaps, just such a contradictory mixture of personal and impersonal expectations of survival as Kahn proposes for Empedocles. Even though no true idea of personality can be attached to what survives—that is, in the return of the constituents of man to nature as described in Empedocles B 9 and B 15— something of the surviving matter is perceived, oddly, as one's own,

35. See Burkert, passim, on the lack of Pythagorean philosophy before Philolaus, e.g., p. 240, where the *acusmata*, the doctrine of transmigration, and the Pythagorean βίος are regarded as elements of Pythagoreanism that "lacked logical foundation or systematic and conceptual coherence." This conclusion must surely affect our view of Pythagorean language.

36. Kahn (1960), pp. 12–27.

possessed of a character or destiny determined by the quality of the life that
has been led.[37] No more than this, if not less, need be implied by any of the
texts considered here as witnesses to early ideas of survival, unless the
Xenophanes fragment is given an exceptionally somber reading. The more
dramatic and moralized picture of the ψυχή in the underworld recorded in
Pindar and in the inscription from Hipponion may have been confined, so
to speak, to the underworld.[38]

Since these documented uses of ψυχή in association with afterlife
survival do not support a case for semantic change, an alternative to the
otherwise natural inference that metempsychosis directly altered the meaning of ψυχή is perhaps called for. I suggest that although the new ideas of
survival and of occult existence undoubtedly helped to create an environment in which the connotations of ψυχή could be greatly enriched as
against earlier beliefs, deeply ingrained traditional attitudes had first to be
overcome for such influences to be felt, and this process may simply not
have occurred in the century after Pythagoras. The well attested Greek
habit of instinctively separating the 'life' uses of ψυχή from those meaning
'shade', traced in part II above, should be recalled. Worth mention here,
therefore, as evidence for something other than an emphatic connection of
the personality with the ψυχή among early believers in metempsychosis,
are the reports in Aristotle in which, for the Orphics, souls are said to come
from everywhere, carried by the winds and penetrating the body when
one breathes (De Anima 410b19), and also his reference to the motes or
ξύσματα (De Anima 404a3), which we are told the Pythagoreans identified
with souls. Both passages imply that as an object of the imagination the
Orphic-Pythagorean soul passed through a phase where it was, like the
souls of the Potidaea inscription or the γνῶμαι of Euripides' Helen, which fly
off into the αἰθήρ, something "curiously impersonal."[39] A related usage
may be attested by the newly discovered Derveni papyrus, a commentary
on traditional Orphic verses dating from the second half of the fourth
century,[40] which seems to refer to the ψυχή in a wholly physiological
sense.[41] In column 15 of the papyrus it is said that "just as beings are
individually called according to what predominates in them, by the same

37. Kahn (1960), pp. 22–23. See also the critique of A. A. Long (1966), pp. 256–76.

38. The lack of literary evidence for new views of the afterlife soul that would reflect the
influence of Orphic-Pythagorean ideas is impressive. In addition to Pi. O. 2 and fragments 131b and
133, Ziegler (col. 1371) cites A. Supp. 230ff. and Eu. 273ff., both of which predict punishment after
death.

39. See Guthrie (1950), p. 263, n. 2, for this phrase.

40. Boyancé, p. 92.

41. The text of the papyrus is published in Merkelbach (1967).

principle all things are called Zeus."[42] There can be no doubt that this statement is meant to explain the Orphic verse Ζεὺς πνοίη πάντων as an allegorical rendering of the ἀήρ-πνεῦμα doctrine of Diogenes of Apollonia,[43] as expressed, for example, in fragment B 5, where knowledge is "what is called air by men, and all men are directed by air, and it rules everything and is justly considered god." Since the connection between air and ψυχή is amply documented for Diogenes, and since thought is something merely contingent on both, it must be assumed that the author of the papyrus is able to connect the Orphic idea of ψυχή with the essentially impersonal 'life-force' ψυχή found in Diogenes. It is not easy to see how a highly personal notion of the surviving Pythagorean or Orphic ψυχή, like that of the *Gorgias*, could coexist with this theory, and it can be argued that Plato himself avoids mention of the animative function of ψυχή in the early dialogues for just this reason. Hence, if the Derveni papyrus attests to anything in the fifth-century Orphic tradition of the soul, what it reports is surprisingly at odds with the Platonic myths.

---

42. ἐπ [εἰ δὲ τὰ ἐό] ντα ἕν ἕκαστον κέκ[λητ] αι ἀπὸ τοῦ ἐπικρατοῦντος, Ζεὺς πάντα κατὰ τὸν αὐτὸν λόγον ἐκλήθη. πάντας γὰρ ὁ ἀὴρ ἐπικρατεῖ τοσοῦτον ὅσον βούλεται.

43. Merkelbach, p. 25; Burkert (1968), pp. 97–98; Boyancé, p. 98.

3

'Life-force' Uses of ψυχή: Anaximenes, Heraclitus, Diogenes[1]

ANAXIMENES

Anaximenes is the only one of the three Milesians of whom there survives what is claimed to be a direct quotation of *ψυχή*: this well-known statement (B 2), taken from Aetius, holds that as the soul, consisting of air, governs and controls men,[2] so *πνεῦμα* and air surround the *κόσμος*. Because of the source problems, the entire passage in Aetius must be quoted:

> Ἀναξιμένης ... ἀρχὴν τῶν ὄντων ἀέρα ἀπεφήνατο· ἐκ γὰρ τούτου πάντα γίγνεσθαι καὶ εἰς αὐτὸν πάλιν ἀναλύεσθαι. 'οἷον ἡ ψυχή, φησίν, ἡ ἡμετέρα ἀὴρ οὖσα συγκρατεῖ ἡμᾶς, καὶ ὅλον τὸν κόσμον πνεῦμα καὶ ἀὴρ περιέχει' (λέγεται δὲ δυνωνύμως ἀὴρ καὶ πνεῦμα). ἁμαρτάνει δὲ καὶ οὗτος ἐξ ἁπλοῦ καὶ μονοειδοῦς ἀέρος καὶ πνεύματος δοκῶν συνεστάναι τὰ ζῷα· ἀδύνατον γὰρ ἀρχὴν μίαν τὴν ὕλην τῶν ὄντων ὑποστῆναι, ἀλλὰ καὶ τὸ ποιοῦν αἴτιον χρὴ ὑποτιθέναι· οἷον ἄργυρος οὐκ ἀρκεῖ πρὸς τὸ ἔκπωμα γενέσθαι, ἐὰν μὴ τὸ ποιοῦν ᾖ, τουτέστιν ὁ ἀργυροκόπος· ὁμοίως καὶ ἐπὶ τοῦ χαλκοῦ καὶ τοῦ ξύλου καὶ τῆς ἄλλης ὕλης.

---

1. Presocratic fragments not discussed here are Epich. B 4 (a hen sitting on eggs causes them to have 'life'), B 45 (the man who gives no goods to his *ψυχή* is not blessed but the guardian of goods for an heir), Anaxag. B 4 and B 12 (both times the phrase ὅσα ψυχὴν ἔχει = whatever is 'alive'). Fragments not quoted in Greek or not using *ψυχή* are Epich. B 9, B 22, Epich. Enni. 48, and Protag. B 11. Lycophron fr. 1 is a summary from Aristotle and is quoted above, p. 105, n. 1.

2. The meaning of anachronistic συγκρατεῖ can be only surmised ("uns beherrschend zusammenhält" [Diels-Kranz]; "holds us together and controls us" [Kirk]). I adopt Kirk's translation here although it may (see Alt, p. 130) overstate the importance of κρατεῖν in the compound.

The authenticity of this quotation rests on the likelihood that the Milesians applied a biological model to the world[3] and also on the indirect notices of ψυχή given for Thales (A 22) and Anaximander (A 29). Of these, the reference to Anaximander will not stand much scrutiny and, even if accurate, reports nothing more than that he held the soul to be composed of air, as did Anaximenes, Anaxagoras, and Archelaus.[4] The theory attributed to Thales, however, that magnetic stone and perhaps also amber possess ψυχή, comes to us directly from Aristotle, is attested by Hippias,[5] and therefore can be presumed authentic. Exactly what Thales meant by this observation, on the other hand, is open to question. Whether the report reflects a simple continuation of primitive animism,[6] an attack on unscientific forms of animism,[7] or the development of a significant analogy of microcosm and macrocosm cannot be decided.[8] But at any rate the tradition obviously attests the generalization of ψυχή beyond its Homeric role as the purely human 'life-force.' If the fragment of Anaximenes is genuine, its importance in this light is, first, that it would allow the analogy of nature and man to be focused specifically on the ψυχή so that the nature and activity of the ψυχή could be explored through the nature and activity of the ἀρχή, and vice versa, as seems to be the case in Heraclitus.[9] Second, the use of συγκρατεῖν in the fragment could imply extension of the functions of soul already at the outset of Presocratic thought beyond those of simple animation.[10] It is of some importance for the history of ψυχή, therefore, that in a recent study Alt[11] has made a strong

---

3. See the concise discussion in Lloyd, pp. 232–36. For Kahn (1960), p. 98, the world for the Milesians is "a geometrical organism suffused with life." A more conservative view is taken in KR, pp. 96–97. Lloyd (p. 234) limits the notion of the world as "a single living organism" to Anaximander and Anaximenes, but the evidence for Anaximenes is taken from B 2.

4. This statement and the commentary of Philoponus on De Anima 405a21 constitute the only testimony apart from B 2 itself that Anaximenes spoke of the soul at all (see Alt, p. 133).

5. Thal. A 1. Cf. KR, p. 94.

6. On animism in early Greece see Nilsson (1925), pp. 105ff., and the sensible remarks in Lloyd, p. 234. Kirk is right (KR, p. 97) that the personified spears of Il. 11.574 are too literary to be used as evidence for early Greek beliefs.

7. I take this as the meaning intended by Burnet (1930), p. 50.

8. See Guthrie (1962), pp. 131–32, and Alt, p. 131, for the dating of the macrocosm-microcosm analogy in Greek thought. Kirk's insistence on the originality of the medical texts of the fifth century in making this analogy (1954), p. 312, is qualified in KR, p. 161, where the analogy is "perhaps unlikely to occur in such a plain form ... so early as Anaximenes." For a useful comment on the two-way nature of the analogy in the Hippocratic texts see Burkert (1972), pp. 44–45, and n. 88.

9. See below, pp. 127ff.

10. That is, if we assume that κρατεῖν implies control over the organism. See Alt, pp. 129–30, for a review of earlier opinion on the diction of the passage and on the weakness of the distinction between paraphrase and quotation in the doxographical tradition.

11. Alt, pp. 129–64.

case for reassigning the fragment from Anaximenes to Diogenes of Apollonia. Since the text stands alone, the question of authenticity is crucial, and since Alt's arguments appear decisive, it is necessary to recapitulate here her extensive philological analysis. This falls into four main points. (1) The fragment and its context in Aetius constitute a single unit, and in that sense, at least, the text is authentic. The fragment is not likely to have appeared for Aetius and his immediate predecessors in any form other than the one in which it is now found, since the combination of ἀήρ and πνεῦμα invalidates the standard criticism of the Presocratics found throughout the περὶ ἀρχῶν chapter of Aetius, namely, that most of the early philosophers named a material but not an efficient cause.[12] In addition, the fragment as it stands is clearly the object of the commentary that follows it, since the commentary idiosyncratically treats ἀήρ and πνεῦμα as synonyms in order to effect its critique of the quotation.[13] (2) Nothing in the quotation itself, the commentary, or the περὶ ἀρχῶν chapter, as opposed to other sections of Aetius, can be shown to be unquestionably post-Peripatetic, and it is certain that much of the chapter comes directly from Aristotle and Theophrastus.[14] (3) Diogenes, in contrast to Anaximenes, not only asserted a doctrine of πνεῦμα but employed, according to the surviving fragments, diction closely allied to that of this text, particularly the doubtful words συγκρατεῖν and κόσμος.[15] No other convincing reference to Anaximenes' supposed doctrine of the soul exists in the doxography, and Aetius seems suspiciously ignorant here of his own later citation of Anaximenes on the conception of god, since there the doctrine of ἀήρ is referred to without mention of πνεῦμα.[16] At chapter I,3,6, moreover, he attributes the theory of rarefaction and condensation solely to Archelaus,[17] an omission suggesting that he has no knowledge of Anaximenes on this point. (4) The structure of the περὶ ἀρχῶν chapter, and of it alone, is that of the biographical Διαδοχαί introduced at the end of the third century B.C. Accordingly, the Presocratic material in it has been reorganized from the categorization by subject followed by Theophrastus into that of the canonical lists of Ionians and Italians.[18]

---

12. Ibid., p. 139.
13. Ibid., pp. 153–54.
14. Ibid., p. 152.
15. Especially B 4: καὶ τοῦτο (sc. ἀήρ) αὐτοῖς καὶ ψυχή ἔστι καὶ νόησις; B 5: ἀναπνεῖν; B 5: καὶ ὑπὸ τούτου τοῦ ἀέρος πάντας καὶ κυβερνᾶσθαι καὶ παντῶν·κρατεῖν. For κόσμος see B 2. Cf. Alt, pp. 159–60.
16. Anaximen. A 8 [= Aet. I,7,13].
17. Alt, p. 156.
18. Ibid., pp. 137–38.

The theory of mistaken attribution is consistent with points (1) to (3), since they prevent the fragment from being broken up, as it usually is, into an Anaximenean core altered by the interpolation of Stoic interest in πνεῦμα. If the fragment stands as a whole and has not undergone late alteration, Diogenes offers the only reasonably acceptable source, although certainty is unattainable. Point (4) in turn suggests a remarkably precise mechanism, as Alt has elegantly demonstrated, by which this reattribution occurred. In *Metaphysics* A and in Theophrastus, Anaximenes and Diogenes are, like Heraclitus and Hippasus, linked as advocates of a common ἀρχή-doctrine, air for the first pair, and fire, of course, for the latter.[19] Whereas Heraclitus and Hippasus continue to be linked and are both included in the sequence following Pythagoras in the reorganized scheme, Diogenes falls into an uncertain place, blocked from his proper position following Anaxagoras by the importance of Archelaus, as the alleged teacher of Socrates, to the overall design.[20] For the relative obscurity and uncertain place of Diogenes in contrast to the fixed position of Anaximenes in the Ionian canon to allow the transfer of material from Diogenes to Anaximenes requires only the existence of a suitable intermediary between Theophrastus and the Διαδοχαί. In this assumed text, Alt argues, a statement of Diogenes on the connection of ψυχή and πνεῦμα must have been juxtaposed with the paraphrase of Anaximenes' doctrine of air as ἀρχή. When the organization of this text by subject was replaced by the biographical design of the Διαδοχαί, the ψυχή fragment might easily have been attributed to the more famous of the paired exponents of an ἀήρ-doctrine. Whether this in fact happened cannot be proved, of course, but Alt's arguments undoubtedly raise to a new level the doubts that have always surrounded the fragment, and with it the claim that systematic interest in the sixth century in the analogy of man and nature centering on ψυχή should be regarded as a general premise of Milesian thought. Why Aristotle would have omitted such a doctrine from his summary in *De Anima*, finally, is not easily explained.

HERACLITUS

The new challenge to the Anaximenean fragment serves to emphasize the remarkable interest in the ψυχή that appears for the first time in Heraclitus. The number of references alone is impressive. The word ψυχή appears in

19. Ibid., p. 158, n. 151.

20. That is, Thales followed by Anaximander, Anaximenes, Anaxagoras, Archelaus, and Socrates. Diogenes appears in Aetius I, 3 only after Zeno.

ten B fragments;[21] reference to it presumably underlies the Latin paraphrase of Chalcidius also quoted by Diels-Kranz as a B fragment.[22] It is
very likely the subject of two additional fragments that happen not to use
the word,[23] and the possible subject of an extensive summary in Sextus,
which has been thought to reflect in part the actual words of Heraclitus.[24]

The doctrine of the soul advanced by these texts was already stated in
the main by Zeller.[25] The general points of agreement are, first, that the
ψυχή is itself fire and undergoes changes of state analogous to those of fire in
the cosmic system. Second, it is distributed throughout the body and is
unmeasurable. Third, its changes of state are manifested by waking, sleeping, and death. These conditions depend on the ratio of moisture to fire in
the soul; so too, in the waking state, the activity and competence of the
sensory faculties and the intelligence are directly dependent on the fieriness
of the ψυχή. Fourth, like cosmic fire, soul fire is in some way nourished by
moisture, although how this happens is not explicitly described. Finally,
following Burnet and Kirk as against others,[26] it seems likely that
Heraclitus envisions two kinds of 'death' for the ψυχή: one by fire for those
cut down by violence in the prime of life and consciousness while still in
possession of ψυχαί that are, at the instant of death, fiery; the other by
water for those whose ψυχαί gradually become moist through disease and
degeneration.

But this consensus does not really address the issues with which we are
concerned here. Although the fragments give unmistakable proof of an
important change in the use of ψυχή, it is not easy to see what exactly has
drawn Heraclitus' interest so markedly to the ψυχή. Nor is it possible, as
always, to know how comprehensive a notion of soul can rightly be
attributed to the more epigrammatic texts—B 118, for example, which

21. Frs. B 12, 36, 45, 77, 85, 98, 107, 117, 118, 136. The joining of the river statement to the
statement on ψυχή in B 12 is condemned by Kirk (*KR*, p. 196; Kirk [1954], pp. 367ff.), and B 77 (Kirk
[1954], p. 253) is taken as a gloss on B 36.

22. B 67a. See the discussion and bibliography in Nussbaum, pp. 6ff.

23. B 26 and B 88.

24. A 16 compares the assimilation of intelligence through breathing to the placing of embers
next to fire. This simile is strikingly appropriate to Heraclitus, and it may therefore be authentic, as
Burnet (1930), p. 171, observed, followed by Kirk (*KR*, p. 209).

25. Zeller (1881), vol. 2, pp. 79ff. For the nourishment of fire by moisture see *KR*, p. 206. Kahn
(1964), p. 199, takes soul as breath or exhalation, not fire, and cites the terminology 'moist' and 'dry' in
B 77, 117, 118, as well as the doxographical reports that soul is an exhalation (above, p. 105, n. 1). In the
view taken here the distinction is not really to the point; it is the ratio of fire to moisture that Heraclitus
is concerned with, and whether this is imagined as a variably moist/dry vapor or as 'fire' directly in
balance with moisture makes no appreciable difference.

26. Kirk (1949), passim.

says that a dry ψυχή is "wisest and best." In recent studies the ψυχή fragments have been variously interpreted as descriptions of a "central faculty [which possesses] the power of connected reasoning and language learning,"[27] a psychophysical self characterized by such qualities as depth and intangibility,[28] and the "human soul as an inner world."[29] Such readings are perhaps valid responses to the evocative language of the surviving fragments. Yet they tend to downgrade or ignore the one part of the Heraclitean doctrine of soul that can be treated less intuitively, namely, the connection between the soul as the physiological animator and the cosmic processes to which, in that capacity, it is plainly analogized.

The nature of this analogy is open to debate. Kirk's view is that a link between the cosmic fragments and the fragments on the soul can be supposed only for the life span of the organism as a whole.[30] He proposes that the oppositions living-dead, sleeping-waking, young-old spoken of in B 88 imply merely "successive states of the living body, namely, sleeping and waking, and on the other [hand] a conviction that the soul, after death, becomes 'alive' and young again."[31] The chief problem with this thesis is that unless one adopts the idiosyncratic view that Heraclitus did not in fact promulgate a doctrine of flux,[32] the analogy between the activity of soul fire and that of cosmic fire is not only distressingly vague but, in a sense, inaccurate. As opposed to the changes of state undergone by cosmic fire, which must be characterized as inevitable and in that sense not injurious, changes of state involving the soul fire are, according to this view, necessarily seen both physically and psychologically as instances of temporary or extended disequilibrium. Sleep, drunkenness, and anger are all states in which soul fire is reduced, and they are to be understood, therefore, as anticipations of the moist condition that will be the fate of the soul at death; intelligence, on the other hand, is a sign that the soul is alive and fiery. It is not hard to find support for this reading in the fragments. The efficient

27. Nussbaum, p. 5. Cf. the view of Vlastos (1955), p. 364, that already in Anaximenes the "ψυχή is identified with the thinking, willing self and hence accorded the power of controlling the body and its functions," a concept of ψυχή then "amply documented" in Heraclitus.

28. Snell (1953), p. 17; Ingenkamp, p. 52.

29. Kahn (1964), p. 201.

30. Kirk (1954), p. 145. Kirk's opinions on this problem are set out in brief, since his main concern is the cosmic scheme. Yet his division into cosmic and psychic fragments is in itself a significant act of interpretation. Cf., for example, Reinhardt, p. 199, and Vlastos (1955), p. 365, who see the analogy of cosmos and soul as an essential heuristic tool for Heraclitus, and especially Cherniss (1951), p. 333, who suggests that for Heraclitus it is possible to discover the "meaning of the world by examining one's own soul, since it is the clearest phase of the ordered cosmic process."

31. Kirk (1954), p. 148.

32. See Guthrie (1962), p. 452; Vlastos (1955), p. 362.

functioning of the soul is made to depend explicitly on the fieriness of the soul in B 117 (the drunkard with a moist soul must be led home stumbling by a young boy) and B 118, for example; in the text of A 16, whose Heraclitean provenance is suggested to scholars, including Kirk, by its imagery,[33] intelligence and memory are said to depend on the contact of mind (νοῦς) with its surroundings.[34] If this late summary of Sextus in fact masks a reference to the ψυχή the point of which is that the good of the soul depends on its contact with external fire, then the soul so conceived must be one whose changes of state are either the prolonged cyclical ones of birth and death or the less lengthy, but still cyclical, states of waking and sleeping. Although the soul may draw nourishment from moisture during the appropriate stages of the cycle or be an exhalation from moisture,[35] the apparent warning against the watery death of the soul in B 36 and B 77, which say that it is death for souls to become water (ὕδωρ) and 'pleasure' or death for souls to become watery (ὑγρός), and the praise of the dry soul in B 117 and B 118 tend to overshadow the positive value of any nutritive role for moisture by making moisture in the soul usually a sign of the disequilibrium that will eventually result in death. If such disequilibrium is what is at issue, Heraclitus' purpose in calling attention to the ψυχή must be largely moral: the human will and the ethical disposition of a man are signs of, or influences upon, the state of the soul that animates him.[36] There is an apparent contradiction in all this, for, on the other hand, the emphasis on the moral importance of these cyclical changes cannot easily be reconciled with the exact parallelism of fragments B 31 and B 36, which makes cosmic changes of state and human changes of state identical except for the substitution of fire for ψυχή.[37] If Heraclitus ignores entirely for the ψυχή, as Kirk believes, the kind of self-regulation that marks the cosmic process, he would seem to remove the soul from the possibility of being analogized to what is surely the most important feature of his cosmic theory, that is, change within measure. Moreover, some attempt to characterize the general purpose of the ψυχή fragments is inescapable: in contrast to the moral or psychological ideas suggested by Kirk, it is possible to suppose that the analogy of microcosm to macrocosm is intended to instruct us in

33. Above, n. 24.

34. Mansfeld (p. 24) believes that A 16 and B 98 point to the contact of the soul with moisture during sleep, a supposed doctrine corrupted by Sextus. Breathing will not preserve contact with surrounding fire, as Sextus implies, but with moisture; that is, the senses are extinguished but the body lives and draws refreshment from sleep.

35. KR, p. 208.

36. Kahn (1964), p. 201.

37. See Marcovitch (pp. 361 and 364) for a clear discussion of this point.

the design of the natural system as a whole, either by the very act of forcing us to make the comparisons in question or, perhaps, by the hope that the changes in state in the microcosm, whose existence depends on its ψυχή, are more intimately accessible to the senses. Taken together, several fragments seem to make this last point.[38] But, in either case, close identity of the two processes is required.

Because it looks for such a close connection between the soul and the cosmic doctrine of constant self-regulating change, the argument of Mansfeld, who has made the most detailed study of this problem, deserves attention, even though it is unconvincing on certain essential points. Against Kirk's assertion that Heraclitus is unlikely to refer to the idea "that the material of [the] body is constantly being renewed and that part of it is being destroyed or 'dying' all the time," Mansfeld suggests that exactly these metabolic processes are at issue. In support of this thesis he tries to show three things: (1) In the river statement (B 12) and elsewhere (B 77) it is essential to distinguish between the soul's beneficial relationship to what is merely moist (ὑγρός) and the extinction of the soul when it undergoes complete transformation into water (ὕδωρ).[39] (2) Thus, sleep and other metabolic processes involving the moistening of the soul are a refreshment as well as a prefigurement of death.[40] (3) The most basic activity carried out by the soul in Heraclitus is therefore digestion, and, as evidence, Plato's description at *Timaeus* 43a of souls confined within a vast river of nourishment is identified as an intentional imitation of the doctrine of Heraclitus. This last point is, of course, not easily proved or disproved, but the parallel is impressive, and such oblique quotation is comparable to Plato's treatment of ψυχή in other dialogues.[41]

38. Fränkel (1938) pointed out that an explicit comparison of sun and soul might be indicated by the fact that after quoting B 45 (that soul is not measurable) Diogenes said that "sun is whatever size it appears to be" (A 1). This suggests that B 3 (εὖρος ποδὸς ἀνθρωπείου) should be taken with B 45 as a comparison of the measurability of sun and soul. The implied connection would extend the point (Kirk [1954], pp. 280–83) that Heraclitus is comparing the apparent size of the sun to the foot which can blot it out as a proof that appearances deceive. Heraclitus may be saying that the sun, which is fire and is nourished by exhalations of moisture (ibid., p. 265) and which undergoes simultaneous kindling and extinguishing (ibid., p. 267), can be analyzed only from a distance and invites naive reliance on appearance. The ψυχή, which behaves in the same way, has a λόγος too deep and invisible to invite such superficial interpretation.

39. Mansfeld, p. 15, following Gigon and Rivier.

40. Mansfeld, p. 20.

41. The Platonic scheme is broadly Heraclitean in that as the nutriment (τροφή) decreases (44b), the one whose soul is in question becomes more intelligent. The comparison with Heraclitus certainly cannot be rejected out of hand but depends on the connection of ψυχή to the river statement, which must remain hypothetical.

Essential parts of Mansfeld's argument, however, are questionable. His proposal that in B 26 ὄψεις carries first the meaning 'eyes' and, second, 'dreams' seen during sleep is extremely hypothetical[42] and ignores the fact that double meanings in Heraclitus (e.g., ἅπτεται in the same fragment) turn on thematically or philosophically important words. The opposition he proposes between ὑγρός and ὕδωρ that allows B 36 and B 77 to be read together to the effect that it is 'death' for the soul to become water, and 'not death'—a fortuitous preservation, if true, of the otherwise bizarre manuscript reading μὴ θάνατον in B 77—for souls to become moist, is simply too obscure, I think, even for Heraclitus. What Heraclitus ordinarily tries to show by wordplay is that single words and expressions can be made to embrace contradictory ideas, not that cognate words embrace philosophically crucial differences. It is rather the unity of contradictory ideas in one word that is Heraclitean. Finally, Mansfeld's reconciliation of καὶ ψυχαὶ δὲ ἀπὸ τῶν ὑγρῶν ἀναθυμιῶνται with the rest of B 12 on the theory that the comparison is between bathers and souls, not rivers and souls, although ingenious, will not resolve for many scholars the vexed problems of the river statement.[43]

There is no easy way to choose between these two fundamentally different views of the analogy between soul and cosmic fire, one of which assumes the priority of the moral and epistemological associations of ψυχή, however these are to be understood, and the other that of the animative 'life-force' in its likeness to cosmic fire. With the stipulation that any interpretation of these fragments is largely speculative, I shall suggest that interest in the ψυχή as 'life-force' is most important to Heraclitus' teaching and that the moral and epistemological fragments must be seen less as statements about the human personality and its cognitive faculties than as corollaries of the knowledge gained by understanding the soul-to-fire analogy. Let me say at once that I am myself persuaded of Mansfeld's conclusion that certain ψυχή fragments attempt to show that the soul's relationship to moisture is twofold. The statements that the soul is an exhalation from moisture (in B 12), a sentiment that is surely Heraclitean even if it is wrongly placed, and that soul comes from water (as B 36 makes explicit) can leave little doubt that there is at least in some sense a beneficial relationship between the soul and moisture.[44] It seems unlikely that

---

42. The possibility of dittography is obviously the strongest argument against the wordplay. Rousseau, p. 506, sees the progression, perhaps more sensibly, as that of sight lost to darkness, followed by sleep in which the 'eyes' are closed.

43. Guthrie (1967), pp. 488–92; Kirk (1954), pp. 367–80; Vlastos (1955), pp. 338ff.

44. Guthrie (1967), pp. 462–63.

Heraclitus would then have been indifferent to the most natural implication which must be drawn from a full exploitation of the analogy between
the changing condition of soul and the unending exchanges of fire, water,
and earth in the cosmic system, namely, in the body too such exchanges are
occurring imperceptibly, constantly, and beneficially as the body main-
tains itself. Formal proof of this point is not easy to come by. Close
consideration of the ψυχή fragments from the point of view of language,
however, offers evidence that has not, to my knowledge, been fully
weighed.[45] By this I mean simply that those ψυχή fragments that concern
the physiology of soul appear to be subtle versions of the general
Heraclitean truth that 'life' and 'death' are terms which can be taken to
illustrate the doctrines of the identity of opposites and, more remotely, of
unity-in-change, as exhibited by the river.[46] A reasonable conclusion,
therefore, is that these doctrines of constant reciprocity are what govern
the physiology of soul fire and its relationship to moisture.

The fragments essential to this argument are the following:

B 88:   ταὐτό τ' ἔνι ζῶν καὶ τεθνηκὸς καὶ [τὸ] ἐγρηγορὸς καὶ καθεῦδων καὶ
        νέον καὶ γηραιόν . . .

B 48:   τῷ οὖν τόξῳ ὄνομα βίος, ἔργον δὲ θάνατος

B 62:   ἀθάνατοι θνητοί, θνητοὶ ἀθάνατοι, ζῶντες τὸν ἐκείνων θάνατον,
        τὸν δὲ ἐκείνων βίον τεθνεῶτες

B 15:   ὠυτὸς δὲ Ἀίδης καὶ Διόνυσος

B 32:   ἕν τὸ σοφὸς μοῦνον λέγεσθαι οὐκ ἐθέλει καὶ ἐθέλει Ζῆνος ὄνομα

Each of these texts demonstrates the ubiquity of the life-death unity in
Heraclitus' surviving fragments. For the sake of brevity I shall pass over
unrelated philological matters except to state, against Kirk,[47] that in
context, B 88 does in fact sustain the idea that living and dying refer to
more than the life and ultimate death of the organism as a whole. To tie this
fragment to alleged folk beliefs about the relationship of infants and old
men in primitive societies, and in so doing to discard the contextual
reference to flux in the passage of pseudo-Plutarch from which the quo-

45. According to Kirk (1954), p. 341, H. Gomperz (in a Festschrift not available to me
[Tessarakontaeteris Th. Borea, Athens 1940]) sees the change of water to earth as *death*, of water to fire
as *life*, an interpretation agreeing with the view taken here insofar as θάνατος and ψυχή are given
technical Heraclitean meanings.
    46. Guthrie (1967), pp. 491–92.
    47. Kirk (1954), pp. 135ff.

tation comes, is unjustified skepticism.[48] The meaning of B 48 is famous enough to need no comment, and it is worth observing that βίος and θάνατος are paired again in B 62, whatever the meaning of this puzzling fragment.[49] B 15 and B 32 show the extraordinary metaphorical range of the life-death unity in Heraclitus. In B 15 it is obvious; for B 32 I adopt Kirk's suggestion that a life-death opposition arises by the pun of Ζῆνος on ζῆν.[50]

The underlying unity of life and death, which this varied group of references surely places close to the center of Heraclitus' thought, has, however, a precise meaning in both the cosmic and psychical systems of Heraclitus. In a word, matter that 'dies' in one form is brought to 'life' in another. Some such meaning must be supposed for the second clause of B 26, a fragment with difficult textual problems: ζῶν δὲ ἅπτεται τεθνεῶτος εὕδων. I take this as a statement that in sleep the soul of the living man nourishes itself by the accretion of moisture the 'death' of which will fuel the soul during the waking hours. This may also be what is meant by the statement of B 75 that "sleepers are workers," not, as others take it, that sleepers simply have dreams.[51] The texts that extend this point to ψυχή are, then, the following:

B 36: ψυχῇσιν θάνατος ὕδωρ γενέσθαι, ὕδατι δὲ θάνατος γῆν γενέσθαι, ἐκ γῆς δὲ ὕδωρ γίνεται, ἐξ ὕδατος δὲ ψυχή

B 31: πυρὸς τροπαὶ πρῶτον θάλασσα, θαλάσσης δὲ τὸ μὲν ἥμισυ γῆ, τὸ δὲ ἥμισυ πρηστήρ

B 21: θάνατος ἐστι ὁκόσα ἐγερθέντες ὁρέομεν, ὁκόσα δὲ εὕδοντες ὕπνος

B 98: αἱ ψυχαὶ ὀσμῶνται καθ᾽ Ἅιδην

B 77: ψυχῇσι τέρψιν ἢ θάνατον ὑγρῇσι γενέσθαι

I interpret these fragments as follows: (1) In B 36 θάνατος has the meaning 'change-of-matter', in keeping with the underlying unity of life and death

---

48. Ibid., pp. 146–47. Kirk's argument against continuous change is founded on his analysis of the meaning of μεταπίπτειν, which he takes to imply sudden reversal, as it does in the passages cited. But this leaves the issue unresolved, for gradual change of the organism over time must be predicated on the cumulative effect of minute instantaneous changes (i.e., at every point some fire is becoming water and vice versa).

49. Cf. the same juxtaposition of death and βίοτος in Ion B 4: καὶ φθίμενος ψυχῇ τερπνὸν ἔχει βίοτον. An oblique association of βίος and ψυχή is possibly found in Plato as well (below, p. 165).

50. Kirk (1954), p. 121. This pun is taken as the "sum of the evidence from the extant fragments that Heraclitus attached special importance to the equation of life with death," a position that is, on the evidence here, unconvincing.

51. KR, p. 208; cf. also the last sentence of B 77 (ζῆν ἡμᾶς τὸν ἐκείνων θάνατον . . .), which repeats B 62.

adduced above by which it can be said that the death of one element is life
for another. This conclusion is made certain by the comparison of B 31 and
B 36, since in B 36 θάνατος is a direct substitute for τροπαί.[52] (B 76 can also
be taken as confirmation of this point but will not be here, owing to its
textual difficulties.[53]) (2) In B 21 θάνατος has the same meaning, an
interpretation that Kirk suggests[54] and that is surely inescapable. To
paraphrase, when we are awake we see occurrences of death, which, of
course, we do not in sleep. At face value this banal assertion has no
philosophical interest. The hidden meaning I take to be that when we are
awake—in the sense that we are alert to the Logos—we perceive θάνατος
in terms of the unity of life and death and the change-of-matter within
measure on which the world order depends. (3) At the same time, however, B 21 is a muted life-death statement itself, ἐγερθέντες implying βίος in
opposition to the θάνατος that those who are awake see. (4) In the three
ψυχή fragments of this group, it is clear that the use of ψυχή is conditioned
by the use of θάνατος so that each statement is, like B 21, a life-death
statement; also, like B 21, each exploits or juxtaposes familiar meanings of
θάνατος with the technical Heraclitean meaning 'change-of-matter'. Thus,
in B 36 the crucial use of ψυχή is the second one, which means primarily
'life' in opposition to the use of θάνατος at the beginning of the fragment,
and then, secondarily, 'soul' as well as 'life': "It is death (in the traditional
sense of cessation of life) for souls to become water, for water it is death to
become earth; but from earth comes water, and from water, life (ψυχή)." If
the technical Heraclitean sense 'change-of-matter' applies to θάνατος, what
is said can be paraphrased to mean that, although it is 'death' for the
elements to undergo a change of state in one direction, it is 'life' for them to
undergo a change of state in the other. In this way θάνατος and ψυχή
become expressions once again of an underlying unity of life and death in
both the familiar sense (perhaps something like the folk wisdom Kirk calls
for)[55] and the Heraclitean sense that 'death' as a change-of-matter and 'life'
as a change-of-matter are patently alike in some sense. The fact that ψυχή
also means 'soul' is not incidental—and is of course consistent with B 12, B
77, B 117, and B 118—but it is not the main point. In B 98 the use of ψυχή is
filtered through an additional level of metaphor, and in a sense, therefore, it
offers even better proof of the importance of this wordplay in Heraclitus'
thoughts about the soul. This fragment has no commonly accepted inter-

52. Kirk (1954), p. 341.
53. Ibid., pp. 342–44, and Kahn Anaximander, p. 152, n. 1.
54. Kirk (1954), p. 341, sees θάνατος in B 21 as "conceivably" change-of-matter.
55. Kirk (1954), p. 148.

pretation: Kirk proposes that the surviving soul in death smells the fire that is drier than itself. But if this reading is right, and all that Heraclitus intends, it relegates the fragment from the mainstream of Heraclitus' thought to the level of incidental commentary. Mansfeld's theory that Hades is meta-phorical for deep sleep and the nutrition of the soul by breathing when all other senses are cut off is intriguing, as is his attempt to see an allusion to this process in the word ῥίζης in A 16.[56] But if we compare B 15 (ὡυτὸς δὲ Ἀίδης καὶ Διόνυσος), the most direct explanation, I think, is that this fragment, like B 36, converts a familiar use of ψυχή into one based again on the unity of life and death and the dual meaning of death in Heraclitus' system. The traditional belief that souls are somehow alive in Hades can now be interpreted to mean cryptically that what has 'life' (ψυχαί) gives evidence of life (ὀσμῶνται) even in death (καθ' Ἅιδην) because life and death are one and because, again, what has life is nourished through θάνατος as 'change-of-matter'. Finally, B 77, if it is genuine,[57] can be read in this manner as a restatement of B 36. Of course, the choice between the reading μή of the manuscripts and the modern correction ᾗ is a textual crux of supreme consequence, but assuming ᾗ and again the dual meaning of θάνατος, the text can be made to yield sense. Like B 36, its point may be that it is death in the familiar sense to the soul to become wet. In addition, it is presumably a harmful pleasure to the soul to become wet (one thinks of B 117, of course). But insofar as θάνατος and ψυχή are also reciprocal terms for change-of-matter, some beneficial relationship between the soul or 'life' and moisture could account for the otherwise ludicrous reading of τέρψις.

I suggest, then, that these three Heraclitean statements about the ψυχή have as their central feature an attempt to express the paradoxical unity of life and death stated not as βίος/θάνατος, as in B 48, but as ψυχή/θάνατος. The remaining fragments are far more psychologically suggestive, and they must now be assessed. I will pass over B 136 (ψυχαὶ ἀρήφατοι καθερ-ώτεραι ἢ ἐνὶ νούσοις), which does not seem to be significant for the problem at hand or to offer difficulties of interpretation that need to be discussed. Kirk's treatment (above, n. 26) seems definitive. Of the remaining frag-ments the most important are those having an epistemological character. Fragment B 107 (κακοὶ μάρτυρες ἀνθρώποισιν ὀφθαλμοὶ κὰ ὦτα βαρβάρους ψυχὰς ἐχόντων) appears to set the soul off as an agent of thought that must interpret the data of the senses. But there is also an unrecognized wordplay in this fragment that affects to some degree the way in which the text is to

56. Mansfeld, p. 25.
57. Kirk (1954), p. 340.

be understood. It should be clear by now that the ψυχή, like cosmic fire, is seen by Heraclitus as a crucial object of knowledge as well as the subject that itself perceives or receives such knowledge. This ambiguity and its linguistic possibilities are not likely to have escaped Heraclitus' attention. B 108 can be compared, since in it the Logos, as something that confers wisdom if known about, is itself 'wise' (ὁκόσων λόγους ἤκουσα, οὐδεὶς ἀφικνεῖται ἐς τοῦτο, ὥστε γινώσκειν ὅτι σοφόν ἐστι πάντων κεχωρισμένον: this can describe nothing other than the Logos itself [cf. B 50 and especially B 72]). It is possible, therefore, that ψυχή acquires the appearance of a 'thinking thing' in Heraclitus in part because it is an aspect of the person that is also a vitally important object of knowledge, and hence, like the Logos, easily personified in Heraclitus' usage.[58] To claim this ambiguity for any other Greek thinker would be absurd, but it is, I think, well within the scope of Heraclitus' exotic style.[59] The word βάρβαρος, moreover, seems to contain a confirming wordplay. To a Greek of 500 B.C. βάρβαρος need not yet have had the pejorative connotations that became commonplace in the late fifth century and that would characterize the βάρβαρος ψυχή as, say, morally degenerate and obtuse. Heraclitus uses βάρβαρος, perhaps, only because of its natural connection with speech, that is, with understanding any λόγος and, then by extension, with understanding the supreme Logos which in Heraclitus' system underlies visible reality. The wordplay in βάρβαρος is therefore crucial, for the word implies not only that the speaker cannot understand a λόγος but that he speaks a λόγος not understood by others.[60] It follows that for Heraclitus a βάρβαρος ψυχή may be both the mental agent that misunderstands the Logos or, as an object of knowledge, that which, if misunderstood, fails to speak the Logos to those who seek it. Here again the overall purpose of Heraclitus' utterances on ψυχή seems at issue. If a part of understanding the Logos is to grasp the analogy of soul to cosmic fire, then it is what we know about the soul, as well as the activity of the soul itself, that makes order out of sense impressions.

58. Vlastos (1955), p. 353: "It would be wholly characteristic of this period to merge thought and thinking things." Guthrie (1962), p. 428: "We have seen evidence that the Logos is both human thought and the governing principle of the Universe." Cf. Snell (1926), p. 353, on ἀκουή as 'hearing' and 'thing heard'. For the general tendency to personification in Heraclitus compare also the use of αἰὼν in B 52.

59. See Kirk (1964), pp. 73–77; Cherniss (1951), p. 333; and the summary of the work of V. V. Karakulakov in Bibl. Class. Orientalis (1967), p. 118.

60. Cf. Nussbaum, p. 12: "A failure [to understand words and make a connected statement] is evidence of a βάρβαρος ψυχή." This is the only statement known to me in which the ambiguous nuances of βάρβαρος are recognized.

These points perhaps apply also to B 118 (αὔη ψυχὴ σοφωτάτη καὶ ἀρίστη), the second epistemological fragment, which undoubtedly contains one of the most innovative linguistic usages of ψυχή in all the Presocratic ipsissima verba. The explicit association of ψυχή with σοφία is not repeated before the end of the fifth century except in Democritus B 31, the *Helen* of Gorgias, and the *Clouds* of Aristophanes. The phrase ψυχὴ σοφωτάτη is, therefore, disconcertingly isolated and subject to the general rule that epigrammatic texts of this kind tend to stimulate evocative readings of a sort which cannot be tested against context. As it stands, the saying offers an astonishingly early anticipation of the Platonic future of ψυχή. But it seems important to refer the use of σοφωτάτη back to the ambiguities of B 107. With the exception of the ironic reference to Homer in B 56 all references to σοφός/σοφίη in Heraclitus concern the understanding of the Logos.[61] If Heraclitus intends us to think of the ψυχή in this fragment, therefore, as one whose wisdom is a product in part of its relationship to the Logos, as it must be since it is itself fire and therefore allows us to know fire as like-to-like, the strong personification and sense of a comprehensive "inner self" conferred by σοφωτάτη may be somewhat misleading—although certainly not the general connection between intelligence and the state of ψυχή that is also implied. The eclectic personifications of B 32 in particular should be considered here: ἓν τὸ σοφὸν μοῦνον λέγεσθαι οὐκ ἐθέλει καὶ ἐθέλει Ζῆνος ὄνομα. In a single sentence, abstract principle, the Logos, the name Zeus, and then the god Zeus fall together directly or by implication in an intentionally paradoxical mixture loosely personified as the subject of ἐθέλει. The uncertain perspective surrounding all nomenclature in Heraclitus, fully demonstrated in B 32 and likely to affect the use of ψυχή in B 107, must also color our reading of ψυχὴ σοφωτάτη. Nevertheless, the fragment is exceptional for its implications.

Two fragments, B 115 (ψυχῆς ἐστι λόγος ἑαυτὸν αὔξων) and B 45 (ψυχῆς πείρατα ἰὼν οὐκ ἂν ἐξεύροιο, πᾶσαν ἐπιπορευόμενος ὁδόν· οὕτω βαθὺν λόγον ἔχει), are identified by Ingenkamp,[62] following Snell, as suggesting for the first time in Greek thought a psychological soul in man that can be characterized by such subtle and intangible qualities as depth and spontaneity and that is able to be perceived only by introspection. For unexplained reasons these fragments seem to him to have no connection with the physiological soul of B 36,[63] and as a result the psychological entity he perceives in them is set apart from whatever is described by the other

61. B 32, 41, 50, 108, 112. The same can be said for φιλόσοφος in B 35. Cf. *KR*, pp. 204–05.

62. Ingenkamp, p. 52.

63. He (rightly) sees the physiological soul as what is described in B 12, 36, 67a, 77, and also, rather remarkably, in B 107 and 117.

statements on ψυχή. A better case can be made for the view that there is a straightforward physiological basis to the use of ψυχή here which has generated what are, or appear to be, new kinds of psychological attributes as well. This is close to Kirk's view of B 45,[64] and B 115, if it is genuine,[65] might well refer most directly of all the fragments to the soul's capacity for physical self-regulation. Indeed, I take B 115 as one of the strongest statements in support of the view that Heraclitus' interest in the ψυχή focuses on constant reciprocal change within the body, as opposed to longer term cyclical change and externally imposed disequilibrium. A comparison of a general nature is warranted between this text and the Latin paraphrase of B 67a, in which the soul is said to hasten to injured parts of the body like a spider running to breaks in its web. For B 45, in addition to compatibility with the physiological sense of B 115, some irony may be supposed. It is quite remarkable that Heraclitus applies to the ψυχή the journey metaphor by which the δαίμων of a Pythagorean would seek knowledge beyond that of ordinary men. One wonders whether there is not in this a reply to all such shamanistic pretensions. The journey that matters to Heraclitus is not the journey *of* the ψυχή but *within* the ψυχή, in the sense that one must try to understand the Logos by which the ψυχή in the self imitates the behavior of fire in general.

Finally, B 85 (θυμῷ μάχεσθαι χαλεπόν· ὁ γὰρ ἂν θέλῃ ψυχῆς ὠνεῖται) and B 117 (ἀνὴρ ὁκόταν μεθυσθῇ, ἄγεται ὑπὸ παιδὸς ἀνήβου σφαλλόμενος οὐκ ἐπαΐων ὅκῃ βαίνει, ὑγρὴν τὴν ψυχὴν ἔχων) can be taken together as moral suasions that complement or parallel the intellectual attributes given the ψυχή in B 107 and B 108, and therefore again help to identify the soul as something "personal" in Heraclitus' thought. But even here what Heraclitus says about the ψυχή seems to have an analytical value for the analogy of soul to fire that must be taken into consideration. Conceivably, neither fragment is concerned with simple disequilibrium but with the complexity of the relationship of fire to moisture. B 117 at least can be read as an illustration of the twofold relationship of soul to moisture. In the form of wine, moisture may account for the soul's activity (the Homeric use of wine as a restorative for the θυμός should be recalled) and for its suppression as well. In the case of the drunkard, wine nourishes the soul in one sense— he is presumably exhilarated for a time—and yet gradually his intelligence and sensation leave him. But the fragment may simply be a general moral suasion combining Heraclitus' asceticism with his systematic treatment of

64. *KR*, p. 206: "The thought here is not so much of self-consciousness as of the soul being a representative portion of the cosmic fire—which, compared with the individual, is obviously of vast extent."

65. Marcovitch, pp. 568–70.

soul. This is probably the case in B 85, where Kirk's reading, following Verdenius,[66] is surely right. Anger is hard to control because it entails the expenditure of fire, on which intelligence depends. There might be a paradoxical ring to this as well in the suggestion that increments of fire lead to contradictory impulses, but it seems unlikely that Heraclitus could admit a negative view of fire under any circumstances.

The ψυχή fragments of Heraclitus unquestionably constitute the most complicated and elusive body of material that must be dealt with in this study, and the one least amenable to a semantic investigation. The fragments embrace both moral and intellectual experience (B 118, 107, 85, 117), they may evoke the notion of an intangible inner self at times (B 117, 45), the ψυχή takes on a highly personified form in some instances (B 107, 118), and finally, the fragments obviously attempt to give an explicit physical basis to common psychological experience. The fragments on ψυχή in Heraclitus do, therefore, in some sense discover the psychological value of ψυχή for Greek thought. At the least, ψυχή is, as all commentators have seen, an entity responsive to a systematic scheme of changes, and on these changes intelligence and the emotional life depend. Yet in order to judge what Heraclitus means when he talks about ψυχή, it is important to extend the definition of context to include some estimate of the purpose of the fragments. I have sufficiently emphasized and will not reiterate what I take to be the importance of the analogy between soul and cosmic fire for the use of ψυχή in fragments B 36, 77, and 98. I do not wish to explain every occurrence of ψυχή in the fragments as a product of the analogy of soul and cosmic fire, nor to depreciate the importance of Heraclitus' contribution to the psychological valuation of the word, but it seems imperative not to separate arbitrarily the physical or 'life-force' uses of ψυχή from those with apparently new psychological scope. That Heraclitus places intellect in the ψυχή and looks to the ψυχή for moral aphorisms about anger and drink may be the result, to some extent, of testing various sayings and beliefs against his new understanding of the physical behavior of ψυχή and of its place in the scheme of nature. It is also possible, as I have suggested, that the personification of soul in some of the fragments—which lends them a comprehensive tone—is, given Heraclitus' ambiguous style, somewhat misleading. Finally, if there is a wordplay on θάνατος and ψυχή that has the implications I have proposed, it can be argued that Heraclitus' interest in ψυχή is, to some degree, based on ideas and linguistic usages that work for him alone.

66. *KR*, pp. 210–11.

DIOGENES OF APOLLONIA

The quoted uses of ψυχή in Diogenes clearly belong semantically to the 'life-force' category. If Anaximenes B 2 should in fact be attributed to Diogenes, we might expect to find attached to the other instances of ψυχή in Diogenes some sense of the controlling power implied in the verb συγκρατεῖν. But the actual connotations of ψυχή as it is used in the ipsissima verba of Diogenes are quite limited. Air, in B 4 and B 5, is the source of intelligence (νόησις), it is what men are governed by (κυβερνᾶσθαι), and it has power over all things (κρατεῖν). In Theophrastus' summary (A 19) air within men is a portion of divinity and that which has perception (αἴσθησις), a fact demonstrated by the cessation, during periods of intro-spection, of sight and hearing, since these are also dependent on air. Thought is caused by air that is pure and dry (A 19), and, as is true for Heraclitus, moisture in the form of sleep, drunkenness, or satiety is said to interfere with intelligence (νοῦς). Animals are therefore inferior to men in intelligence because they breathe the moist air nearer the surface of the earth. The ψυχή also originates in air, and intelligence is thus contingent on ψυχή. In B 4 both ψυχή and νόησις are air (καὶ τοῦτο αὐτοῖς καὶ ψυχή ἐστι καὶ νόησις), and if air is taken away a man dies and his ψυχή leaves him. In B 5 the ψυχή is said to be the same for all living creatures, consisting of internal air, which is warmer than external air. Differences in intelligence and way of life between men and other animate beings are accounted for by differences in the warmth of the internal air. Aristotle's summary clearly distorts the meaning of Diogenes' use of ψυχή.

> Diogenes and certain others think the soul is air, believing it to consist of the finest particles and to be the first principle [ἀρχή]; and therefore the soul both knows and causes motion. It knows by virtue of being primary and the source of all else; it causes motion by virtue of its rarity [405a21].

Diogenes' own words are quoted extensively and coherently enough in Theophrastus and in the fragments given by Simplicius that the difference can be readily seen. In the quotations, the semantic treatment of ψυχή is utterly straightforward and physiological. It is taken to be a noetic sub-stance, true enough, but beyond that nothing in the surviving quotations or in the *testimonia* suggests that Diogenes would refer to the soul as a moral or cognitive faculty, or as the seat of the psychical functions that Aristotle attributes to the soul generally in *De Anima* (403a16ff.). Quite the contrary, that Diogenes uses ψυχή as 'life-force' in the way he does and limits his discussion of intelligence to the role of air (following the evidence of Theophrastus) without mention of the ψυχή should caution us against thinking that the ψυχή is here any more systematically or fully endowed with the function of knowledge than it is earlier, that its imagined functions have dramatically enlarged through its speculative relationship to the ἀρχή and to knowledge, or that it has assumed a more comprehensive nature. Knowledge seems contingent on ψυχή, as are all life functions. The more personified and comprehensive character of ψυχή in Anaximenes B 2—assuming the fragment should in fact be attributed to Diogenes—as opposed to the meaning required in Diogenes B 4 and B 5, can be explained as the result of doxographical interpretation. Thus, in the discussion of Diogenes at *De Anima* 405a23, ψυχή is made the subject of γιγνώσκειν and is therefore felt to be a personified agent, whatever the actual nuances of Diogenes' ideas may have been.

4

Non-Socratic Soul–Body Uses of ψυχή: Democritus, Gorgias, the Medical Texts

Although most occurrences of ψυχή in late fifth-century prose denote either 'life'[1] or 'courage',[2] or can be seen as imitations of tragic diction,[3] two important innovative references to ψυχή reflect the appearance at last in popular usage of the dichotomy of σῶμα and ψυχή. In Antiphon V (415–411 B.C.) the ψυχή is morally contrasted to the body: for a defendant sure of his own innocence, although the body may have surrendered, the ψυχή has saved him by its willingness to struggle "through knowledge of its innocence." But for the guilty, even a strong body is of no avail, since the ψυχή fails him (ψυχὴ προαπολείπει), "believing the vengeance coming to him is for his impieties." ψυχή here suggests the familiar quality of courage, but the deliberate division of body and soul in a general context of this kind is significant. At Lysias 24.3 (403 B.C.) we encounter the first reference in Greek thought to the notion of leading a life of the ψυχή as opposed to a life of the body: the destitute man must heal the body's misfortunes with the pursuits (ἐπιτηδεύματα) of the ψυχή, since to keep his thoughts (ἡ διάναια) on a plane with his misfortunes would reduce him to

---

1. Antiphon II 4, II 5, III 6, V 82; Lys. 6.43; Isoc. 63.

2. Lys. 20.14, 20.24, 20.25, 20.29. It is worth noting that at 20.14 (ca. 410 B.C.) ψυχὴν πονηρός still implies just courage, not moral worth.

3. At Lys. 6.23 (399 B.C.) Andocides is asked what ψυχή he had when he committed the 'shameful' act of informing against his relatives, and in 32.12 (ca. 400 B.C.) a mother is reported to have asked the dishonest guardian of her children what ψυχή he had that allowed him so to abuse the children. These statements can be directly compared with Or. 526, where Tyndareus asks Orestes what ψυχή he had when his mother bared her breast to him in supplication. In Tetralogies 14a7 the jury is asked to punish the hubris of a drunken murderer by depriving him of the ψυχή that planned the act (ὑμᾶς δὲ χρὴ ... τὴν βουλεύσασαν ψυχὴν ἀνταφέλεσθαι αὐτόν). Webster (p. 151) unduly emphasizes the rationality implied by the planning aspect of this use of ψυχή. Although the usage is not found in tragedy, the pun on 'life' and the circumstances of the drunken, hence irrational, behavior suggest rhetorical adaptation of traditional poetic usage.

the level of his accuser. The attachment of the dichotomy of soul and body
to the living man is unparalleled either in popular usage or in the
Presocratic material considered so far. It appears as a commonplace, however, in two early Hippocratic treatises and in the ethical fragments of
Democritus, and it perhaps underlies the extensive use of ψυχή in the brief
but exciting rhetorical display piece of Gorgias, the *Encomium on Helen*.
How these texts can be related to one another, to the quotations just given,
and to the evidence for the Socratic use of ψυχή is obviously crucial for the
history of the word, and the problem to be addressed in this section. No
chronological ordering of the works in question is possible.[4] and therefore
the order in which they are taken up is not intended to suggest a historical
sequence of ideas. We shall be looking essentially for implicit connections
among works that are thought to fall in the late fifth century.

DEMOCRITUS

The fragments of Democritus illustrate the need for an empirical approach
to ψυχή. The materialism of Democritus, as Burnet pointed out long ago,
makes him perhaps the least likely of all the Presocratics to have had
anything to do with the development of the Socratic use of ψυχή. Yet, it is
clear at once that the statements on ψυχή attributed to Democritus are
Socratic in tone and offer for the first time an ethical program founded
explicitly on the well-being of the ψυχή. Happiness and unhappiness are
matters of the ψυχή (B 170 εὐδαιμονίη ψυχῆς καὶ κακοδαιμονίη); happiness
does not come from material possessions but from the condition of the
ψυχή (B 171 ψυχή οἰκητήριον δαίμονος); it is better to make a λόγος about the
ψυχή than about the body, for soul sets the body right, not body the soul
(B 187 ψυχῆς μὲν γὰρ τελεότης σκήνεος μοχθηρίην ὀρθοῖ, σκήνεος δὲ ἰσχὺς ἄνευ
λογισμοῦ ψυχὴν οὐδέν τι ἀμείνω τίθησιν); one must respect oneself (B 264
ἑωυτὸν αἰδεῖσθαι) and set that as a νόμος for one's ψυχή. In all these
statements the moral valuation of soul is explicit and impressive, and
in contrast to Heraclitus, placed unambiguously in a context of general
moral admonition. Moreover, this striking interest in the ψυχή cannot be
doubted, as can much of the ethical miscellany that has come down under

4. On Antiphon V see Dover (1944), pp. 44–60, who favors a date of 414 B.C. on stylistic
grounds. The date of the *Helen* is impossible to ascertain. Suggestions range from 440 to 394 B.C.
(Untersteiner, p. 99, n. 59). The fragments of Democritus cannot be dated except by reference to
404 B.C. as the earliest possible date for his death (Freeman, p. 290). R. Joly, pp. 203–09, dates *Regimen* I
to the beginning of the fourth century.

the names of Democritus and Democrites, since the most important text, B 191, is corroborated by Diogenes[5] and can be interpreted in terms of atomist theory. Although several fragments are of questionable authenticity—among which I would include B 37, where it is said that the goods of the soul are divine, those of the body merely human[6]—it is certain that a doctrine of ψυχή figured centrally in Democritus' ethical views.

The moral attributes of ψυχή in Democritus cannot be separated from the role of soul as the animator of the body, or from the problems associated with accounting for thought within the material scheme of the atomists. The spherical atoms of the soul that animates the body are breathed in from the air and distributed throughout the body,[7] and in concentrated mass these soul atoms constitute mind.[8] Thought is contingent on the reception of stimuli by the atoms of the mind, although how passive an agent mind is, and how we are to account for the two kinds of knowledge—sensory and rational—referred to in B 11 is never made clear.[9] If Vlastos's well-known study of Democritean ethics and physics is right, the ethical behavior of soul must be related explicitly to these materialist doctrines of mind and soul.[10] According to this view, what is described by the ethical activity of ψυχή in Democritus is the physical arrangement or patterning (ῥυσμός) of soul atoms as they are altered by external "forces" like reason and passion (cf. B 290)—a thesis most clearly

---

5. In D.L. 9.45 the end of the ethical system is said to be contentment, a condition dependent on the stable order of the soul.

6. Both B 37 and B 72 are attributed to Democrites. B 247 (ἀνδρὶ σοφῷ πᾶσα γῆ βατή· ψυχῆς γὰρ ἀγαθῆς πατρὶς ὁ ξύμπας κόσμος), preserved in Stobaeus with the genuine sayings, was already challenged by Freudenthal (p. 38) in 1886 as a specimen of reconstructable trimeter. In addition, σοφός suggests the philosopher of the fourth century, not the 'intellectual' or 'skilled person' of the fifth century. We are also obliged to accept this as the first certain appearance of the morally 'good' soul. Together, these objections and, of course, the implausibility of the whole idea within the materialism of Democritus— the soul cannot live apart from the body after death—create a strong case for rejecting the fragment as a later forgery. I omit also B 278, which uses the phrase πάντων ... ὅσα ψυχὴν ἔχει to mean merely "of all living creatures," and B 298a, classified by Diels as dubious.

7. B 1, if authentic, gives direct evidence of at least one use of ψυχή by Democritus to denote only animation. Death is not a "quenching of all life within the body, but when the body endures a blow of some kind, the bonds (δεσμοί) of the ψυχή remain vigorous about the muscle and the καρδία keeps the spark of life."

8. Guthrie (1965), p. 452.

9. Guthrie (1965), p. 462: "No extant text explains for us exactly the relationship between sensible experience and rational thought in Leucippus or Democritus."

10. Vlastos (1945), pp. 582–85. Vlastos was anticipated by von Fritz in *Philosophie und Sprachlicher Ausdruck bei Demokrit, Plato und Aristoteles* (Leipzig [n.d.]), pp. 35ff. especially. Cf. also Luria, pp. 14–15.

stated in B 33 as the case for teaching (ἡ διδαχὴ μεταρυσμοῖ τὸν ἄνθρωπον, μεταρυσμοῦσα δὲ φυσιοποιεῖ). This general theory offers a basis for moral suasion linked to a ψυχή that is manifestly and directly physical in its connotations; in essence, the physical condition of the soul, concretely imagined in terms of the motion of the soul atoms, accounts for moral well-being. Proof of this interpretation turns on the long fragment B 191, which says that cheerfulness (εὐθυμίη) can be achieved only through moderation and the avoidance of great disturbances, since the latter render souls neither stable nor cheerful (ἀνθρώποισι γὰρ εὐθυμίη γίνεται μετριότητι τέρψιος καὶ βίου συμμετρίῃ· τὰ δ᾽ ἐλλείποντα καὶ ὑπερβάλλοντα μεταπίπτειν τε φιλεῖ καὶ μεγάλας κινήσιας ἐμποιεῖν τῇ ψυχῇ. αἱ δ᾽ ἐκ μεγάλων διαστημάτων κινούμεναι τῶν ψυχέων οὔτε εὐσταθέες εἰσιν οὔτε εὔθυμοι). The significance of this quotation is taken from the equation in B 4 of εὐθυμία with εὐεστώ, to which Vlastos gives, on the basis of antecedent uses, literal rather than figurative meaning: "We can then understand why motions of wide amplitude, i.e., envy, etc., are precluded: because they are prejudicial to the order and integrity of the atomic soul cluster. This is never explicitly stated in the surviving fragments. But there are strong indications that this is just what Democritus had in mind."[11] This physical definition of emotion is, then, in the remainder of B 191, tied to more abstract ethical suasion: one must concentrate on the possible, forgo envy, reflect on the lives of those less fortunate and thus suffer less in one's ψυχή (καὶ μηκέτι πλειόνων ἐπιθυμέοντι [sc. σοι] συμβαίνῃ κακοπαθεῖν τῇ ψυχῇ), and be content with what one has. Unfortunately, no other ethical fragment using ψυχή offers direct evidence of this proposed physical scheme, and so it is impossible to verify absolutely the systematic implications of εὐεστώ. That the fragments do not do so is a fair objection.[12] B 191 is the most extensive and reflective ethical fragment we have, however, and to doubt the intention of the physical language assumes that an atomist could make casual use of εὐεστώ or discuss the κινήσεις of the soul without thinking of its atomic composition.

In another sense, however, our attempt to get at the substance of Democritus' use of ψυχή is hindered rather than helped by this explicit

11. Vlastos (1945), p. 583.

12. Taylor, pp. 10ff., makes an extensive attempt to refute Vlastos, but his attack on Vlastos's interpretation of εὐεστώ (p. 11) suffers from the effort to disprove a technical usage, and presumably coinage, of Democritus by reference to ordinary diction. Antiphon's ἀειεστώ shows that compounds of ἐστώ had philosophical currency and therefore justifies the attempt to give εὐεστώ a systematic meaning. Guthrie's acknowledgment, quoting von Fritz (1965), pp. 496–97, that the language of B 191 "can hardly be metaphorical" although it is not possible to "explain . . . how successful he was in attempting a systematic integration" of physics and ethics, is judicious. Cf. Burkert (1972), p. 256, n. 87, on ἐστώ words in the fifth century.

materialist interpretation. If the soul is material, and soul and mind are composed of similar atoms, a prima facie connection is created between soul and mind[13] that obscures the more subtle semantic nuances we are trying to uncover here. In all contexts involving knowledge in the surviving fragments, words other than ψυχή are used to designate mental agents,[14] most notably in B 125, where, in making the distinction between the senses and the agent that uses them, Democritus uses (and personifies) the latter as φρήν. The role of the ψυχή in the mental life of the individual, judging from the actual fragments, is again more limited. A useful example appears even in B 264, the injunction to respect oneself and base moral behavior on self-judgment rather than on the opinions of others, "setting this as the νόμος for the ψυχή, so as not to act reprehensibly." This text contains, along with Antiphon B 44, perhaps the earliest explicit renunciation of shame values in Greek thought and is as "Socratic" in tone and thought as anything in the Democritean corpus. It is tempting, therefore, to identify the ψυχή with that 'self' in the fragment (ἑωυτόν) which seems to imply a genuine conscience. Although it can be assumed from B 191 that the ψυχή must be in a condition of εὐθυμίη for its possessor to act in a manner consistent with justice, it is clearly not the νόμος of the ψυχή itself that is obeyed; rather, the ψυχή is something able to fulfill a νόμος placed upon it by a 'self' that wishes to act morally.

One would not care to draw extensive conclusions on the basis of this single detail. I stress it here simply because it shows that even B 264, for all its Socratic character, restricts the word ψυχή itself to a usage consistent with those of the other major fragments. The thrust of B 191, for example, is extraordinarily pragmatic; deficiencies (τὰ ἐλλείποντα) and excesses (τὰ ὑπερβάλλοντα) cause commotions in the soul; the Democritean man must direct his γνώμη to things that are possible (ἐπὶ τοῖς δυνάτοις), being content with what is at hand. If he reflects on the lives of others who are in distress he will make his own possessions and situation seem great and enviable. The fragment goes on at length in this vein and need not be reproduced in full. It is quite clear that in context—as opposed to the deduction one might draw from the association of soul atoms with mind—ψυχή is concerned with practical rules of reason and morality as they apply to the simple passions and to the need for social self-control. Although the soul's achievement of εὐθυμίη is essential to happiness—and to be valued more

13. Cherniss (1935), p. 389, n. 3, notes that the similarity of fire and soul atoms does not produce similar characteristics, which depend rather on the nature of the combination. This point must apply for mind and soul as well.

14. Cf. B 119 (φρόνησις); B 129 (φρενὶ θεῖα νοῦνται); B 183 (ξύνεσις).

than possessions (B 170 εὐδαιμονίη ψυχῆς καὶ κακοδαιμονίη; B 171 εὐδαιμονίη
οὐκ ἐν βοσκήμασιν οἰκεῖ οὐδὲ ἐν χρυσῷ· ψυχὴ οἰκητήριον δαίμονος)—the
comparisons with the soul as self in the Socratic or Platonic sense seem to go
no further. The self of B 264 is, in context, merely a socially private self,
not an "inner" self; the microcosm that is man in B 34 is the man as a
whole, body and soul; so, too, the peaceful ψυχή of B 191 is not the self
searching out some higher order of experience centering on its capacity to
discover truth, but the soul as it is known to us through its influence over
the body and over day-to-day feelings of greed and jealousy. If these
occurrences of ψυχή in Democritus are set against the many others we have
examined, they still suggest very much the animative 'life-force' of the
body and its emotional traits. ψυχή continues to have, it seems, a natural
disposition to excess typical of the archaic 'life-force', but, in contrast to
archaic usage, its energy is now assumed to be amenable to external reason
and control. This is what I take to be the significance of B 159: if the body
brought suit against the soul for the pain it had suffered, and Democritus
were to judge, he would condemn the soul because it had destroyed the
body (ἀπώλεσε) with neglect, dissolved it (ἐξέλυσε) with drunkenness,
ruined it (κατέφθειρε), and torn it to shreds (διέσπασε) with its love of
pleasure—as one would blame the careless user and not the tool (ὄργανον).
Although this passage sounds as though it could have been spoken by the
Platonic Socrates, it differs importantly from Platonic doctrine in its intent.
Whereas in Plato immorality of soul may well have physical concomitants,
it is the effect of the soul's immorality on the *soul* that concerns Plato. In
Democritus, on the other hand, not only is the line between morality and
physical health more ambiguous, but some of the fragments make physical
health the actual goal of care for the soul. A sense of a progression toward
explicit treatment of health can be seen in a sequence of four fragments. I
take B 290 (grief can be driven from the numbed ψυχή by reason: λύπην
ἀδέσποτον ψυχῆς ναρκώσης λογισμῷ ἔκκρουε) to show an interest in ties
between demonstrably emotional or psychological states and concretely
imagined states of the physical 'life-force'. A more explicitly physical
fragment is B 212, which attributes an abnormal bodily condition
(daytime sleep) to bodily disorder, disorder of the physical 'life-force', an
inherent character defect, or lack of training (ἡμερήσιοι ὕπνοι σώματος
ὄχλησιν ἢ ψυχῆς ἀδημοσύνην ἢ ἀργίην ἢ ἀπαιδευσίην σημαίνουσι).[15] Even
more direct in its connection of soul with health is B 174, where the man
who is εὔθυμος is said to be driven to just and lawful works, to rejoice day

15. Cf. ἀδημονῆσαι τὰς ψυχάς at X. HG 4.4.3.

and night, and to be strong (ἔρρωται) and without care. If εὐθυμία results from the condition of the soul, then it is reasonable to see the bodily strength implied in ἔρρωται not as metaphorical but as an aim and consequence of attention to the soul. Most striking of all the Democritean fragments in this regard is B 234: men pray to the gods for health (ὑγιείη), not realizing that they have this power (δύναμις) in themselves. Because they do the opposite on account of lack of control they become the betrayers of health to their desires (ἀκρασίῃ δὲ τἀναντία πρήσσοντες αὐτοὶ προδόται τῆς ὑγιείης τῇσιν ἐπιθυμίῃσιν γίνονται). This text can be read, I think, only as a restatement of the doctrine of B 191: the "power that men have in themselves," at least the only one we know of in Democritus, is that of realizing a proper condition of ψυχή, and this condition in turn will result in self-control and lawfulness. But the ultimate and explicit objective of this activity is health itself.

Although these fragments on ψυχή seem at first compatible with the beliefs of Socrates, those that actually give us empirical information about the activity and value of the ψυχή in Democritus (B 191, 159, 240, 212—as well as 174 and 234, which I include even though they do not use the word) seem to advocate attention to the ψυχή less for the achievement of something that might be identified as a psychical order of experience—able to unify the cognitive and moral life of the man as in Plato—than for the welfare of the man as a whole and, explicitly, for physical health. It seems appropriate to bring forward at this point the odd report in Aulus Gellius (4.13) that Democritus attempted to cure snakebite by flute playing. This historical note is perhaps sufficiently bizarre to be true, or at least based on truth, and would suggest again that Democritean soul therapy had a specific interest in physical health. One might also compare here the intriguing reports that Damon, the legendary teacher of Socrates, attempted to shape moral character with specific melodies[16] and that in Corinth Antiphon conceived a τέχνη ἀλυπίας comparable to medicine by which he tried to cure the sick with words.[17] How seriously we are to take these notices is open to question, but as given they suggest that early forms of soul treatment were contrived to resemble medical specifics for the treatment of either health or emotion. It is of particular interest in the case of Democritus, therefore, that close examination of the fragments themselves seems to make the moral dichotomy of soul and body a pragmatic relationship in which soul care has as its end therapy of the body in some

---

16. Damon B 7.
17. Antiphon A 6; cf. fr. B 2, where mind (γνώμη) leads body to health, disease, and all else.

form.[18] I will not argue that this is always or exclusively the case, but that this utilitarian claim is central to Democritean soul therapy is, I hope, evident.

The two fragments of Democritus that deal explicitly with the contrasting of soul and body must be seen against this background. In B 187 Democritus says that perfection of ψυχή can heal bodily distress but that the converse is not true (ἀνθρώποις ἁρμόδιον ψυχῆς μᾶλλον ἢ σώματος λόγον ποιεῖσθαι· ψυχῆς μὲν γὰρ τελεότης σκήνεος μοχθηρίην ὀρθοῖ, σκήνεος δὲ ἰσχὺς ἄνευ λογισμοῦ ψυχὴν οὐδέν τι ἀμείνω τίθησιν). The ability of the soul to 'heal' the body can no longer seem peripheral to the relative merits of soul and body but is a very real virtue of soul for Democritus. In B 31, which calls for a σοφίη of soul to match treatment of the body by medicine (ἰατρικὴ μὲν γὰρ σώματος νόσους ἀκέεται, σοφίη δὲ ψυχὴν παθῶν ἀφαίρεται), we are justified in looking less for 'wisdom' and intellective experience as the soul's province than for the kind of practical doctrine of moderation and self-control explicitly advocated for ψυχή in B 191. By calling for a σοφίη of this kind for the soul comparable to medicine for the body, Democritus means, I think, to make soul therapy, like medicine, a τέχνη. And if soul becomes the object of a τέχνη, that τέχνη is likely to be predicated on very limited, universally recognized responses of soul—namely, sex (B 159), passion (B 235), anger (B 236), and greed (B 228)—which have concomitant somatic manifestations. The focusing of soul on these psychosomatic or practical matters may account for the constant emphasis on training and habit that runs throughout Democritus (e.g., B 242 more men become good through practice [ἄσκησις] than by nature).

GORGIAS

In the *Encomium of Helen*, the word ψυχή occurs on a scale unprecedented in fifth-century literature. Since Gorgias lived well into the fourth century it would be helpful to know when this document was composed, but unfortunately there are no internal criteria for dating. The way in which Gorgias uses ψυχή, however, seems analogous to the kind of strongly psychophysical 'life-force' references we have just traced in Democritus and will see again in the Hippocratic texts. I therefore include the *Helen* as relevant to an inquiry into the early use of ψυχή, despite the uncertainty of date.

---

18. For obvious reasons I reject B 189, at least the concluding sentence. It is of a piece with B 37, and one must either reject it or give up hope of understanding Democritus on the subject of the soul.

The thirteen references to ψυχή in the *Helen* virtually eliminate all other comparable psychological language. For this reason alone there can be no doubt that the ψυχή is perceived by Gorgias as the chief psychological entity in human beings. It is explicitly associated with intelligence in the sense that it incorporates δόξα into itself (10), but δόξα, which is its only form of knowledge (11), is ridiculed for its inherent weakness because men lack memory, knowledge of the present, and foreknowledge. That there are two τέχναι of witchcraft and magic (10), one the ψυχῆς ἁμαρτήματα, the other δόξης ἀπατήματα, suggests that δόξα is, like λόγος (8), πειθώ (13), and ὄψις (15), imagined as something external to the soul and to which the soul is vulnerable. On most subjects (11) the mass of men take δόξα as an adviser to the soul (σύμβουλον τῇ ψυχῇ). These statements are hard to reconcile with the opening sentence of the speech, in which the virtues of city, body, soul, deed, and speech are enumerated as, respectively, manliness, beauty, wisdom, virtue, and truth (κόσμος πόλει μὲν εὐανδρία, σώματι δὲ κάλλος, ψυχῇ δὲ σοφία, πράγματι δὲ ἀρετή, λόγῳ δὲ ἀλήθεια). If the final pairing suggests irony, as it must in this Gorgianic setting, the connection of soul with wisdom is undoubtedly problematical as well, but for our purposes it is significant that the connection is made at all. Obviously the audience of Gorgias included some who would speak in this way about the ψυχή.

Whether the opinion belongs to Gorgias or not, the underlying premise that the soul should respond to wisdom is taken by him as the starting point for a wholly affective, psychophysical theory of soul and rhetoric comparable to ideas found elsewhere in the fragments. In B 23, which Untersteiner[19] takes to be a model for the epistemology of *Helen*, the ἀπάτη of tragedy makes the deceiver more just (δικαιότερος) than the nondeceiver, and the deceived wiser (σοφώτερος) than the undeceived (the use of σοφία in *Helen* (1) just quoted should be compared, of course). A comparable but less paradoxical statement is made in *Helen* (12), where it is said that it is the persuader who is wrong, and the persuaded who is unjustly accused. Gorgias' cynicism creates obvious differences in the moral valuation assigned to ψυχή, and he is more consistently interested in emotion than in somatic health, but the ψυχή is thus treated in much the same way as it is in Democritus. It is of interest to Gorgias because of its influence over visible behavior and somatic responses, and it is perceived as a wholly passive entity, onto which rationality is externally imposed. Gorgias tells us directly that any sensory or mental stimulus will bend the ψυχή to its purposes, and when that happens (19) the ψυχή cannot be held responsible.

19. Untersteiner, p. 116.

This abdication of moral responsibility is, of course, impossible from a Platonic point of view and differs as well from the attitude toward ψυχή in Democritean texts like B 159. Gorgias stresses particularly (15) the impression (τυποῦται) on the soul made by the sight of the beloved. Since sight can produce disease (17) as well as madness and pointless struggle, it is clear that for Gorgias, as for Democritus, psychic manipulation can be aimed at specific somatic manifestations. Poetry (9) can be used as a tool, therefore, to manipulate the emotions of listeners in ways that will often produce somatic reaction. Thus, they are affected by shuddering (φρίκη περίφοβος), tears (ἔλεος πολύδακρυς), and painful yearning (πόθος φιλοπενθής). In this way Gorgias' statement that incantations of words can drive out grief and induce pleasure (8) may be compared directly to Democritus B 290 and, more generally, to the reports of verbal and musical therapy, mentioned above, attributed to Democritus, Damon, and Antiphon.

MEDICAL TEXTS

An important analogy to these uses of ψυχή in Gorgias and Democritus occurs in the medical texts, where, for probably the first time, σῶμα and ψυχή are paired in a direct quotation surviving from the fifth century. In *Airs, Waters, Places* the use of ψυχή seems to have only incidental importance to the author, but in comparison to traditional attitudes his treatment of it reflects crucial changes in scope and meaning. In *Regimen* I, the only other early text in which ψυχή is found, the role of ψυχή is perhaps more idiosyncratic, but the assumptions behind its use may still be pertinent to understanding the fifth-century development of the word.

Since the passages in question are quite extensive, they can only be summarized here. For *Airs* it is clear that (insofar as it has a psychological aspect) the ψυχή described is essentially that which possesses 'courage'. Thus, after the writer has concluded in chapter 23 that human stature is affected by seasonal change because the "coagulation of the seed" is corrupted by frequent climatic variations, he asserts that character (ἦθος) is affected by climate as well. Changing climates produce wildness by causing frequent disturbances of the mind (ἐκπλήξιες τῆς γνώμης) and account for endurance in body and soul (αἱ ταλαιπωρίαι τῷ σώματι καὶ τῇ ψυχῇ). Where there are kings, as in Asia, there, too, are cowards because the souls of men become enslaved (αἱ ψυχαὶ δεδούλωνται), and thus institutions like monarchy can be said to affect the bravery (εὐψυχία) of the citizens. In the ensuing chapter these theories are reiterated for specific tribes. Those in regions of sharp climatic change will possess endurance and courage naturally (καὶ πρὸς τὸ ταλαίπωρον καὶ τὸ ἀνδρεῖον εὖ πεφυκότα). Inhabitants of the hot lowlands are of a sort in whom courage and endurance do not belong by nature but must be instilled by law (τὸ δὲ ἀνδρεῖον καὶ τὸ ταλαίπωρον ἐν τῇ ψυχῇ φύσει μὲν οὐκ ἂν ... ἐνείη, νόμος δὲ προσγενόμενος ἀπεργάζοιτ’ ἂν). These statements tell us little about the nature of ψυχή other than that it is material and that it manifests itself in human courage, an interpretation made certain by the use of εὐψυχότερος and εὐψυχία. No particular importance is attached to the pairing of ψυχή with σῶμα, and why the combination has emerged here for the first time is not made clear by any statement in the text. The writer's usual summarizing term for the psychological character of a man is ἦθος, as opposed to εἶδος for physical appearance.[20] More important, where this or an earlier writer is attempting to describe mental process in Sacred Disease (17), he does not mention ψυχή, or even φρένες, but attributes such activity only to the brain. Later, in Airs 24, when ψυχή is used for the last time, it again has a fairly specific reference to cowardice, as can be seen if we compare the use of κακός with ψυχή in tragedy: in a benign climate men are fleshy, ill-jointed, moist, lazy, and 'generally weak' in ψυχή (ἀταλαίπωροι καὶ τὴν ψυχὴν κακοὶ ὡς ἐπὶ τὸ πολύ).

The discussion in Regimen I.35 is far more detailed and assigns a larger range of psychological activities to the ψυχή. In a scheme that undoubtedly draws on Heraclitus,[21] the writer contends that with respect to the "so-called intelligence" of the ψυχή (περὶ δὲ φρονήσιος ψυχῆς ὀνομαζομένης), the soul is a blending (κρῆσις) of fire and moisture whose qualities of perception and thought are determined by the quality and quantities of the mixture. Walks are recommended, along with the dietary regimen, as a way of controlling the moisture of ψυχή, and even vomiting is held to produce benefits for the ψυχή in this fashion. A smaller proportion of fire to water produces a ψυχή that is slow (βραδυτέρη) and people who are half-wits (ἠλίθιοι). Such persons can manage the sensations of touch, which are slow in nature, but not those of sight and hearing, which require the speed of fire. Dry foods, steam baths, and vomiting will improve the abilities of such ψυχαί. True idiocy (μανίη) is the result of having a ψυχή that is completely watery, but one that is fiery, in turn, is intelligent (φρόνιμος),

20. E.g., 24.36ff. Wherever seasonal change is greatest, there too is the greatest variety in physical appearance, character, and nature (ἐκεῖ καὶ τὰ εἴδεα καὶ τὰ ἤθεα καὶ τὰς φύσιας εὑρήσεις πλεῖστον διαφερούσας). φύσις is used repeatedly for 'character' in this section.

21. Heraclitean influence over Regimen I cannot be contested, but Joly, p. 26, and Kirk (1954), p. 338, rightly stress its eclecticism.

and "such a nature is that of a good soul" (ψυχῆς ἀγαθῆς). The blending of fire and water, however, is the governing principle only of intelligence. Traits of character such as kindness, anger, and craft are functions of the passages through which ψυχή moves, and they are unalterable.[22]

The connection between medical theory and practice and the ψυχή must be approached cautiously. The text of *Regimen* I implies that physicians designed actual therapeutic programs for the health of the ψυχή. A record of such treatment appears for the early Pythagoreans in Iamblichus and could conceivably be the remnant of a fifth-century tradition, otherwise lost to us, about the ψυχή.[23] The Pythagoreans, Aristoxenus tells us, practiced early training to protect and purify the young against bodily or self-aggrandizing desires, which originate in the ψυχή.[24] Unfortunately, this account is too schematic and rationalistic to be trustworthy, and, as in the case of all such later material, it must be doubted as a source of explicit information, particularly of a semantic nature, about the ψυχή. But some interest in the ψυχή, whatever its specific focus, is convincingly attested for Pythagorean medicine. Burkert's reassessment of the importance of Philolaus,[25] if accepted, allows an explicit medical tradition involving the ψυχή to be reconstructed. Alcmaeon's doctrine of health as a harmonious

22. Similar notions of ψυχή are found in *Regimen* IV, which is omitted here for lack of date, although it perhaps provides better evidence than does *Regimen* I for reciprocal interaction of ψυχή and σῶμα. Briefly, the ψυχή is the servant of the body (τῷ σώματι ὑπηρετέουσα) when the body is awake, but when it is asleep the ψυχή takes over the functions of body and soul: it hears, walks, sees, feels, etc. (IV.86). Dreams that repeat the day's activities indicate health and the fact that the soul is not 'surfeited', 'overpowered', or 'depleted' (IV.88). Bad dreams indicate that the body has undergone a disturbance, and a corresponding disturbance of soul has been caused by a "secretion arising from some surfeit" (πλησμονῆς τινος ἐγγενομένης ἀπόκρισίς τις γενομένη), a physical condition which in its turn may be treated by emetic, exercise, and the like, so that we are returned to the theory of blended fire and water put forward in *Regimen* I.35.

23. The attribution of this report to fifth-century Pythagoreans raises the issue of the reliability of Aristoxenus. Modern opinion in general is cited in Burkert (1972), p. 103, n. 54 esp., but without discussion of the medical material. Wehrli's negative opinion (p. 61) on frs. 37–38 is to my mind not decisive, since he skirts the matters of dietetic detail, abstinence, exercise, and the like, which are the heart of the account, and merely takes the general discussion of desire in *Philebus* and *Nicomachean Ethics* as evidence that the text uses only fourth-century antecedents. Edelstein (p. 17) treats this material as genuine and also takes early medicine as Pythagorean in character. Against this view see Burkert (1972), pp. 292ff. That the material in Aristoxenus in some way reflects a transformation of the Pythagorean βίος, however much rationalized, seems possible.

24. E.g., *VP* 206: the young must be trained in order to be purified of desire for excess, luxurious food, clothing, bed, and dwelling. These desires originate in the ψυχή and are not of a nature to stop, but they expand indefinitely. Each type of food introduced into the body (208) will produce a unique mental disposition. Music and incantations are used for health (164), and the sayings of Homer and Hesiod are used for betterment of the ψυχή.

25. Burkert (1972), p. 234.

mixing of hot-cold, wet-dry, bitter-sweet, and the like (B 4) reappears in Menon, the pupil of Aristotle who cites Philolaus, with the relevant observation that ψυχή is derived from ψύχειν because it creates a balance of warm flesh and cool breath.[26] Equally important, it is to Echecrates, another pupil of Philolaus, that Plato gives the outburst of excitement at *Phaedo* 88c–d when he hears that the ψυχή is a harmony of the body, and this can point only to a medical milieu for ψυχή.[27] It is therefore reasonable to assume that the earlier notion of the bodily φύσις as a harmony became linked in some way to ψυχή in the writing of Philolaus, who was both interested in medical matters and is said to have written a περὶ ψυχῆς.[28] But the extension of this interest in the ψυχή to psychological associations is not demonstrated by the authentic uses of ψυχή in the surviving fragments, as I have shown earlier, and we can safely assume only that for Philolaus the ψυχή has to do with physical health. Its contribution to psychological activity may again be only that thought and sensation are, as in Alcmaeon, dependent on ψυχή. The case for giving the soul explicit psychological and moral value in early medicine, which could be taken up by others, rests, then, on the Hippocratic treatises just summarized, and it is a delicate question how we are to understand the connection between the obviously similar uses of ψυχή that appear in the medical and nonmedical texts discussed in this section. Whether the psychological use of ψυχή in *Airs* and *Regimen* I should be regarded as eclectic and atypical of earlier Greek medicine, as it would be for later Greek medicine, or whether we are looking at uses of the word which had actual historical influence on its development are questions that cannot be resolved easily on the evidence available.

What matters for our purposes is, first, that these texts share with Democritus and Gorgias a common identification of ψυχή as a naturalistic 'life-force' whose psychological properties can be scientifically understood and manipulated, and made amenable to externally imposed therapies; and, second, that the object of this τέχνη of soul is as likely to be somatic as it is psychological. In theory, at least, great significance can be attached to this context, in which the meaning of ψυχή would presumably range from that of a virtual synonym for the φύσις of the body—as in *Epidemics* VI, where 'natures' are said to be the real physicians, or *On Humors*, where, like the ψυχή of *Airs*, φύσις varies according to climate[29]—to something a good

---

26. Ibid., p. 271.
27. Ibid., p. 272.
28. Ibid., pp. 242 and 227.
29. Refs. from Guthrie (1965), p. 352.

deal vaguer whose emotional and moral condition will nevertheless affect
health. Most important, doctrines placing rationality and moral intelligence in the ψυχή would do so less because of abstract speculation about the
soul's ability to know than from the tendency to analogize the soul in its
psychological aspects, whatever they are, to the medical conception of
body as something treatable by a scientific σοφία or τέχνη. The chief
possibilities here I take to be that (1) like diseases of the body, soul
disturbances no longer are defined as demonic and external, even though
external forces may influence them, but as disorders of something "internal" and normally harmonious; (2) as in medicine, this disturbance is not
the fault of the patient, although he is responsible for participating in his
own therapy; (3) the φύσις to which therapy is directed must be perceived
as fundamental and single. In brief, if a concept of psychological soul
gradually emerged in response to the medical character of the claims for
soul therapy, it is likely to have implied that the soul is something internal,
a single unified center of the man responsive to persuasion (rational or
otherwise) and an entity around whose welfare the subject must somehow
regulate his life.[30] Even though these ideas would turn, as in Democritus,
Gorgias, and the medical writers, on the prosperity only of the body or at
best the psychophysical soul, not the soul as an ontologically higher order
of existence, each of these connotations is in some form indispensable for
the Socratic doctrine of soul.

It is the implicit tone of such attitudes toward the ψυχή, as well as the
explicit ideas traced earlier, that I take to be apparent in both the *Helen* and
the fragments of Democritus. Two points of interpretation that illustrate
this are worth particular mention. First, although it seems obvious in the
Helen that Gorgias intends to compare his skill with that of others who
claim to have a τέχνη for the treatment of soul, and that this idea must
coincide with the use of ψυχή in the other texts we have dealt with here, it is
also clear that Gorgias' own τέχνη is intentionally archaic. The result is
almost certainly ironic in some degree: the ψυχή as Gorgias conceives it can
only be the product of scientific attitudes to the soul, yet when Gorgias
claims that his words are ἐπῳδαί able to charm the soul (10), he chooses to
align himself explicitly with devices of superstitious medicine of the sort
that therapy of the soul would, for others, be intended to eliminate. The
contradiction between the nature of the therapy and the nature of the soul
is doubtless in accord with Gorgias' wish to arrogate divine powers to

---

30. Entralgo, pp. 143–46; Schumacher, pp. 202–03; cf. Kahn *Anaximander*, pp. 126–29;
Guthrie (1962), p. 356, (1965), pp. 351–53; Burkert (1972), p. 272, n. 163.

rhetoric (the therapy), but its occurrence here should warn us not to assume too direct a connection with medicine. I am tempted to suggest that Gorgias uses ψυχή here to make a play on δαίμων, since in prescientific medicine the ἐπῳδαί were directed not to the ψυχή but to the δαίμων. The point of this is not easily seen, but Democritus B 171, ψυχὴ οἰκητήριον δαίμονος, might be compared.

Against this background, secondly, it is possible to see a somewhat different nuance in Democritus B 187, which urges that men make a λόγος about soul instead of body and which claims that perfection of ψυχή can cure μοχθηρία of the body (for 'body' Democritus uses the designation σκῆνος, a word appearing elsewhere only in the Hippocratic corpus). We may compare this with the paideutic character of early medicine as Edelstein, for example, describes it in the case of the humors: "It is not possible to demonstrate experimentally how the balance of fluids in the human body is disturbed nor how this imbalance evokes diseases. But it is possible to claim so . . . and to attempt verification of the claim by means of arguments, analogies, sophistry. . . . This medicine by 'hypothesis' is the real achievement of ancient medicine." [31] Edelstein's account is well illustrated by *Laws* 857c–d, where the doctor who discusses his prescriptions with slaves is said to be laughable, although such discussions are a common device in the medical therapy of others. Therapeutic interest in the ψυχή of either a medical or quasi-medical kind must have produced similar attempts to instruct, so to speak, on the basis of knowledge about the tangible effects that various psychical states could induce. In the fragment of Democritus we hear, I suggest, exactly the sort of "therapeutic" speech Plato attributes to the practice of medicine. As such, therefore, it should perhaps be regarded less as a claim for the superiority of soul to body than as a claim for the superiority of the therapy of soul to the therapy of body.

31. Edelstein, p. 105.

5

Socratic–Platonic Uses of ψυχή

Evidence for this last and most critical phase in the development of ψυχή from its Homeric origins to its preeminent role in the philosophical thought of the fourth century is insufficient in some respects, overabundant in others. Direct contemporary testimony for the use of ψυχή by Socrates is found only in Aristophanes, and although he seems to verify the connection, the evidence is scarcely decisive. The occurrences of ψυχή in the early dialogues of Plato, on the other hand, are so extensive and varied that it may easily seem fruitless to search them for anything other than the conceptual foundations of the Platonic doctrine of the soul, the Socratic contribution to which can never be known with any certainty. This is the approach taken by Robinson in his otherwise excellent study of the meanings of ψυχή in Plato, when he dismisses the pre-Platonic uses of ψυχή as merely a chaotic miscellany of ideas about body and soul. But it is difficult to argue that the semantic and thematic affinities among occurrences of ψυχή within the Platonic corpus matter, while those between Plato and his antecedents do not. This returns us again to the form, at least, of the purely conceptual history of ψυχή offered by Aristotle. I shall try to demonstrate the existence of important similarities of language and detail joining the fifth-century uses of ψυχή with those of Plato and then suggest that these similarities offer evidence of the historical context in which the Socratic doctrine was formed. I make no claim, of course, to show any direct evidence for the Socratic doctrine itself. After a brief survey of the Socratic material in Aristophanes and Xenophon, I shall turn to this most essential comparison.

NON-PLATONIC EVIDENCE FOR THE SOCRATIC USE
OF ψυχή

Of the twenty-six occurrences of ψυχή in Aristophanes no fewer than six are found in *Clouds*, and a seventh occurs in one of the two Aristophanic references to Socrates outside *Clouds*: at *Birds* 1553 the chorus relates that on its recent journey it has seen Socrates calling up spirits in company with the coward Peisander, who wishes to know if he can see again the ψυχή that has left him (πρὸς δὲ τοῖς Σκιάποσιν λί- | μνη τις ἔστ᾽ ἄλουτος οὗ | ψυχαγωγεῖ Σωκράτης· | ἔνθα καὶ Πείσανδρος ἦλθε | δεόμενος ψυχὴν ἰδεῖν ἣ | ζῶντ᾽ ἐκεῖνον προὔλιπε). It has been suggested that this association of ψυχή with Socrates refers principally to the ghostlike character of his followers:[1] Socrates as the leader of earthly ψυχαί ('ghosts') can restore to Peisander the ψυχή ('courage') that has deserted him by summoning the ψυχαί of the under-world. There is doubtless some truth in this reading—Chairephon, who is ἡμιθνής at *Clouds* 504, appears here (1564) as a 'bat'—but given the lack of contextual preparation, as at *Clouds* 94, where a play on Socratic ψυχαί as 'ghosts' is deliberately made,[2] it is perhaps excessively conservative. We must assume that the spectral appearance of Socrates and his followers had become a standing joke with the Athenians, an assumption at odds with the constant Socratic emphasis on health in *Memorabilia*.[3]

For five of the six instances of ψυχή in *Clouds*, Socratic allusions can be defended.[4] Two of these, remarkably, attribute σοφία to the ψυχή, an association that, with the exception of Heraclitus B 118 and the Gorgianic *Helen*, is original to this play. In the first, Strepsiades describes the dwelling place of Socrates and his disciples as ψυχῶν σοφῶν φροντιστήριον (94), and in the second (414–15), he is told by the chorus that he will fulfill his desire to achieve σοφία if he has a good memory, is intelligent, endures in his ψυχή (εἰ μνήμων εἶ καὶ φροντιστὴς καὶ τὸ ταλαίπωρον ἔνεστιν | ἐν τῇ ψυχῇ), and prac-tices bodily asceticism. To this recommendation Strepsiades responds that he has a stubborn ψυχή, uneasy care, and a properly frugal stomach (ψυχῆς στερρᾶς δυσκολοκοίτον τε μερίμνης | καὶ φειδωλοῦ καὶ τρυσιβίου γαστρὸς καὶ θυμβρεπιδείπνου). What exactly is meant by ψυχῶν σοφῶν φροντιστήριον can

---

1. Handley, p. 213, acknowledges a secondary sense of 'mind leading' or 'persuading', however, basing the latter on the possibility that ψυχαγωγεῖν in a rhetorical context is Gorgianic.

2. Dover (1968), p. 106: "Souls are unsubstantial and, as we shall see, the philosophers are not 'real men' but pale and feeble."

3. E.g., *Mem.* 3.12.

4. I omit ἄριστον ψυχήν ('courage') at 1048.

be debated. It is certainly possible to suggest tragic periphrasis.[5] A direct play in the speaker's mind on 'ghosts',[6] as has been suggested, must break the dramatic illusion by forcing Strepsiades to step out of character in one line in order to ridicule the men he venerates in the next line as a part of his scheme to motivate Pheidippes to seek out Socratic instruction. If there is a pertinent idea for Strepsiades in the use of ψυχή that can account for the phrase as something other than tragic periphrasis, it may be that, like φροντιστήριον, it is a word Strepsiades does not really understand but one he can be imagined to have heard associated with the Socratic sect. The connection of σοφός with ψυχή, and the use in this phrase of σοφός as philosophically 'wise',[7] may well point beyond simple parody of traditional meanings.[8] The later connection of σοφία with the ψυχή in Strepsiades' response to the chorus tends to confirm the importance and comic value of the first reference for the Aristophanic audience. More important, however, it provides direct evidence that the language of the medical texts—ταλαιπωρία / ταλαίπωρον ἐν τῇ ψυχῇ occurs twice in Airs— which implies that ψυχή is the physical 'life-force', could be used in a context of instruction that is at least sophistic, if not conclusively Socratic. Strepsiades' reply by referring to ψυχή, sleep, and diet tends to confirm the medical or therapeutic context of this reference.[9] In effect, Strepsiades instinctively interprets the chorus's appeal to him to achieve σοφία through psychic discipline as requiring a regime of somatic self-discipline in which ψυχή is in some way involved.

The remaining instances of ψυχή are imitations of tragedy and can be attributed to a philosophic or Socratic use of ψυχή only through the heavy screen of parody. The ψυχή of Strepsiades, like that of Agave (Ba. 1268), takes wing at the thundering of the clouds and wants to engage thereafter in subtle discourse (315 ff. ἡ ψυχή μου πεπότηται / καὶ λεπτολεγεῖν ἤδη ζητεῖ καὶ περὶ καπνοῦ στενολεσχεῖν). A sophistic frenzy, as it were, overpowers Strepsiades just as a Dionysian frenzy overcame Agave, and the religious metaphor is carried out in his contemplation of the mysteries of rhetoric

5. Handley, p. 213, cites the scholiast's periphrastic interpretation ἀνδρῶν φιλοσοφῶν.

6. Dover (1968), p. 106.

7. The semantics of σοφός/σοφία in the fifth century are discussed in Snell (1924) and Havelock (1963), p. 162 and pp. 287–88 especially.

8. Parody of intellectual jargon is, of course, frequent in Clouds and indicates such use of ψυχή here: e.g., φροντιστής (266), μερίμνη (420 and 951—see Dover's note at 1.101), μεριμνοφροντισταί (101), αὐτὸς καθ᾽ αὑτόν (194), θυμόσοφος (877). Strepsiades himself joins in with μεριμνοφροντισταί at 101, when he speaks of Socratic λόγοι as though they were physical objects (112), and when he begins to create φροντ- words in imitation of his mentors. See Havelock (1972).

9. See above, p. 151.

and argument that are revealed to him. Finally, at 712 ff. Strepsiades first complains that bedbugs are drinking up his ψυχή (ψυχὴν ἐκπίνουσιν), just as Clytemnestra complains of Electra in the Sophoclean *Electra* (785), and then that his ψυχή (719) as well as his other valuables have been taken from him (φροῦδα τὰ χρήματα, φρούδη χροιά / φρούδη ψυχή, φρούδη δ᾿ ἐμβάς)[10] within the φροντιστήριον. Unlike the use of ψυχὴν ἄριστος elsewhere in the play, each of these is an exotic and pointed occurrence of ψυχή whose comic value would be substantially increased if there existed a genuine Socratic association of ψυχή with σοφία or σωφροσύνη suitable for parody. Socratic insistence on the rational training of ψυχή would thus be mocked by the ecstatic transport of Strepsiades at thunder, by the enumeration of ψυχή with the testicles and rectum as parts of the body under attack, and finally by the transformation of ψυχή into a "thing" that can be stolen by the Socratics.

As we have seen earlier, ψυχή is regularly regarded by Aristophanes as a useful word for comic exploitation and therefore appears in the plays with some frequency. Nevertheless, the references to ψυχή in connection with Socrates are substantially more plentiful than one would expect on the basis of the other plays, and they seem to be directed toward parody of a rational notion of ψυχή. The association of ψυχή with σοφία offers strong evidence for the fact of Socratic teaching about the ψυχή.

In Xenophon, interest in the ψυχή is considered an explicit part of Socratic teaching. Since Xenophon is so questionable a witness to Socrates' life, this evidence cannot be taken at face value. Against the background of the other texts we have examined, however, information provided obliquely by Xenophon may be of value, for it seems apparent that the relationship of σῶμα and ψυχή of the medical texts, Democritus, and Gorgias is most frequently in the air when Xenophon's Socrates speaks. By contrast, references to ψυχή that imply a strict dualism, although numerous, are for the most part obvious imitations of Plato—the speech of Socrates in *Symposium* 8, in which loves of body and soul are divided, respectively, between the Pandemian and Uranian Aphrodites (8, 10), contains twelve uses of ψυχή that can be defined as dualistic[11]—or depend

---

10. Handley, p. 212, cites *Hec.* 160ff. for repeated φροῦδος in tragedy.

11. That is, the ψυχή becomes more worthy of love as it progresses toward wisdom (8.14); affection of the soul is ἀγνή (8.15); we would rather trust our practical affairs to those whose love is of the ψυχή, not the body (8.36). *Smp.* 1.9 can also be included here (everyone present feels something in his ψυχή as Autolycus enters), although the traditional erotic ψυχή is also meant. Cf. *Smp.* 4.2, where Callias is asked by Antisthenes whether justice is found in the ψυχαί of men.

upon an imposed or dogmatic juxtaposition of σῶμα and ψυχή that has the ring of ill-defined jargon. By this I mean the strongly dichotomous sense of ψυχή that is implied wherever carnal and psychic love are juxtaposed, or passages like *Memorabilia* 3.10.1ff., where Socrates asks a painter whether he tries to reproduce the character of the soul (τῆς ψυχῆς ἦθος) as well as the image of the body, and this psychic character (3.10.4–5) is manifested for Socrates in the eyes of the subject as they exhibit such qualities as kindliness, moderation, intelligence, or arrogance.[12] But aside from these instances,[13] ψυχή is rarely alluded to as the seat of moral character without a specific sense of bodily identity.[14] Only twice is it introduced for the sake of a function that is specifically intellectual: at *Memorabilia* 1.4.17 the ψυχή, like the φρόνησις of the gods, can ponder (φροντίζειν) things in Egypt and Sicily, and at 1.2.53 the ψυχή that departs from the dead man is alone what has intelligence (φρόνησις), Finally, Xenophon twice attributes a highly Platonic formulation of ψυχή to Socrates; it is invisible, shares in the divine more than does any other human thing, and rules the body.[15]

If we omit instances that are obviously traditional,[16] every remaining use of ψυχή in Xenophon, however, assumes a psychosomatic relationship of σῶμα and ψυχή. As in the forms of soul therapy described above, this division of ψυχή and σῶμα does not seem to denote a separation of immaterial intellect and bodily emotion, or anything like it, but is intended instead to account for the overall well-being of the man, σῶμα and ψυχή together, by assuming that whatever emotion is owed to ψυχή can be controlled through training. At the core of this attitude to σῶμα-ψυχή is an explicit regimen of training aimed not at denial of the body in the interests of ψυχή but at general social and personal σωφροσύνη. Of course, Plato also assumes the favorable—more often, unfavorable—effect of bodily activities on ψυχή. But in Xenophon bodily regimen is not a side issue; it is perceived as the principal way to influence soul, and so we are justified in seeing the soul and the mental life of the soul that results from this tenet as having to do again with pragmatic psychosomatic forms of self-control. However, although this view comes through in the substance of what is

12. Cf. 3.10.6–8, in which the same line of argument is directed toward sculpture.

13. *Mem.* 2.6.30, 2.6.36, 3.11.10, 4.1.2.

14. E.g., *Ap.* 7, where remembrance of friends attends a man who died while still in possession of a healthy body and a kindly soul (ψυχὴν δυναμένην φιλοφρονεῖσθαι). Other examples of this usage are rare: perhaps *Smp.* 4.43 and 4.2 (above, n. 11).

15. *Mem.* 1.4.8–9 and 4.3.14. The idea of divinity is implied in the first passage, directly stated in the second (τοῦ θείου μετέχει).

16. *Smp.* 1.16 and 4.64. The meaning of the latter is obscure, but possibly there is a play on Socrates' words at 4.43 and the archaic idea of gratifying the ψυχή.

said, it is often at odds with the Platonic touches in Xenophon's language. Thus at *Memorabilia* 1.3.5 Socrates is said to have trained body and soul by a regime that, barring accident, allows a confident, safe, and inexpensive life (διαίτῃ δὲ τήν τε ψυχήν ἐπαίδευσε καὶ τὸ σῶμα, ᾗ χρώμενος ἄν τις, εἰ μή τι δαιμόνιον εἴη, θαρραλέως καὶ ἀσφαλῶς διάγοι). As a consequence he ate only enough to guarantee pleasure, drank only when thirsty, and at feasts advised others to avoid eating what would encourage further excess, holding such foods to be harmful to stomachs, brains and ψυχαί (τὰ λυμαινόμενα γαστέρας καὶ κεφαλὰς καὶ ψυχῆς).[17] Again (*Mem.* 1.2.1–5), he was in control of his sexual and gastronomic passions, able to endure heat and cold; he was generally moderate in his needs, making others cease from the corresponding vices by giving them confidence to care for themselves (ἂν ἑαυτῶν ἐπιμελῶνται). He exercised only as much as would be good for the ψυχή (ὅσα γ' ἡδέως ἡ ψυχὴ δέχεται), in the belief that such exercise was good for health and no obstacle to care of the soul (καὶ τὴν τῆς ψυχῆς ἐπιμέλειαν οὐκ ἐμποδίζειν). The final qualification here gives psychosomatic training a Platonic ending and betrays, perhaps, the uncertain path that Xenophon is following. Thus, in one of the fullest descriptions of ψυχή (*Mem.* 1.4.13–14), it is said that the god has given man a ψυχή able to recognize the existence of the gods, to protect itself against hunger, thirst, heat, cold, disease, and weakness, to exert itself for knowledge, and to remember what it has seen, heard, and learned—a frankly astonishing mixture of themes obviously influenced by knowledge of Plato but insensitive to the wariness Plato himself exhibits throughout the early dialogues toward such eclectic combinations of the various powers of soul.

What has an uncorrupted ring to it in Xenophon is the use of ψυχή in the many instances where the relationship of σῶμα and ψυχή arises in the context of a bodily regimen or the achievement of ἐγκράτεια in body and soul. Indolence and hedonism (*Mem.* 2.1.20) cannot put any worthwhile knowledge (ἐπιστήμην ἀξιόλογον) into the ψυχή.[18] Drunkards and lovers are less able to care about proper behavior (*Mem.* 2.1.22–23) because the soul forgets σωφροσύνη, succumbing to those pleasures implanted in the body along with ψυχή. If sexual desire cannot be forestalled (*Mem.* 1.3.14), one should at least avoid whatever the ψυχή would not accept without

---

17. Cf. also *Ap.* 18 and Antisthenes at *Smp.* 4.41, where ψυχή is used in the defense against poverty and physical duress.

18. Cf. *Mem.* 2.1.31 (omitted here as not Socratic), where, in the usual recital of luxurious practices, overeating, drinking, wantonness, and excessive sleeping are said to make the young ἀδύνατοι in body and the old ἀνόητοι in ψυχή. This should be seen, perhaps, in terms of the functions appropriate to youth and old age rather than in terms of σῶμα and ψυχή.

bodily need; Socrates has therefore trained himself to shun the fair in form. In a pun on εὐωχεῖσθαι (*Mem.* 3.14.7) the compounding element εὖ is held to imply eating what can harm neither body nor ψυχή. Wine (*Smp.* 2.24) moistens souls (ἄρδων τὰς ψυχάς) and in excess makes both σῶμα and ψυχή stumble. ἐγκράτεια must be laid down as a foundation in the ψυχή (*Mem.* 1.5.4–5), for whoever is the servant of his pleasures is poorly off in body and soul.[19]

Dualistic uses of ψυχή in Xenophon thus seem weak and suspiciously imitative. While ψυχή in contrast to σῶμα always implies for Xenophon amenability to reason and a general sense of moral character, in most cases it would be impossible, and even contradictory, to identify ψυχή directly with rationality or to see it as that which "contains" rationality apart from the body. Rather, it is an energy contiguous with the body, directly influenced by the same things that influence the body, and important because of its bodily identity and thus for its role in the achievement of overall ἐγκράτεια in the affairs, demands, and temptations of one's life. The inconsistency of Xenophon's usages of ψυχή must be emphasized, but such inconsistency may well provide a better reflection of late fifth-century ideas of ψυχή and their linguistic context than would more sophisticated texts. A particularly striking occurrence of ψυχή in Xenophon's *Apology* (30) perhaps best illustrates the difficult transition for Xenophon, if not for Socrates, between the archaic 'life-force' and the Platonic soul as 'self'. Socrates once associated with the son of Anytus; he thought him not weak in ψυχή (οὐκ ἄρρωστος τὴν ψυχὴν εἶναι) and thus unlikely to remain employed in a servile trade, as he had been compelled to do by his father. Lack of a good adviser, in Socrates' opinion, destined him therefore to vice, a prediction Xenophon reports to have been borne out by the youth's subsequent career as a drunkard. This and a similar passage[20] display directly Xenophon's tendency to think instinctively of the ψυχή as an impersonal energy that is inherently neither good nor bad (if anything, perhaps naturally prone more to irrational than rational behavior, like the archaic 'life-force') but by its strength a source only of the largeness of

19. References to self-control not mentioning ψυχή are frequent: e.g., *Mem.* 1.3.8, 1.6.4–10, 2.6.1, 3.12.1–8, 3.13.2ff., 4.7.9; *Ap.* 19. *Mem.* 2.1.1–6 shows that the achievement of ἐγκράτεια allows a man to be rational in that, for example (2.1.5), overcoming sexual passion allows one to be sensible toward the law. If ἐγκράτεια involves ψυχή here, as it does elsewhere in Xenophon's thought, then the passage implies an indirect transference of rationality to the ψυχή from overall achievement of σωφροσύνη in body and soul, not that ψυχή is naturally the origin of rationality.

20. *Mem.* 4.1.4: Youths who are ἐρρωμενέστατοι ταῖς ψυχαῖς can succeed at any undertaking if trained. Untrained, they become more evil and uncontrollable through their very propensity to excess (μεγαλείους τε καὶ σφοδροὺς ὄντας). Cf. *Mem.* 3.9.1–3 for ψυχή and ἐρρωμένος implying 'courage'.

goodness or evil which one exhibits in life. As in Democritus and Gorgias, it seems to be imagined as the 'life-force' to which rationality must be applied from without by training.[21] Thus, when Socrates displays strength of soul (τῆς ψυχῆς τὴν ῥώμην) in the last days of his life, what is meant for Xenophon is not separable from 'courage' and other 'life-force' manifestations.

ψυχή IN THE EARLY DIALOGUES OF PLATO

The most remarkable feature of Plato's use of ψυχή in the early dialogues[22] is the absence, until arguments for immortality in *Phaedo*,[23] of any direct reference to the traditional function of the ψυχή as animator familiar to ordinary Greek usage. In light of the semantic history we have so far traced, it is reasonable to surmise that this silence results from recognition of the inherent contradiction between ψυχή as the 'life-force' and ψυχή as that which, for Plato, is able to ground human life in knowledge of non-phenomenal reality,[24] and not from religious or philosophical indifference to the noncognitive functions of soul. That the existence of this contradiction was first recognized by Plato only in the discussion of soul as a harmony in *Phaedo* is unlikely.[25] Worth noting here is the fact that phrases analogous to εὖ ζῆν, which Plato explicitly incorporates into a doctrine of soul in *Republic* and *Timaeus*,[26] and which in turn underlie the treatment of ψυχή in *Laws* as the psychical source of physical movements,[27] already appear in juxtaposition in the earlier texts.[28] But whether or not the later

---

21. Cf. *Mem.* 1.2.19. As in Democritus (B 187), there must be training of soul like that of body. It is unclear, from Xenophon's account of Socrates, how they would differ in nature.

22. I have included here all the dialogues commonly regarded as early (Guthrie [1975], p. 312), adding only the *Euthydemus* and *Menexenus* from the middle group as dialogues in which ψυχή is not central—and therefore beyond the scope of this work—as it is in *Meno, Phaedo, Republic, Symposium,* and *Phaedrus.*

23. *Ph.* 69e–72d; 102aff. See the discussion in Robinson, pp. 26ff.

24. Robinson, p. 30.

25. Burkert (1972), p. 272: "One has the impression that Plato, in this passage of the *Phaedo*, was the first to point out an embarrassing implication in the idea of the soul as a harmony."

26. See *R.* 353dff. and the discussion in Robinson, pp. 35–37: the virtues of soul are to deliberate, to live (τὸ ζῆν), and to live well (τὸ εὖ ζῆν). Cf. *Ti.* 30b, which argues, (1) the rational is fairer than the irrational, (2) reason cannot exist apart from ψυχή, (3) the god therefore put reason into soul and soul into body as he fashioned τὸ πᾶν, (4) the cosmos is therefore living (ζῷον), ensouled (ἔμψυχον), and rational (ἔννουν). This clearly bridges the gap between the ψυχή as a principle of 'life' and as the center of the rational faculty.

27. *Lg.* 897a.

28. *Cri.* 48b; *La.* 187e.

doctrines are anticipated early on, the extraordinary efforts Plato makes in
the later dialogues to unify systematically the 'life' functions of soul with
the moral and cognitive "Socratic" interest in ψυχή are consistent in
manner, if not substance, with his treatment of ψυχή in and before *Phaedo*.
Although earlier uses are not nearly as startling as, say, that of *Laws*
896c–897b, where the 'life' functions of ψυχή in the broad sense of all the
manifest activities of bodies are made to depend on the soul's capacity for
thought and feeling, almost every early occurrence of ψυχή in Plato
attempts to conserve historical contexts of the word by revaluation of pre-
Platonic usages into something compatible with Platonic theory. When
this phenomenon is examined closely it becomes fairly clear that both
Burnet's portrayal of Socrates as inventor of the moral-intellectual ψυχή
and the alternative view, that Plato is simply attempting to provide a
systematic ethical basis for inherited religious or dualistic ideas of ψυχή,
have little to do with the actual occurrences of the word in the early
dialogues. These must now be examined.

EUTHYPHRO, APOLOGY, CRITO

ψυχή appears only twice, at *Apology* 30b, where Socrates describes his
lifework in the familiar words as that of urging the Athenians to care for
the soul (ἐπιμελεῖσθαι ... τῆς ψυχῆς) more than for the body or possessions,
and at 40c, where death is described as either the absence of consciousness or
a μετοίκησις of the ψυχή to another place. There is no reason to doubt that
soul care, whatever was meant by ψυχή, was the core of the Socratic
teaching,[29] or to deny the connection between the explicit soul care of
Apology 30b and the remarkable circumlocution of *Crito* 47d–e, where it is
said that just as the athlete follows the trainer, in matters of right and wrong
we ought to follow the person concerned with "that part of us which is
made better by justice but ruined by injustice" (ὃ τῷ μὲν δικαίῳ βέλτιον
ἐγίγετο, τῷ δὲ ἀδίκῳ ἀπώλλυτο). But it is difficult to accept Burnet's notion
that this uncertainty of diction in *Crito* is a literal reflection of the innovative character of Socratic usage. The circumlocution in question is in fact
not common in the early dialogues, as Burnet implies, and the question
cannot be avoided why here, of all places, it should be employed. The
context is that of soul training as something akin to body training and
horse training, a juxtaposition that recurs elsewhere, of course,[30] and that

29. Meier, p. 333, n. 3; Guthrie (1971), pp. 147ff.
30. E.g., *La.* 185e.

predominates, as we have seen, in Xenophon's account of Socrates. If there was, as I have argued, a tradition of soul training which identified ψυχή as 'life-force', there is some reason, perhaps, to regard the circumlocution of ψυχή here as a purposeful evasion based on dialectical considerations. That the passage is constructed ironically and not as a record of Socratic usage is indicated, moreover, by 48b, which, continuing the thought of 47e, asks whether we ought to be most concerned not about living (τὸ ζῆν) but about living well (τὸ εὖ ζῆν), a phrase pointing again to underlying thoughts about ψυχή as that which accounts for physical life. For the similar usage of εὖ ζῆν at *Republic* 353ff., Robinson[31] shows decisively that Plato constructs a deliberate fallacy in an effort to unify on some basis at least the moral and 'life' functions of ψυχή, and it is reasonable to treat the reference in *Crito*, where our attention has already been drawn perhaps to the concept of the soul, if not the word ψυχή, by the odd circumlocutions of 47d–e, as a significant anticipation of this later reconciliation. The omission of ψυχή here, therefore, is more likely to be a stylistic device on Plato's part than a reflection of actual dubitation by Socrates. Whether its purpose is to shield Socrates from association with other practitioners of soul training or to avoid inquiry, at this point, into the systematic issues that Plato will only later bring forward, or something else altogether, cannot be ascertained from the context. Another possibly oblique reference to the soul, comparable to this, occurs at *Apology* 37c.

ION, LACHES

In slightly different ways these dialogues illustrate concisely the chief rhetorical feature of almost all early use of ψυχή in Plato, that is, the conservation and revaluation of traditional or unwanted uses of ψυχή into ones that work on a higher ethical plane. Thus, *Ion* employs a traditional context of ψυχή quite straightforwardly in order to attack the archaic view of the poet's relationship to his work. We are reminded at once of ψυχή in *Bacchae* and *Peace*,[32] and of other instances of poetic ecstasis. Possessed by its art, the soul of the lyric poet begins, like that of the bacchants, to make songs (534a); the poet is inspired and out of his senses (ἔνθεος . . . ἔκφρων . . . ὁ νοῦς μηκέτι ἐν αὐτῷ [534b]); when someone recites from Homer, Ion's soul dances and is with the scene he is describing (534c); when the poet sings the god draws the ψυχαί of the rhapsodes wherever he pleases (536a), a thought

31. Above, n. 26.
32. *Ba.* 72–76; *Peace* 827ff.

that brings to mind once again, as do many of the earlier uses of ψυχή in Plato, the Gorgianic *Helen*.[33] In *Laches*, however, a more complicated scheme is worked out, and the cruder traditional associations of ψυχή with courage are revalued so pointedly that the argument of the dialogue depends on the ability of the reader to grasp this method of explication while at least one of the speakers fails to. The dialogue takes up education of the young and begins with the specific question whether the art of fighting in armor will improve the young. After the more prosaic benefits of such exercise have been mentioned, Socrates introduces question-and-answer and the subject of ψυχή simultaneously. The adviser to be consulted about such training must be skilled in the end as well as the means. The lesson to be learned, then, is for the ψυχή of the young men (185e), and the question becomes one of identifying those who are skilled in soul θεραπεία or who have had good (ἀγαθοί: punning on 'brave') teachers. Lysimachus and Melesias have come with the desire to make the ψυχαί of their sons best. They must be told of teachers who, themselves ἀγαθοί, have trained (τεθεραπευκότες) the ψυχαί of the young and taught those present. Socrates has never had such a teacher (186c), since he himself has never had funds sufficient for such a course. In response to the point (187e) that Socrates will soon bring any subject around to a discussion of the way his interlocutor now lives (ὅντινα τρόπον νῦν τε ζῇ), and used to live (ὅντινα τὸν παρεληλυθότα βίον βεβίωκεν), Laches says that he has personally no objection to hearing a man speak of ἀρετή if he deserves to do so. He has himself had no doubts about the ἀρετή of Socrates since the day Socrates fought alongside him at Delium (189b). Socrates asserts that ἀρετή cannot be attached to the ψυχαί of the young unless it can be defined (190b), and the discussion is then centered on that one part of ἀρετή, courage, which Laches defines (192b) as καρτερία τῆς ψυχῆς. When this line of discussion fails, Nicias volunteers that each man is ἀγαθός in whatever respects he is σοφός; κακός, in whatever respects he is ἀμαθής (194d). Predictably, if the brave man (ἀνδρεῖος) is good (ἀγαθός), he must also be wise, and courage thus becomes a form of knowledge. The discussion concludes aporetically on the need to define knowledge from this beginning.

An odd feature of the dialogue is the repeated mention of Damon.[34] Laches has introduced Nicias to Damon not only as a music teacher but as the best sort of companion for young men; again, at the end of the dialogue, the wisdom of Damon is appealed to ironically as a source from

33. *Helen* (13) and (14).
34. 180d; 197d; 200a–b.

which to find a solution for the argument. The connection of Damon with the training of character through music, as noted earlier, is attested in fragment B 7,[35] and the bizarre transformation of fighting in armor into an enlightened form of soul treatment is plausibly directed at Damon's alleged skills. Certainly the dialogue's equation of character with musical modalities[36] must be so taken. Indeed, that the practice of soul therapy of a medical or Sophistic nature is in question is here made almost explicit by the exchange from 185b to 185e: the question at hand is to find the person who is τεχνικώτατος with respect to a contest, and this choice requires one to know the real end for which training is intended. If the subject at hand is not really fighting in armor but the ψυχαί of the boys who are to be trained, as Socrates alleges, then it is necessary to consider (185e) whether one of those engaged in the discussion is technically skilled in therapy of the soul (τεχνικώτατος περὶ ψυχῆς θεραπείαν). But most of all, the dialogue poses a clear and deliberate revaluation of ψυχή by juxtaposing one speaker, Laches, who is portrayed as incapable of understanding not only ψυχή but ἀγαθός and ἀρετή except in the traditional military way, to others, Socrates and Nicias, who divert these traditional meanings to ones charged with innovative moral value. This is exceptionally obvious at 185e, just quoted, where ψυχή is gratuitously introduced by Socrates, as it is elsewhere,[37] but in effect the whole dialogue supports this view. Laches' use of καρτερία τῆς ψυχῆς, moreover, recalls ταλαιπωρία τῇ ψυχῇ used in Airs, Waters, Places and by Strepsiades at Clouds 415, as well as ἐγκράτεια in the soul at Memorabilia 1.5.4−5. Finally, it may be suggested, if only suggested, that the references to mode of life (ζῇ / βίον βεβίωκεν) toward which, it is said, Socrates tries to direct every discussion, are to be seen as oblique allusions to the notion of ψυχή along the lines of Crito 48b.

LYSIS, HIPPIAS MAJOR, HIPPIAS MINOR

ψυχή appears twice in Lysis with simple reference to the duality of σῶμα and ψυχή (218c and 220c); both times it is used in a way reminiscent of Xenophon as that which is neither good nor bad in itself. If the comparison with Xenophon is valid, these phrases therefore bear overtones of the psychosomatic ψυχή. At 221e love is said to be for one's deficiencies,

35. Cf. also B 4, in which playing the lyre advances one in courage, moderation, and justice; B 6, in which music creates like moods in the soul; A 8 (from Galen), in which different modalities are used to treat drunkenness and madness.

36. 188b; 193d−e.

37. Cf. Prt. 313a.

hence for things of one's own. The lovers are οἰκεῖοι φύσει, and so the lover must belong to the beloved in soul or in some aspect of soul (κατὰ τὴν ψυχὴν ἢ κατά τι τῆς ψυχῆς ἦθος ἢ τρόπος ἢ εἶδος), usages at least superficially recalling the erotic ψυχή of lyric poetry and fifth-century tragedy but at the same time looking to the identification of ψυχή with φύσις—a connotation more significant than that of the erotic ψυχή. At *Hippias Major* (296d) Socrates gratuitously incorporates ψυχή into his speech, asking whether the previous argument was that which "our ψυχή wished to say." This odd use of ψυχή, neither anticipated nor followed by any explanatory context, has no real parallel in early Plato and could therefore be construed as evidence to be added to the argument against the authenticity of the dialogue. *Hippias Minor*, by contrast, clearly exploits the use of ψυχή, but in a sequence of bizarre contexts that may epitomize somewhat the eclecticism with which Plato treats the meaning of ψυχή in the early dialogues. At issue (371e) is the superiority of voluntary error to involuntary. Socrates is drawn by the arguments for voluntary error but suspects he may be wrong (372d–e). Describing his ignorance metaphorically as a medical seizure (καταβολή 372e), he begs his interlocutors, Hippias and Eudicus, not to begrudge curing his soul (μὴ φθονήσῃς ἰάσασθαι τὴν ψυχήν). It will do him more good to cure his soul of ignorance than his body of disease. When the argument resumes, Socrates forces admission that the better practitioner of any bodily skill is the one who can err voluntarily (373c–374b), that the better bodily quality or part is that which can err voluntarily (374b–374e), that the better instruments are those which allow their users to err voluntarily; these include rudder, bow, lyre, flutes, and a horse with the sort of ψυχή by which one might willingly ride badly (375a). Last, Socrates asks whether it is not preferable in the case of an archer to have a ψυχή that voluntarily misses the mark than one that does so involuntarily. The ψυχή that errs voluntarily, he concludes, will therefore be better—in medicine, music, and in all the arts and sciences (374b–c)—and we should prefer to have slaves with such ψυχαί. If we wish, then, to have our own ψυχή as well off as possible, we should want it to do evil voluntarily rather than involuntarily (375c–d). Since the more power and wisdom a soul has the more just it is, it follows that the voluntary performance of shameful acts is within the province of the good man, and the involuntary within that of the bad man (375d–376b).

These passages need little comment. Socrates' desire to cure the soul of ignorance rather than the body of disease is in keeping with other dialogues.[38] Here it serves to introduce obliquely the subject of ψυχή by

38. *Chrm.* 155d.

questioning the effect of the dialogue on the ψυχαί of the listeners, a point that recalls, for example, the opening scene of the *Protagoras* (312c). The introduction of the horse as an instrument of voluntary or involuntary error according to the nature of its ψυχή is notable for giving ψυχή to animals as well as humans, and this solecism, if taken seriously, threatens once again to raise the issue of the congruency of the animative and cognitive powers of ψυχή. That this is an arbitrary, and perhaps satiric, use of ψυχή (based perhaps on the popular use of ψυχή as 'spirit' or 'courage'), in keeping with the arrogant use of fallacy in the argument itself, is borne out by Socrates' attribution of skill in archery to the ψυχή. Attributing this power to the ψυχή is truly odd, unlike anything in the history of the word, or anything else in Plato, and the abrupt transition from technical to moral knowledge both focused on ψυχή illustrates in a rough and forthright way the same kind of idiosyncratic revaluation of ψυχή from nonmoral to moral use that appears in *Laches*. But here, of course, the antecedent nonmoral use is wholly invented, not traditional.

ALCIBIADES I, CHARMIDES

Perhaps the most precise example of Platonic revaluation is offered by the passage in *Alcibiades I*,[39] beginning at 129e, that Burnet took as fundamental for the definition of ψυχή in Plato. As user and that which is used differ, so the man himself must be other than his body, for he uses and rules the body. Man must therefore be either soul, body, or both. But if body does not rule itself it is unlikely to share in the rule of the man; hence man is either nothing or nothing other than ψυχή (μηδὲν ἄλλο τὸν ἄνθρωπον ἢ ψυχήν). This assertion, which must have startled the neophyte Platonist for whom, possibly, *Alcibiades I* is intended, almost certainly draws on medical antecedents and perhaps specifically on the arguments discounted in *Nature of Man*, a text that may belong in part to the fifth century.[40] Much like the author of *Ancient Medicine*, the writer of this text first disagrees with those natural philosophers who say that man is air, fire, water, or earth, or anything else that is not manifest in man (οὔτε γὰρ τὸ πάμπαν ἠέρα λέγω τὸν ἄνθρωπον εἶναι, οὔτε πῦρ, οὔτε ὕδωρ, οὔτε γῆν οὔτ' ἄλλο οὐδὲν ὅ τι μὴ φανερόν ἐστιν ἐνεὸν ἐν τῷ ἀνθρώπῳ),[41] and then turns to physicians, dismissing those who say that a man is blood, bile, or phlegm (ὡς ὤνθρωπος αἷμα ἐστιν)[42] in

---

39. The question of authenticity is a problem. No decisive answer is possible. Cf. Guthrie (1975), p. 169, and Lesky (1966), p. 512.

40. Jones, *Hippocrates* vol. 4, pp. xxvi ff.

41. *Nature of Man* 1.

42. *Nature of Man* 2.

favor of those who acknowledge that man is a mixture of constituents. These mistakes arise from conclusions drawn in the observation of death; when they see someone die from bleeding, certain doctors conclude that blood is the ψυχή in man.[43] Thus a medical context in which "man is the ψυχή" and ψυχή is, in turn, blood or one of the other humors, is transformed in *Alcibiades* I into the highly dualistic and unprecedented formulation "man is nothing other than ψυχή." If this has in fact happened and if the dialogue is genuine and early, nothing could indicate more clearly that Plato intends to separate himself from medical interest in the ψυχή as the 'life-force' that animates the body.

A similar medical setting is found in what might well be regarded from the point of view taken here as the most important passage in the early dialogues for understanding the Socratic history of the soul, namely, *Charmides* 155d and following, in which Socrates proposes to cure Charmides of a headache by applying the wisdom of Zalmoxis. Socrates is alleged to know the cure for headache (155d), which consists of a certain leaf accompanied by the use of an ἐπῳδή. The charm cannot cure only the head (156b) but must be used as physicians ordinarily use cures. For physicians understand that the eyes cannot be treated apart from the head, nor the head apart from the body as a whole. Thus it is essential to treat and heal the part together with the whole (156c). Socrates' charm, we are told, was learned from one of the Thracian physicians taught by Zalmoxis,[44] who are sometimes said to be able to confer immortality (156d). But this engaging allusion to the ψυχή that survives at death is not followed up; we are told instead that Zalmoxis believes the relationship of eye to head and head to body applies as well to body and soul. Greek physicians fail in healing the body because they do not understand the real nature of the whole (that is, body and soul), and despite their efforts they treat only the part (that is, body). Since all good and evil in the body and in the man as a whole arises from the soul, according to Zalmoxis, the soul must therefore be treated first (157a), and this treatment will consist of certain charms composed of καλοὶ λόγοι through which the soul is to gain σωφροσύνη, and

43. *Nature of Man* 6.

44. The Zalmoxis tradition is reexamined in Burkert (1972), pp. 157ff., who shows the intimate connections with shamanism and the confusion with the Pythagorean legend. Socrates' transformation of this figure into a physician of souls shows as much as any Platonic text the deliberate use to which historical antecedents of ψυχή can be put. For the Greek of the fourth century this passage entails contextual associations with both the immortal ψυχή of Pythagorean legend and the ψυχή as an object of medical therapy. When these have, in effect, canceled each other, Socrates introduces the notion of ψυχή as the moral self.

the head and body health. Socrates is therefore instructed not to apply the headache cure until he has first treated the soul with this charm (157b).

The levels of reference in this passage need some sorting out. At the lowest level, I assume, are those doctors who actually do what Socrates says they do, that is, treat the parts of the body by treating the body as a whole. But there are also close parallels between the doctrine of soul and body set out here and the doctrines of the fifth-century texts I have described above as having a psychosomatic notion of ψυχή, in particular the recommended use of ἐπῳδαί in *Helen* and the apparent injunction to make health the object of soul therapy in Democritus B 234 and B 187. What is attributed to Zalmoxis—whose name appears here, one suspects, because as a Pythagorean shaman he can be taken to unify medicine with some transcendental interest in the ψυχή—is, on the other hand, almost certainly a Platonic invention, not a historical theory. At issue then is the purpose of the doctrine of this "Zalmoxis." In his reading of the passage in its immediate context Robinson proposes that Plato is attempting to describe the relationship of soul and body as an entailment in which, like the relationship of eye to head, body is a part of soul, while soul can claim to be in some sense the whole man. But this rather extreme statement of soul doctrine appears nowhere else in Plato, apart from the passing reference in *Alcibiades* I. And it seems unlikely that Plato would risk or adulterate the doctrine of the soul, already in *Charmides* and *Laches* a means by which mankind is able to participate in moral absolutes, for pragmatic or explicit medical specifics of this kind. It is important, therefore, to see that, whatever else Plato may intend, the passage as it stands offers a profound rebuttal to any naive psychosomaticism centering on the ψυχή. Plato, Zalmoxis, and the Thracian physicians argue that the body cannot be treated without the soul, but in their scheme, as opposed to that of genuine psychosomatic doctrine, the soul matters primarily because it is the locus of generalized good and evil. To such physicians, therefore, the health of the body cannot really be the object of soul therapy but merely an epiphenomenon accompanying the health of the soul, which is a good in its own right, and since all else depends upon it, the only good with which we need concern ourselves.

It is unnecessary to discount entirely the positive doctrine of entailment that Socrates advocates in *Charmides*. As in *Apology* and *Crito*, there may well be in the remarkable monism of body and soul that Socrates proposes another early attempt to anticipate the reconciliation of the life-soul and the psychological soul. At the same time, however, the close tie to fifth-century antecedents more genuinely or directly concerned with the soul's effect on health, not to mention the alleged authority of the revered Zalmoxis, cannot fail to give the argument as a whole an ironic quality. It is likely, I think, that Socrates has assumed the mantle of pragmatic soul science here, as he assumes the posture of a teacher of physical courage in *Laches*, not to advocate such things but to transform them by revising the notion of ψυχή on which they depend. Although the argument here is more abstract, as in *Laches* the process of defining the soul is again not simply the assertion of positive doctrines but the unraveling of doctrines, definitions, and usages of the past. It may therefore be worth recalling here, for a candid glimpse into this method of explication, Socrates' statement at *Protagoras* 343c (a statement that applies more aptly to Socrates' treatment of Simonides than to Simonides' treatment of Pittacus) that Simonides had incorporated the saying χαλεπὸν ἐσθλὸν ἔμμεναι into his poem so as "craftily to abuse it" (ἐπιβουλεύων κολοῦσαι). That Plato has himself made comparable use of the wisdom of Zalmoxis seems more than plausible.

PROTAGORAS

Protagoras B 11 tells us, unfortunately in a textually questionable fragment, that education "takes root in the soul." The main sequence of references to ψυχή in the dialogue may recall, therefore, Protagorean education of the soul, but again the context in question seems akin to the psychosomatic soul therapy of Gorgias and the other late fifth-century sources we have identified with this use of ψυχή. Here, too, irony and stylistic problems are not lacking. At 312c Hippocrates is to submit his ψυχή to a sophist for treatment (θεραπεῦσαι), not knowing what a sophist is. He does not know (313a) at what hazard he is risking his ψυχή, a pun on 'life' that forms the basis, perhaps, at the end of the dialogue for a connection of βίος and ψυχή: at 356d Socrates asserts that if to be well off depends on knowledge of relative sizes, the art of measurement would be the σωτηρία τοῦ βίου by bringing the soul into peaceful conformity with truth—a point repeated four times (356e [twice], 357a [twice]). Again this can be thought to imply, along with *Crito* and the other references above in which βίος and ψυχή are juxtaposed, an allusion to the potential identity of the biological and cognitive souls. At 313a the soul is more important than the body, the source of good and evil in all matters concerning the man; the sophist is (313c) a merchant in the wares by which the soul is nurtured; sophists are ready to sell anything although they are as ignorant as their buyers about what is good and bad, unless one of them happens to be a doctor περὶ τὴν ψυχήν, like the doctor or trainer of the body. Unlike someone who purchases food that he can carry away and reconsider, the man who listens to a sophist must of necessity take the doctrine into the ψυχή itself, and having learned it depart harmed or helped, a statement very much in line with the Protagorean fragment on education. In the great speech of Protagoras (325c–326c) the sophist is made to assert that all men take care for the virtue of their sons and that all are therefore teachers of ἀρετή. If the child learns what is just and unjust, well and good; if not, the parent works on him as one tries to straighten a bent piece of wood. Pupils learn the compositions of good poets and are exposed to the encomia of noble ancestors; their instructors in music give them training beneficial to ἀρετή, causing the right rhythms and scales to take hold in their souls in order that they may become good at words and deeds. They are trained in body so that the body will be able to serve the διάνοια and so that they may not be forced by the body to act the part of a coward. Thus, at 351b, Protagoras is able to ascribe courage to φύσις and to the εὐτροφία τῶν ψυχῶν.

Every occurrence of ψυχή in *Protagoras* seems connected, therefore, to the claims of psychosomatic soul therapy and training, and Socrates treats Protagoras' interest in ψυχή with considerable regard. The point that all such discussions of ψυχή lead to, e.g., in *Charmides* and, shortly, in *Gorgias*, namely that the soul itself must acquire moral knowledge and thus become self-regulating, is made here without direct reference to ψυχή but with motifs that could come directly from the Gorgianic *Helen*. Thus Protagoras is asked (352b) to talk about ἐπιστήμη. Does he share the common view that it is not "strong or guiding" but that even those who have it are ruled by something else—θυμός, ἡδονή, λύπη, ἔρως, φόβος? The common opinion of knowledge, it is said, is the opinion held of slaves: knowledge can be dragged about by any other thing. To this, *Helen* (16) may be compared.

EUTHYDEMUS

In the main the Platonic uses of ψυχή so far can be seen as (1) revaluations of popular ideas, and (2) attempts to correct more technical notions of soul therapy. Since both antecedents depend on a strong sense of reference to the animative 'life-force', Plato's purposes are served by suppressing as much as possible reference to the biological connotations of ψυχή. In contrast to this pattern, the three occurrences of ψυχή in *Euthydemus* are quite extraordinary and point clearly to the middle dialogues. On the assumption that serious doctrines underlie the eristic exchanges,[45] it is clear

45. Guthrie (1975), pp. 278ff.

that the epistemology of *Meno* is anticipated in the dialogue, as well as the attempt in *Phaedo* to reconcile the animative and cognitive functions of soul. Euthydemus attempts to force Socrates into the admission that if he knows something he must know everything, and since he "always knows" (296d) he must have known all things before his own birth and before heaven and earth came into being. Socrates attempts to resist these ludicrous questions by gratuitously qualifying his answer to the question whether "he knows with something" or "not with something"—he must answer yes or no for the eristic to succeed—by saying that he knows whatever he knows by means of his ψυχή. If this juxtaposition of question and answer is taken seriously, Socrates can be said to have knowledge based on prior existence and to have such knowledge through the agency of his ψυχή, an argument he will himself demonstrate for the slave boy in *Meno*. The next reference occurs at 302b, where Socrates is forced to say that animals (ζῷα) have life (ψυχή), and then (302d–e), that because gods have ψυχή gods must be animals. I take this to refer, on the side of Socrates at least, to the divinity of the soul and thus to the fact that it is proper for immortal gods to possess soul. Hence there is here again a rough juxtaposition of the lower and higher functions of ψυχή, in this case 'life' contrasted with 'soul' in the sense of immortal δαίμων. Finally, ψυχή occurs in a startling exchange between Dionysiodorus and Socrates at 287d. Dionysiodorus asks whether things that 'mean' (τὰ νοοῦντα) have life (ψυχὴν ἔχοντα) when they do so and whether the same case can be made for things that are ἄψυχα. Socrates limits 'meaning' (or 'thinking' in Dionysiodorus' eristic) to things in possession of ψυχή. Since inanimate phrases cannot have ψυχή, Socrates is said to be in the wrong for asking what the phrase of Dionysiodorus meant. There is, obviously, in this exchange a decisive pun on the division of animative and cognitive aspects of ψυχή. In *Timaeus* Plato will argue that whatever is biologically ἔμψυχον has a share of intelligence and cognition.[46]

MENEXENUS, GORGIAS

Menexenus 235a purports to show Socrates introducing the funeral speech of Aspasia by praising the skill of orators who enchant the souls of their listeners (γοητεύουσιν ἡμῶν τὰς ψυχάς), a phrase that recalls the description of verbal ἐπῳδαί in *Charmides* and, once again, the Gorgianic *Helen*. Socrates goes on to say that the orator's voice so rang in his ears that he can

46. Above, n. 26.

but barely recall himself (ἀναμιμνήσκομαι ἐμαυτοῦ) on the fourth or fifth day afterward from the fantasy that he now lives among those who dwell on the Islands of the Blest (235b–c). In his choice of words Socrates plays loosely with both afterlife and ecstatic notions of ψυχή, but he also seems to respond to the specific psychosomatic claims for the effect of rhetoric on the soul alleged by Gorgias. Also striking is the resemblance of the idea of self-oblivion to the opening lines of the *Apology* (... ὀλίγου ἐμαυτοῦ ἐπαλαθόμην) and to the closing lines of *Crito*, where, at the end of the powerful suasion spoken by the personified Laws, Socrates claims that the sound of their words buzz in his ears as loudly as the sound of flutes in the ears of the Corybantes. Both passages may be oblique references to the ecstasy inherent in the effect of words on the ψυχή and, particularly in the case of *Crito*, suggest a greater interest in the soul in the trial dialogues than the references to ψυχή alone indicate.

But the chief importance of the *Menexenus* here is as an introduction to *Gorgias*, to which it is plausibly aligned in date as well as subject matter.[47] There can be no question that the use of ψυχή in *Gorgias* incorporates the Gorgianic attitude toward ψυχή and perhaps rests on actual knowledge of the *Helen*. When Socrates proposes (504b) to introduce κόσμος into the soul he uses, in κόσμος, a word common to Pythagorean theories of the natural world—in keeping, I assume, with the Pythagorean eschatology of the dialogue—and to the medical notion of health as a mixture of bodily constituents. This may also recall, however, the striking use of κόσμος as the first word of the Gorgianic *Helen*, where it denotes a quality able to unify the proper virtues of city, body, soul, and speech. That the virtue of soul in the *Helen* is wisdom, however Gorgias intends the relationship to be understood, might well have attracted Plato's attention. In any case the connection of κόσμος and ψυχή in the *Helen* stands as a direct antecedent to the view of the soul in *Gorgias*.[48] This connection is shown explicitly at 501b and following, where, in order to develop the contrast of cookery and medicine with rhetoric and justice, Socrates asks whether there are not περὶ τὴν ψυχήν certain other πραγματεῖαι—some τεχνικαί, others merely devoted to gross forms of self-indulgence—like medicine and cookery with respect to the body. Such indulgent treatments of the soul can aim at gratifying souls collectively rather than singly (501d), a point that recalls the sense of impersonality associated with the psychosomatic ψυχή in Xenophon. These treatments

47. Guthrie (1975), p. 313.
48. Guthrie (1975), p. 300.

(ἐπιτηδεύσεις) aimed at simple gratification rather than improvement are
then instanced by flute playing, harp playing, dramatic choruses, and
dithyrambs—a group of examples that leads forward to the practice of
rhetoric itself in the dialogue, and backward to the use of irrational ἐπῳδαί
in contexts like that of the *Helen*. Since it is the tone of the passage, not just
its ideas, that matter, I will quote it in full:

> I said that in my opinion cookery is not an art [τέχνη] but a matter of
> experience [ἐμπειρία], whereas medicine is an art, and considers the
> nature of the person it treats [θεραπεύει] and the reason for what it
> does, and has an account to give of each of these things. Cookery
> turns to the pleasure with which its whole care [θεραπεία] is con-
> cerned, doing so entirely without art [ἀτέχνως], considering neither
> the nature nor cause of pleasure, completely without reason [ἀλόγως],
> so to speak, measuring nothing, trusting to habit and experience for
> mere recollection of what customarily happens, and so furnishes its
> pleasures. Consider, then, whether this is satisfactorily said, and
> whether there are not certain other occupations [πραγματεῖαι] con-
> cerning the *soul*, some [like medicine] scientific [τεχνικαί], having
> forethought of some sort for what is best for the soul, and others [like
> cookery] that neglect this, considering here too as before only the
> pleasure of the soul and how to get it for her. These occupations are
> not concerned to know which pleasure is better and which worse,
> caring for nothing other than the fact of gratification. I think there
> are such occupations, Callicles, and I say this is flattery both in the case
> of the body and of the soul and of anything else whose pleasure one
> serves without concern for the better and the worse. [501a–c]

This passage is, I believe, crucial. If the background to the doctrine of
soul in *Gorgias* is as specific as this text implies, and not simply the general
notion of soul as a moral and cognitive principle suggested by Robinson,[49]
it can be argued that the dialogue exhibits as decisive a movement in the
development of the Platonic doctrine of soul as do the *Meno* and *Phaedo*,
although one that is less overt. The analogy between the health of the body
and the health of the soul, repeated throughout the earlier dialogues, is
again the central problem, but it now brought to a resolution. The essential
point is that whether or not Socrates believes the knowledge of right and
wrong—here as in *Charmides* the only thing that can cure the soul—to be a

---

49. Robinson, p. 20.

τέχνη and whether or not he believes that he himself possesses it as an expert, that knowledge is not to be regarded as a τέχνη of any ordinary sort. Here, explicitly, as he has implied already in the earlier dialogue, the analogy of medicine with soul therapy works only if medicine is purged of all preoccupation with means and ἐμπειρία as opposed to ends and a theory of the whole. This view Socrates attributes directly to Hippocrates, of course, at *Phaedrus* 270c (the argument that it is not possible to know the nature of the body without knowing the nature of τὸ ὅλον), where, whatever the underlying Hippocratic doctrine really was, it is used once again to link the soul and its treatment to knowledge of reality, not to appearance or practical suasion. That Socrates' report of Hippocratic theory has been distorted or purified, so to speak, in order to make the analogy work in this way, and so too has been distorted in the earlier uses of the analogy, seems not impossible, and one might suggest this as a somewhat unorthodox approach to the debate over the meaning of τὸ ὅλον in *Phaedrus*.[50] This conclusion at least is one that might be drawn from *Ancient Medicine* 20, the canonical passage for the Hippocratic theory of medical science. Here the writer rejects, in a polemical fashion, the demand that physicians gain knowledge about the ultimate nature of man through philosophy and advocates that they gain knowledge about "what man is" from the practice of medicine:

> This is what a doctor must know—really know—if he is going to do his duties, what a man is with respect to foods and drinks and to other habits, and what will happen to each from each thing, not simply that cheese is bad and gives pain in excess, but what pain and why and what part of the man is disturbed.

The medical art described here obviously falls somewhere between the grounding in absolute principle that Plato calls for in *Gorgias* and the reliance on ἐμπειρία that he loathes. But the pragmatism of *Ancient Medicine* is evident enough to suggest that in the characterization of medicine in *Gorgias* as an exemplary τέχνη for the treatment of the soul, it is medicine that is being likened to the new "Socratic" form of soul therapy as much as soul therapy is to medicine.

Accurate or not, Socrates' view of medicine forms a basis for claiming that the relationship of soul and body is now at last, in this dialogue, decisively transformed as against the fifth century and that the *Gorgias* is, in

---

50. See Cherniss (1959), n. 700, for a summary of opinions.

terms of its relationship to the earlier use of ψυχή, much more than simply a
transitional text of some kind between a more or less erratic mixture of
early statements on ψυχή in Plato and the tripartite scheme of the *Republic*.
As I have argued, the doctrine of soul subscribed to by Gorgias himself in
the *Helen*, and by whatever other adherents there were to similar psychosomatic ideas, stressed a productive, therapeutic analogy between soul and
body such that ψυχή—and thus bodily behavior, social character, and even
health—could be treated by an external skill or craft analogous to medicine, itself understood as an empirically founded τέχνη. In Plato this
pragmatic analogy is, as early as *Charmides*, moralized beyond recognition,
with the result that the analogy becomes purely an abstract one, while
those things that were once regarded as practical treatments for the psychosomatic soul are relegated to the role of cookery in treating the body. The
arguments of *Gorgias* by which this design is carried out (above and
463e–480a) put a decisive end to any practical interest in real psychosomatic or pragmatic use of the soul-body analogy at the same time that they
exploit and embellish the comparison with medicine as a tool for inquiry
into more abstract ideas of soul.

    This careful revaluation of the analogy of soul to body in *Gorgias*, I
believe, can be claimed as the first unmistakable antithesis in Plato of soul as
master and body as subject. But the main point of interest is that the
antithesis has come about not by separating soul and body on religious or
ontological grounds—as we expect and find, for example, in the *Phaedo*—
but by constructing an extended discussion which assumes, in contrast to
earlier ideas, that body and soul are served by utterly different therapies,
not by a common, or nearly common, therapy addressed to a psychosomatic mixture of body and soul. Between the therapy of body and the
therapy of soul there is no longer a sense of practical connection, but in
Gorgias, as already anticipated in *Charmides*, an analogy of merely theore-
tical and heuristic value. Moreover, Plato now exploits the medical
exemplar to the full by the extraordinary new way in which he analogizes
the very nature of soul to body. As is true when he compares therapies,
Plato's success in creating an abstract analogy again entails criticism of the
pragmatic and empirical approach of the *Helen*. For, although external
discipline may still benefit the soul (just as the verbal devices of Gorgias can
induce, psychosomatically, changes in the soul of Helen), it is the soul's
capacity for *self*-regulation, through its own achievement of internal
regularity and order, that gives it the capacity to achieve σωφροσύνη, and
this self-regulation is compared at once to the regularity supposed for the
body's constituent parts by scientific medicine.

"What is the name given to that which derives from order and regularity [ἐκ τῆς τάξεώς τε καὶ τοῦ κόσμου] in the body?"

"Health and strength, probably."

"And in the soul, for that which derives from order and regularity?"

[504b–c]

The soul's condition is no longer dependent on chance or external influence (506d), as in *Helen*, but on its inherent possession of proper or improper order, that is, we can assume, on the relationship between reason and whatever else the soul may contain:

"But the virtue of each thing—tool or body or soul or any living thing—does not come to be at random but by order and rightness and art, which is granted for each of them ..."

"Then the order [κόσμος] in a thing that is proper to it [ὁ ἑκάστου οἰκεῖος] makes good each of the things that are?"

"Yes."

"And so a soul that has an order of its own [κόσμον ... τὸν ἑαυτῆς] is better than one which is not ordered?"

In contrast to the psychosomatic theory of soul, it follows at once that the soul that is a self-regulating balance of constituents can never be as wholly and helplessly vulnerable to external forces acting upon it as the soul portrayed in the doctrine of Gorgias the sophist, which assumed, if we can judge from *Helen*, a far less enlightened notion of medical practice.

I do not wish to suggest that this is why Plato gives us in *Gorgias* the first real or detailed view of the conscious soul as something able to approximate the notion of "everything mental,"[51] and with it the first detailed description of the afterlife soul as the survival of this "mental" yet personal entity. Obviously these doctrines are the result of the development of, or are to be coordinated with the emergence of (depending on one's view of the dialogues), the ontology of the Forms. But the *Gorgias* seems to occupy a crucial place in Plato's description of the soul, for it establishes decisively the essential congruity of the soul with the individual human personality, a belief that will be threatened at once by the demonstration of prior cognition based on the universal knowledge of mathematics in *Meno* and by the explicit incorporation at last into the Platonic soul of the impersonal 'life' functions in *Phaedo*. Before undertaking these arduous

51. Crombie, p. 301.

discussions, however, Plato gives us in the *Gorgias* a dialogue in which both
the psychosomatic soul of the fifth-century doctors and sophists, and the
afterlife soul of the Orphics and Pythagoreans, are fused and transformed
into an entity far more personal and comprehensive than any of its
predecessors. The relatively volatile psychosomatic ψυχή becomes, by a
truly subtle analogy with scientific medicine and the body, self-regulating,
hierarchical, and responsive to moral discipline in a wholly self-reliant
way. Obviously this analogy has antecedents in the fifth century—in
Democritus' stable atoms,[52] in the remarkably prescient doctrines of
Heraclitus, and to a degree in any medically inspired idea of soul therapy—
but here at last it has worked so deeply and centrally into the doctrine of its
advocate that of itself it defines a separate order of existence. The κόσμος
Socrates now calls for in the ψυχή is plainly not one that any physical entity
could hope to achieve, however much the scheme is based on medical
notions of body. In turn, the afterlife soul, if I may draw summarily upon
the splendid suggestion of Halbwachs,[53] reaches the same goal, so to speak,
by passing from an Orphic or Pythagorean model into what is, in the
great myth that closes the dialogue, a beautiful and unexpected re-creation
of the Homeric 'shade'. No longer, however, is this 'shade' the corporeal
shade of Homer but a new "psychic" shade—the survival of "everything
mental," in a word—for which there is no real antecedent in Greek
thought, except perhaps the soul as a balance of reason and desire, created
by analogy to the Hippocratic theory of humors, which Plato himself has
just introduced in the preceding arguments of the *Gorgias*.

I therefore view the doctrine of soul in the *Gorgias* as equal in
importance to the political and rhetorical themes of the dialogue, for it
furnishes an essential base on which all the later soul theory of Plato rests.
There is never a clear resolution of the contradictions between personal and
impersonal views of the soul in Plato, despite the attempts to reach such a
resolution in the later dialogues. The chief accomplishment of the *Gorgias*,
then, is to establish unequivocally, before these problems are fully attacked,
the identity of soul as a comprehensive personal self and to use that doctrine
as a way of clearing the air of what are by comparison the shallow and
morally unacceptable versions of both the animative and afterlife soul that
Plato has inherited from others. Viewed against these antecedents, therefore, the *Gorgias* can be seen as a turning point in the development and
exposition of Plato's doctrine of the soul.

52. Vlastos (1945), pp. 584–85.
53. Halbwachs, p. 529.

Conclusion

Despite the erratic quality of the evidence on which judgment must be based and the inherent difficulty of analyzing a culturally bound term like ψυχή, two specific conclusions are suggested by this study.

(1) The development of ψυχή as a psychological agent in popular usage after Homer does not seem to be owed to the introduction into Greece of new conceptions of the afterlife or to the development of some new sense of psychological self-conception after Homer. Rather, from the beginning, ψυχή is a word whose psychological qualities depend on its ability to be felt as a 'life-force' word, much like θυμός, ἦτορ, κῆρ, and μένος in Homer. If a conclusion can be drawn on the basis of the literary evidence, the absence of ψυχή from psychological contexts in Homer is possibly a consequence of the Homeric preoccupation with the ψυχή as 'shade'; conversely, the appearance of ψυχή in such contexts elsewhere can be seen as a result of the reduced importance accorded to the ψυχή as 'shade' outside the Homeric tradition. Whether or not this explanation is correct, it is clear that ψυχή does not become a psychological agent after Homer because of any specific linguistic analogy or, on the other hand, because of its ability to assimilate ideas of a religious or philosophical character. In late tragedy ψυχή succeeds as a psychological agent at the expense of the other 'soul' words by its capacity to preserve fully the psychosomatic connotations of the archaic 'life-force', and it seems likely that this success is to be coordinated mainly with the complete elimination of other 'life-force' words from contexts in which they denote the physical 'life' of the man that is lost at death. Although ψυχή appears with greater frequency in late tragedy, most uses of the word to the end of the fifth century remain, therefore, traditional. It is probably this traditional and even archaizing quality, suitable to tragedy, that prevents ψυχή from

having an important role in Herodotus and Thucydides and accounts for its apparent decline, along with the other Homeric 'soul' words, in ordinary speech. Those occurrences of the word in popular usage that can be seen as innovative are plausibly derived not from speculation about something psychological per se but from a more naturalistic view of the psychological concomitants of ψυχή as the physical 'life'.

(2) Outside of popular usage the development of ψυχή is less easily traced. Texts that might offer direct or indirect information about the effect of Pythagorean and Orphic ideas on the use of ψυχή are almost entirely lacking. Perhaps this omission has resulted from the vagaries of textual transmission. Yet the silence of fifth-century witnesses to instances of ψυχή that might reflect subtle coloring by the new doctrines of survival and occult existence is impressive. Naturalistic views of the ψυχή, on the other hand, seem to have been more directly connected to the development of the ψυχή as self. As opposed to direct or explicit interest in the cognitive functions of ψυχή, the most important thread here may well have been the development of an oblique analogy between body and soul by which rationalistic ideas of the body and its φύσις are transferred to the soul. The argument given above can be recapitulated as follows: (a) The contingent relationship in the Presocratics between the ψυχή and "knowing" is treated loosely by Aristotle as a series of doctrines in which the soul is itself that which "knows." (b) Only in Heraclitus do instances of ψυχή appear in which such comprehensive ideas of soul are possible, and these fragments, important as they are for the development of the word, nevertheless depend in large measure on linguistic and ideological features peculiar to Heraclitus. (c) Consistent interest in the moral value of ψυχή and the earliest treatment of ψυχή as the correlative of σῶμα appear in Democritus, Gorgias, and the early medical texts. Here the character of the ψυχή plainly does not derive from the attachment to it of rational powers arising from epistemological speculation or from a growing tendency to separate 'soul' or 'mind' from body. The ψυχή acquires moral and personal connotations because it is regarded as the psychosomatic φύσις of a man, amenable to therapy and doctrines like those furnished by scientific medicine for the body. The goal of such therapy is emphatically the whole man, if not simply health. (d) This sense of ψυχή predominates in Xenophon's account of Socrates and appears with significant frequency as background to the earlier dialogues of Plato. (e) The Platonic use of ψυχή in the earlier dialogues involves the moralization and revaluation of many traditional contexts of ψυχή, but the decisive early use is here taken to be moralization of the psychosomatic ψυχή of fifth-century medical and sophistic soul

therapy. In the *Charmides*, first, and then in the *Gorgias*, Plato treats the analogy of soul and body in such a way as to destroy any practical psychosomatic connection between soul and body and to re-create the therapy of the soul—and thus the soul itself—in the image of an idealized form of medical theory. In doing so Plato brings about, perhaps, the first genuine separation of ψυχή and body in Greek thought, and this achievement can be coordinated with the appearance in the *Gorgias*, for the first time, of a fully realized psychological version of the Pythagorean soul.

Both of these conclusions differ markedly from Burnet's assertion of the Socratic "invention" of the idea of the soul. The Platonic use of ψυχή in the early dialogues is in fact radically at odds with traditional usages, and Plato himself repeatedly makes us aware of this. It is also true, however, that by the late fifth century an important confluence was beginning to be formed between ψυχή as the archaic 'life-force' with its traditional psychological characteristics and ψυχή as a naturalistic 'life-force' whose psychological behavior could be rationally predicted and controlled. On the whole the literary evidence shows that by the time of Socrates this merger had not yet gained sufficient currency in popular usage to affect the language of poetry. Yet it must have been constantly at hand in the oral speech of late fifth-century Athens, and as such constituted a significant antecedent to the Socratic doctrine of the soul.

Bibliography

INDICES

Allen, J. T., and Italie, G. *A Concordance to Euripides*. Berkeley, 1954.

Diels, H. *Die Fragmente der Vorsokratiker*, Edited by W. Kranz. 12th ed. Dublin, 1967.

Dittenberger, W. *Sylloge Inscriptionum Graecarum*. 3d ed. vol. 4. Leipzig, 1924.

Ebeling, H. *Lexicon Homericum*. Leipzig, 1885.

Ellendt, F. *Lexicon Sophocleum*. Hildesheim, 1965.

Fatouros, G. *Index Verborum zur frühgriechischen Lyrik*. Heidelberg, 1966.

Forman, L. L. *Index Andocideus, Lycurgeus, Dinarcheus*. Oxford, 1898.

Holmes, D. H. *Index Lysiacus*. Bonn, 1895.

Italie, G. *Index Aeschyleus*. Leiden, 1964.

Jacobi, H. *Comicae Dictionis Index*. Berlin, 1857.

Nauck, A. *Tragicae Dictionis Index Spectans ad Tragicorum Graecorum Fragmenta* Hildesheim, 1962.

Paulson, J. *Index Hesiodeus*. Lund, 1890.

Powell, J. E. *Lexicon to Herodotus*. Cambridge, 1938.

Preuss, S. *Index Isocrateus*. Leipzig, 1904.

Todd, O. J. *Index Aristophaneus*. Hildesheim, 1962.

van Cleef, F. L. *Index Antiphonteus*, Cornell Studies in Classical Philology, vol. 5 Ithaca, 1895.

von Essen, M. H. N. *Index Thucydideus*. Berlin, 1887.

TEXTS

Aeschylus: *Aeschyli Septem Quae Supersunt Tragoediae*. Ed. D. Page. Oxford, 1972.

Antiphon: *Antiphon: Discours Suivis des Fragments d'Antiphon le Sophiste*. Ed. L. Gernet. Paris, 1923.

Aristophanes: *Aristophanis Comoediae*. Ed. F. W. Hall and W. M. Geldart. 2d ed. Oxford, 1906–07.

Aristotle: Aristotle, *De Anima*. Ed. and trans. R. D. Hicks. Amsterdam, 1965. Unaltered reprint of 1907 edition.

Bacchylides: *Bacchylidis Carmina cum Fragmentis*. Ed. B. Snell. 8th ed. Leipzig, 1961.

Comic Fragments: *Comicorum Atticorum Fragmenta*. Ed. T. Kock. Leipzig, 1880–88.

Euripides: *Euripidis Fabulae*. Ed. G. Murray. Oxford, 1902–13.

Herodotus: *Herodoti Historiae*, Ed. C. Hude. 3d ed. Oxford, 1927.

Hesiod: *Hesiod, the Homeric Hymns and Homerica*. Ed. and trans. H. G. Evelyn-White. Cambridge, Mass., 1936.

———. *Fragmenta Hesiodea*. Ed. R. Merkelbach and M. L. West. Oxford, 1967.

Homer: *Homeri Opera*. Ed. D. B. Monro and T. W. Allen. 3d ed. Oxford, 1920, vols. 1 and 2.

———. *Homeri Opera*. Ed. T. W. Allen. 2d ed. Oxford, 1917–19. vols. 3 and 4.

Iamblichus: *De Vita Pythagorica Liber*. Ed. and trans. M. von Albrecht. Zurich, 1963.

Inscriptions: W. Dittenberger. *Sylloge Inscriptionum Graecarum*. 3d ed. Leipzig, 1915–24.

———. E. Schwyzer. *Dialectorum Graecarum Exempla Epigraphica Potiora*. Leipzig, 1923.

Lyric Poets: *Anthologia Lyrica Graeca*. Ed. E. Diehl. Leipzig, 1954.

———. *Poetae Melici Graeci*. Ed. D. L. Page. Oxford, 1967.

———. *Poetarum Lesbiorum Fragmenta*. Ed. E. Lobel and D. Page. Oxford, 1963.

———. *Iambi et Elegi Graeci ante Alexandrum Cantati*. Ed. M. L. West (Oxford, 1971–72).

Lysias: *Lysias: Discours*. Ed. L. Gernet. Paris, 1924–26.

Medical Writers: *Hippocrates*, vol. 1. Ed. W. H. S. Jones. London, 1923.

———. *Hippocrates*, vol. 4. Ed. W. H. S. Jones. Cambridge, Mass., 1959.

Pindar: *Pindari Carmina cum Fragmentis*. Ed. B. Snell. Leipzig, 1955.

Presocratics: H. Diels. *Die Fragmente der Vorsokratiker*. Ed. W. Kranz. 12th ed. Dublin, 1967.

Sophocles: *Sophoclis Fabulae*. Ed. A. C. Pearson. Oxford, 1924.

Thucydides: *Thucydidis Historiae*. Ed. H. S. Jones. Oxford, 1942.

Tragic Fragments: *Tragicorum Graecorum Fragmenta*. Ed. A. Nauck, with Supplement ed. B. Snell (Hildesheim, 1964).

BOOKS AND ARTICLES CITED IN THE NOTES

Adkins, A. W. H. *Merit and Responsibility*. Oxford, 1960.

――――. *From the Many to the One*. London, 1970.

Alt, K. "Zum Satz des Anaximenes über die Seele." *Hermes* 101 (1973): 129–64.

Assmann, M. M. "De Vocabulis Quibus Herodotus in Singulis Operis Sui Partibus Mentem Animumque Significat." *Mnemosyne* 54 (1926): 118–29.

――――. *Mens et Animus*. Amsterdam, 1917.

Barrett, W. S. *Euripides' Hippolytus*. Oxford, 1964.

Bayet, J. "Les Plus Anciennes Conceptions du Psychisme chez les Grecs et chez les Latins." *Critique* 61 (June 1952): 506–21.

Benveniste, E. "Grec ψυχή." *Bulletin de la Société de Linguistique de Paris* 33 (1932): 165–68.

――――. "Expressions indoeuropéenes de l'éternité." *Bulletin de la Société de Linguistique de Paris* (1937): 102–12.

Bickel, E. "Homerischer Seelenglaube: Geschichtliche Grundzüge Menschlicher Seelenvorstellungen." *Schriften der Königsberger Gelehrten Gesellschaft* (1925).

Bluck, R. S. "Plato, Pindar and Metempsychosis." *American Journal of Philology* (1958): 405–14.

Böhme, J. *Die Seele und das Ich im homerischen Epos*. Leipzig, 1929.

Boisacq, E. *Dictionnaire Etymologique de la Langue Grecque*. Heidelberg, 1950.

Boyancé, P. "Remarques sur le papyrus de Derveni." *Revue des Etudes Grecques* 87 (1970): 91–110.

Burkert, W. "Orpheus und die Vorsokratiker. Bemerkungen zum Derveni-Papyrus und zur pythagoreischen Zahlenlehre." *Antike und Abendland* (1968): 93–114.

――――. *Weisheit und Wissenschaft: Studien zu Pythagoras, Philolaus und Platon*. 1962. Quoted in English translation by E. L. Minar, Jr., *Lore and Science in Ancient Pythagoreanism* (revised by the author). Cambridge, Mass., 1972.

Burnet, J. "The Socratic Doctrine of the Soul." *Proceedings of the British Academy* (1916): 235–59.

――――. *Early Greek Philosophy*. 4th ed. London, 1930.

Caratelli, G. P., and Foti, G. "Un sepolcro di Hipponion e un nuovo testo Orphico." *Parola del Passato* (1974): 91–126.

Chantraine, P. *Dictionnaire Etymologique de la Langue Grecque*. Paris, 1968.

――――. *La Formation des Noms en Grec Ancien*. Paris, 1933.

Cherniss, H. *Aristotle's Criticism of Presocratic Philosophy*. Baltimore, 1935.

――――. "The Characteristics and Effects of Presocratic Philosophy." *Journal of the History of Ideas* 12 (1951): 319–45.

Cornford, F. M. "Was the Ionian Philosophy Scientific?" *Studies in Presocratic Philosophy*, vol. 1. London, 1970.

Degani, E. *AIΩN da Omero ad Aristotele*. Padua, 1961.

Détienne, M. *La Notion de Daimon dans le Pythagorisme Ancien*. Paris, 1963.

De Vogel, C. J. *Pythagoras and Early Pythagoreanism*. Assen, 1966.

Dodds, E. R. *The Greeks and the Irrational*. Berkeley, 1951.

Dover, K. J. *Aristophanes' Clouds*. Oxford, 1968.

———. "The Chronology of Antiphon's Speeches." *Classical Quarterly* 44 (1950):44–60.

Edelstein, L. *Ancient Medicine: Selected Papers of Ludwig Edelstein*. Baltimore, 1967.

Entralgo, P. L. *Therapy of the Word in Classical Antiquity*. New Haven, 1970.

Evans-Pritchard, E. E. *Theories of Primitive Religion*. Oxford, 1965.

Farnell, L. R. *Critical Commentary to the Works of Pindar*. Amsterdam, 1961. Reprint of *The Works of Pindar*, vol. 2 (London, 1932).

Fränkel, H. "A Thought Pattern in Heraclitus." *American Journal of Philology* 59 (1938):309–37.

———. *Dichtung und Philosophie des frühen Griechentums*, 2d ed. Munich, 1962.

Freeman, K. *The Presocratic Philosophers: A Companion to Diels*. Oxford, 1946.

Freudenthal, J. *Über die Theologie des Xenophanes*. Breslau, 1886.

Frisk, H. *Griechisches Etymologisches Wörterbuch*. Heidelberg, 1954–70.

Furley, D. J. "The Early History of the Concept of the Soul." *Bulletin of the Institute of Classical Studies, Univ. of London*, no. 3 (1956):1–18.

Gigon, O. *Untersuchungen zu Heraklit*. Leipzig, 1935.

———. *Der Ursprung der griechischen Philosophie*. Basel, 1945.

Gulley, N. *The Philosophy of Socrates*. London, 1968.

Guthrie, W. K. C. *The Greeks and Their Gods*. Boston, 1950.

———. *A History of Greek Philosophy*. 3 vols. Cambridge, 1962, 1965, and 1969.

———. *Orpheus and Greek Religion*. London, 1952.

Halbwachs, M. "La Représentation de l'Ame chez les Grecs." *Revue de Metaphysique et de Morale* 37 (1930):493–534.

Handley, E. W. "Words for 'Soul', 'Heart', and 'Mind' in Aristophanes." *Rheinisches Museum* 99 (1956):205–25.

Harrison, E. L. "Notes on Homeric Psychology." *Phoenix* 14 (1960):63–80.

Havelock, E. A. "The Socratic Self." *Yale Classical Studies* 22 (1972):1–18.

———. *Preface to Plato*. Cambridge, Mass., 1963.

Ingenkamp, H. G. "Inneres Selbst und Lebensträger." *Rheinisches Museum* 118 (1975):48–61.

Jarcho, V. N. "Zum Menschenbild der nachhomerischen Dichtung." *Philologus* 112 (1968):147–72.

Jaeger, W. *Theology of the Early Greek Philosophers*. Oxford, 1947.

Jebb, R. C. *Sophocles: The Plays and Fragments with Critical Notes, Commentary, and Translation into English Prose.* Reprint. Amsterdam, 1962–67.

Joly, R. *Recherches sur le Traité Pseudo-Hippocratique du Régime.* Paris, 1960.

Kahn, C. H. *Anaximander and the Origins of Greek Cosmology.* New York, 1960.

———. "A New Look at Heraclitus." *American Philosophical Quarterly* 1 (1964): 189–203.

———. "Religion and Natural Philosophy in Empedocles' Doctrine of the Soul." *Archiv für Geschichte der Philosophie* 52 (1960): 3–35.

Karakulakov, V. V. "Das Problem der Sprache bei Heraklit." Résumé in *Bibliotheca Classica Orientalis* (1967): 118.

Kirk, G. S. "Heraclitus and Death in Battle." *American Journal of Philology* 70 (1949): 384–93.

———. "Heraclitus' Contribution to the Development of a Language for Philosophy." *Archiv für Begriffsgeschichte* 9 (1964): 73–77.

———. *Heraclitus: The Cosmic Fragments.* Cambridge, 1954.

———. "Natural Change in Heraclitus." *Mind* 60 (1951): 35–42. Reprinted in A. P. D. Mourelatos *The Presocratics.* New York, 1974.

Kirk, G. S., and Raven, J. E. *The Presocratic Philosophers.* Cambridge, 1957.

Krafft, F. *Vergleichende Untersuchungen zu Homer und Hesiod.* Hypomnemata, 6. Göttingen, 1963.

Larock, V. "Les Premières Conceptions Psychologiques des Grecs." *Revue Belge de Philologie et d'Histoire* 9 (1930): 377–406.

Lesky, A. "Psychologie bei Euripides." *Fondation Hardt, Entretiens* 6 (1960): 125–68.

Lloyd, G. E. R. *Polarity and Analogy: Two Types of Argumentation in Early Greek Thought.* Cambridge, 1971.

Long, A. A. "Thinking and Sense Perception in Empedocles: Mysticism or Materialism." *Classical Quarterly* (1966): 256–76.

Long, H. S. *A Study of the Doctrine of Metempsychosis in Greece from Pythagoras to Plato.* Princeton, 1948.

Luria, S. *Zur Frage der materialistischen Begründung der Ethik bei Demokrit.* Deutsche Akademie der Wissenschaften zu Berlin, 44. Berlin, 1964.

Maier, H. *Sokrates, sein Werk und seine geschichtliche Stellung.* Tübingen, 1913.

Mansfield, J. "Heraclitus on the Psychology and Physiology of Sleep and on Rivers." *Mnemosyne* (4th ser.), 20 (1967): 1–29.

Meissner, B. "Mythisches und Rationales in der Psychologie der euripideischen Tragödie." Dissertation, Göttingen, 1951.

Merkelbach, R. "Der Orphische Papyrus von Derveni." *Zeitschrift für Papyrologie und Epigraphik*, vol. 1 (1967), pp. 21–32.

Müller, G. *Sophokles Antigone*. Heidelberg, 1967.

Nehring, A. "Homer's Descriptions of Syncopes." *Classical Philology* 42 (1947):106–21.

Nilsson, M. P. "Early Orphism and Kindred Religious Movements." *Harvard Theological Review* 28 (1928):181–230.

———. *Geschichte der Griechischen Religion*. 2d ed. Munich, 1955

———. *Greek Popular Religion*. New York, 1940.

———. *A History of Greek Religion*. Oxford, 1925.

———. "The Immortality of the Soul in Greek Religion." *Eranos* 39 (1941):1–16.

———. "Letter to Professor Nock on Some Fundamental Concepts in the Science of Religion." *Harvard Theological Review* 42 (1949):71–107.

Nussbaum, M. "ψυχή in Heraclitus." *Phronesis* 17 (1972):1–15, 153–70.

Onians, R. B. *The Origins of European Thought about the Body, the Soul, the World, Time, and Fate*. 2d ed. Cambridge, 1954.

Otto, W. F. *Die Manen oder von den Urformen des Totenglaubens*. Darmstadt, 1962. Reprint of first edition of 1923.

Philip, J. A. *Pythagoras and Early Pythagoreanism*. Toronto, 1966.

Rahn, H. "Tier und Mensch in der homerischen Auffassung der Wirklichkeit." *Paideuma: Mitteilungen zur Kulturkunde*, vol. 5, no. 6 (June 1953):277–97, and vol. 5, no. 7/8 (April 1954):431–80.

Randall, J. H., Jr. *Aristotle*. New York, 1960.

Regenbogen, O. "δαιμόνιον ψυχῆς φῶς: Erwin Rohdes Psyche und die neuere kritik." *Synopsis: Festgabe für Alfred Weber*. Edited by E. Salin. Heidelberg [1948?]. pp. 361–96.

Reinhardt, K. *Parmenides und die Geschichte der Griechischen Philosophie*. 2d ed. Frankfurt, 1959.

Robinson, T. M. *Plato's Psychology*. Toronto, 1970.

Rohde, E. *Psyche: The Cult of Souls and Belief in Immortality among the Greeks*. Trans. W. B. Hillis. 8th ed. New York [Harper Torchbooks], 1966.

Rose, H. J. "On the Original Significance of the Genius." *Classical Quarterly* 92 (1923):57–60.

Rousseau, P. "Le Sommeil de la vie et la veille de la mort." *Etudes Philosophiques* (1970):499–506.

Rüsche, F. *Blut, Leben und Seele*. Paderborn, 1930.

Russo, J., and Simon, B. "Homeric Psychology and the Oral Epic Tradition." *Journal of the History of Ideas* 29 (1968):483–98.

Schnauffer, A. Frühgriechischen Totenglaube. *Spudasmata* 20 (1972).

Schumacher, J. *Antike Medizin*. Berlin, 1963.

Snell, B. *Die Ausdrücke für den Begriff des Wissens in der vorplatonischen Philosophie.* Philologische Untersuchungen, 29. Berlin, 1924.

———. *The Discovery of the Mind.* Trans. T. G. Rosenmeyer. Cambridge, Mass., 1953.

———. *Scenes from Greek Drama.* Berkeley, 1964.

———. "Die Sprache Heraklits." *Hermes* 61 (1926): 353–81.

———. *Tyrtaios und die Sprache des Epos.* Göttingen, 1969.

Taylor, A. E. *A Commentary on Plato's Timaeus.* Oxford, 1928.

Taylor, C. C. W. "Pleasure, Knowledge and Sensation in Democritus." *Phronesis* 12 (1967): 6–27.

Treu, M. "Griechische Ewigkeitswörter." *Glotta* (1965): 1–24.

Untersteiner, M. *The Sophists.* Trans. K. Freeman. Oxford, 1954.

Verdenius, W. J. "Der Logosbegriff bei Heraklit und Parmenides." *Phronesis* 11 (1966): 81–98.

Vlastos, G. "Ethics and Physics in Democritus." *Philosophical Review* 54 (1945): 578–92; 55 (1946): 53–64.

———. "On Heraclitus." *American Journal of Philology* 76 (1955): 337–68.

von Fritz, K. "*NOOΣ* and *NOEIN* in the Homeric poems." *Classical Philogy* 38 (1943): 79–93.

———. "*NOYΣ, NOEIN*, and Their Derivatives in Presocratic Philosophy (excluding Anaxagoras): Part 1. From the Beginnings to Parmenides." *Classical Philology* 40 (1945): 223–42. Part 2. "The Post-Parmenidean Period." *Classical Philology* 41 (1946): 12–34.

———. *Philosophie und Sprachlicher Ausdruck bei Demokrit, Plato und Aristoteles.* Leipzig, n.d.

———. "Pythagoras." *RE* 47 (1963), cols. 171–209.

von Wilamowitz-Moellendorff, U. *Der Glaube der Hellenen.* Berlin, 1931.

———. *Die Heimkehr des Odysseus.* Berlin, 1927.

Warden, J. "ψυχή in Homeric Death Descriptions." *Phoenix* 25 (1971): 95–103.

Webster, T. B. L. "Some Psychological Terms in Greek Tragedy." *Journal of Hellenic Studies* (1957). 149–54.

Wehrli, F. *Die Schule des Aristoteles: Aristoxenos.* Basel, 1967.

Zeller, E. *A History of Greek Philosophy.* Trans. S. F. Alleyne. London, 1881.

Ziegler, K. "Orphische Dichtung." *RE* 18, cols. 1370–73. (Orphische Eschatologie), cols. 1373–83 (Orphische Seelenlehre bei Platon), cols. 1386–91 (Die Orphische-pythagoreischen Goldplattchen).

Index to Citations of
ψυχή

General Index